Master TOEFL Junior

Intermediate

1

Listening Comprehension

Preface

Each book in the **Master TOEFL Junior** series includes a carefully researched and detailed guide to each part of the TOEFL Junior Test. This series was designed to give test-takers the skills and knowledge needed to obtain a high score on the TOEFL Junior Test.

I have geared this guide towards students who wish to assess their grasp of the communication skills necessary for participating in an English language learning environment. The TOEFL Junior Test provides parents and educators with objective information about improvements in a student's English ability over time. It also serves as a comprehensive measurement that can be helpful in gaining students admission to selective educational programs. This book will be a great asset for EFL students who wish to enter middle schools and exchange programs across America.

I wish to acknowledge the enthusiastic efforts of my writing assistants: Adam Whibley, and Emma Siemasko.

Lastly, I'd like to thank my family for being there while this **Master TOEFL Junior** series was being put together. I could not have done it without the love and support of my wife, Bora Lee, and our new baby, Si-woo Hahn.

Richie Hahn

Contents

Introduction to the TOEFL Junior Test

What is the TOEFL Junior Test?

Basic Overview

The TOEFL Junior test was made to measure a non-native, English speaker's ability to understand the English used in a North American educational environment (age range of 12~17). The test is divided into three sections: Listening Comprehension (42 questions), Language Form and Meaning (42 questions), and Reading Comprehension (42 questions). It is a 115-minute multiple-choice test.

What You Can Expect During the Test

- The test will be done at a secure testing center. The testing center will have one or two testers who will watch test takers. The testers will check your identification to be sure you are who you say you are. The testers will then explain how to do the test, and give you the materials to do the test. The testers cannot help answer any questions as you do the test.
- Test takers can take notes on their test papers during the test. At the end of the test, the testers will take your papers. Students who are caught trying to bring notes from outside into the testing center will be punished. Also, students may not leave the test center with any notes or information found in the test booklet. Consequences may include not getting a test score. These rules exist so students do not give TOEFL Junior exam information to future test takers.
- Test takers cannot have any electrical devices on during the test. Leave them at home or turned off in your bag. If a test taker is caught using an electrical device, they could be kicked out of the test center. Electrical devices include cell phones, MP3 players, radios, calculators, pocket computers and electronic dictionaries.
- At the start of each section students will be given instructions for that section. All the information needed to finish the test is in the written instructions provided by the test center.
- Go to the bathroom before the test. You cannot leave the test room until your break.

The Structure of the TOEFL Junior Test

- Total 126 Questions = 3 Sections × 42 Questions
- Time Given = 115 Minutes
- The TOEFL Junior is a Paper-based Test.

Section	Word Count	# of Passages	# of Questions	Time Given (minutes)	Possible Score
Listening Comprehension	55 ~ 65	10	1	40	200 ~ 300
	210 ~ 360	8	4		
Language Form and Meaning	60 ~ 120	3	4	25	200 ~ 300
	120 ~ 170	4	6 ~ 8		
Reading Comprehension	120 ~ 200	2 ~ 3	4 ~ 7	50	200 ~ 300
	200 ~ 420	3 ~ 4	5 ~ 11		

Why Take the TOEFL Junior Test?

The TOEFL Junior test provides test takers with the following:

- Offers an objective measure of a student's English proficiency.
- Scores can be used as a placement tool for students on exchange programs or entering into other programs aimed at increasing English proficiency.
- Provides test takers with the fundamentals of the much more difficult TOEFL iBT test.
- Can indicate where a student requires more practice in a particular area of English.
- Helps with decisions regarding readiness to study abroad.
- Informs educators of where a student needs to be instructed.
- Gauges a test taker's improvement over time.

Overview of LC

The Listening Portion of the TOEFL Junior

The TOEFL Junior listening test is used to judge whether or not a non-native English speaking student has the listening skills necessary for learning in mid-level English learning environments. Mid-level English learning environments include middle school and high school in North America.

1 One of the purposes for the TOEFL Junior listening test is to measure a test taker's ability to understand commonplace conversations (every day topics, day to day events) that occur in a school environment. The test taker should be able to understand main ideas and important details, be capable of making inferences or predictions, and understand the meanings behind prosodic use / intonation.

2 Test takers must also have the ability to listen for the purposes of learning. The TOEFL Junior contains both lectures and instructional dialogues similar to the level of English used in mid-level learning environments. Students must be able to understand school staff members in and outside of the classroom (in class, during school trips, in the lunch room, intercom messages, in the auditorium) while being capable of understanding a variety of roles that dialogues may have (school notices, reminders, warnings, or invitations). Test takers must understand main ideas, important details and have the ability to infer information or make predictions based on the material. Lastly, test takers should know a speaker's purpose and understand any rhetorical devices used.

This book will cover all the need-to-know information mentioned above in detail. Each question type is covered in its own unit in the following chapters.

The Structure of the Listening Test

<table>
<tr><td rowspan="6">Passage Type</td><td rowspan="2">Academic</td><td>Academic Listening</td><td>4 Scripts</td><td>Word Count</td></tr>
<tr><td>Lecture / Discussion
100~150 sec.</td><td>4 Questions / Script</td><td>210~360</td></tr>
<tr><td rowspan="4">Non-academic</td><td>Classroom Instructions</td><td>10 Scripts</td><td>Word Count</td></tr>
<tr><td>Monologue
(Announcement / Talk)
20~45 sec.</td><td>1 Question / Script</td><td>55~65</td></tr>
<tr><td>Short Conversations</td><td>4 Scripts</td><td>Word Count</td></tr>
<tr><td>Conversation between two people
90~120 sec.</td><td>4 Questions / Script</td><td>210~360</td></tr>
<tr><td colspan="2" rowspan="7">Question Type</td><td>Main Idea</td><td colspan="2">What is the speaker mainly talking about?</td></tr>
<tr><td>Details</td><td colspan="2">• What does the teacher instruct the students to do?
• What point does the boy make about the big test?</td></tr>
<tr><td>Prediction</td><td colspan="2">What will the girl probably do next?</td></tr>
<tr><td>Inference</td><td colspan="2">What is the class probably doing?</td></tr>
<tr><td>Speaker's Purpose</td><td colspan="2">What is the purpose of the talk?</td></tr>
<tr><td>Rhetorical Device</td><td colspan="2">Why does the teacher mention that there will be many students working on the project?</td></tr>
<tr><td>Prosody</td><td colspan="2">What does the girl mean when she says, "I'm not sure I'll be very much help"?</td></tr>
<tr><td colspan="3">Time Given</td><td colspan="2">40 minutes</td></tr>
<tr><td colspan="3">Possible Score</td><td colspan="2">200 ~ 300</td></tr>
</table>

Question Types Summarized

There are seven different types of questions on the listening test, grouped into three different categories. This book will look at each type of question, provide strategies on how to answer each question type, and test material to practice with. For now, here is a summary of the question types:

A. Basic Understanding

These questions focus on the main topic and factual information of the scripts in the following ways:

1. **Main Idea** _ The main topic of the announcement / talk, conversation, and lecture
2. **Details** _ Specific information in the material (words, names, or definitions)

B. Logical Reasoning

These questions focus on using the information given while asking you to logically decide the speaker's meaning or next plan of action.

3. **Inference** _ Unsaid suggestions or ideas made by a speaker
4. **Prediction** _ The logical thing a speaker may do or say next
5. **Prosody** _ A speaker's meaning based on how they sound

C. Practical Meaning

These questions ask about details in a question in a non-specific way and test your understanding of the material's theme.

6. **Speaker's Purpose** _ The function of a dialogue or specific phrase
7. **Rhetorical Device** _ The goal in using a specific phrase

What's in This Book?

This book contains eight parts.

1 The Orientation ~ This portion of the book

2 The Diagnostic Test ~ This section of the book will assess your current listening ability. The diagnostic test tells you your listening strengths and also what you should focus on to improve your skills. Additionally the diagnostic test gives you a grade you can refer back to once you take the practice tests to see how much your listening skill has improved since you began this book.

3 The Question Types ~ This segment of the book gives you a detailed look at each question type on the TOEFL Junior.

4 The Strategies ~ Here is where you will learn tricks and hints to help you answer each question type successfully. This section also includes methods you can use to recognize specific question types and explains the test's traps used to trick you into answering incorrectly.

5 The Example Questions ~ This portion of each strategy unit illustrates how a specific question type appears in a listening dialogue. Each example question is an opportunity to practice answering a specific question type on its own before you encounter them mixed with the various other question types. Each example question is followed by a full explanation, providing the correct answer and reasons why the other choices are incorrect.

6 The Dictation Questions ~ This section's main purpose is to give you an opportunity to practice listening for key phrases. Key phrases are necessary in understanding each dialogue and answering the question given in each dictation section. The dictation portion of each unit also acts as a second example question so you can practice a specific question type before tackling the practice tests.

7 The Practice Tests ~ Each question type unit has a practice test to give you a chance to answer specific question types on their own before trying out the actual test at the end of this book. The practice tests will show your improvements on each question type as you study their specific units.

8 The Sample Actual Test ~ The last section of this book is your chance to see what you learned and how much you have improved. It will give you a feeling for what you should expect on the real TOEFL Junior listening test.

Official Examinee Score Report

Internationally Verified Report Card

The TOEFL Junior test provides test takers with both an English and Korean report card that indicates their placement in relation to the domestic test score standard. The English version of the report is verified internationally: therefore you can use it when applying to primarily English based secondary schools.

Global Index Report

This segment of the report allows you to compare your TOEFL Junior score against a sample of ETS native English speaking scores.

Lexile Measures

The Lexile Measure is the standard method of assessing reading ability all over the world. It measures the general abilities of a test taker in understanding and translating English passages created by Metametrix.

CEFR: Common European Framework of Reference

The TOEFL Junior test is now used in accord with the Common European Framework of Reference. The TOEFL Junior was endorsed in 2000 by the European Council for use within Europe. The TOEFL Junior provides test takers with a total index and details of their score based on each section of the test (listening, language form and meaning, and reading).

Rating Certificate

This is an official level rating certificate. The first 3 levels classify a test taker's English ability as gold (1), silver (2) or bronze (3). The last two levels do not reward a medal grade.

Global Standard

* Shows a student's likely level in the U.S. Grading System and CEFR
* Scores are widely accepted for studying abroad.

All-around English Ability Test

* Tests logical thinking and reading comprehension skills
* Tests the test taker's English speaking ability in secondary school

Test optimized for Junior High level Students

* English standard akin to that of Dae-won International Middle School
* Test scores accepted and recognized both domestically and internationally
* Widely accepted as an objective measure of a student's English ability

Provides an Individual Reading Ability Index

* Provides students with an English reading ability index
* Recommends customized reading books to improve a student's reading ability

TOEFL Junior

Diagnostic Test

Diagnostic Test

Track 1~14

Listening Comprehension

The listening section has 13 questions. Follow along as you listen to the directions to the listening section.

Directions

In this section of the test, you will hear a teacher or other school staff member talking to students. Each talk is followed by one question. Choose the best answer to each question and mark the letter of the correct answer on your answer sheet. You will hear each talk only one time.

Here is an example: 

What does the teacher want the students to do?

(A) Choose buddies
(B) Make new friends
(C) Behave on the bus
(D) Empty their backpacks

The correct answer is (A), "Choose buddies."

Here is another example: 

What will the students probably do next?

(A) Find lab partners
(B) Use the microscopes
(C) Explore the supplies
(D) Choose a pair of safety goggles

The correct answer is (D), "Choose a pair of safety goggles."

Go on to the next page, and the test will begin with question number one.

GO ON TO THE NEXT PAGE

PART 1

1. What does the teacher instruct the students to do?

(A) Come to the science fair
(B) Talk with the eighth graders
(C) Work for three or four months
(D) Work on their science projects

2. What can be inferred about the last game played against Brooksly?

(A) It was lost.
(B) It was easily won.
(C) It was not exciting.
(D) It had a lot of fouls.

3. What is the purpose of the talk?

(A) To prove that the library is big
(B) To warn students about getting lost
(C) To give students directions for writing
(D) To explain where students will find books

4. What will the volunteer probably do next?

(A) Look at the stars with the students
(B) Tell the students where to buy lunch
(C) Show the students the new planetarium
(D) Explain why they must go with a staff member

5. What is the teacher mainly talking about?

(A) Being a lover of music
(B) Practicing twice a week
(C) Trying out for the orchestra
(D) Having an interest in performance

GO ON TO THE NEXT PAGE

PART 1

Now you will hear some conversations. Each conversation is followed by three or more questions. Choose the best answer to each question and mark the letter of the correct answer on your answer sheet. You will hear each conversation only one time.

6. What are the students mainly talking about?

(A) Mr. Horowitz's difficult assignments

(B) The girl's decision to attend the trip

(C) The boy being the most talented writer in the class

(D) The boy worrying about the trip to Tuck's Point

7. What does the boy say about the trip?

(A) No one will want to go.

(B) Mr. Horowitz will not go.

(C) There aren't a lot of spots.

(D) It won't be good without the girl.

8. What does the boy imply when he says "Maybe, but there are a lot of other good writers."?

(A) He isn't sure that he's a very good writer.

(B) He thinks the girl is a better writer than he is.

(C) He doesn't think the other students are nervous.

(D) He believes other students could write better essays.

9. What will the boy probably do after school?

(A) Visit Tuck's Point with his parents

(B) Ask the girl to help him write his essay

(C) E-mail Mr. Horowitz about his concerns

(D) Start his essay about why he wants to go to Tuck's Point

GO ON TO THE NEXT PAGE

Answer Key pp. 3~6

PART 1

10. What is the girl's problem?

(A) She doesn't have an e-mail account.

(B) Her singing group needs a music teacher.

(C) Her friends don't want to be in the singing group.

(D) She needs a teacher to sponsor her singing group.

11. What does the teacher ask the girl to do?

(A) Ask another teacher to sponsor the group

(B) Find some more members to join the group

(C) Give the teacher the concert dates in advance

(D) Send her an e-mail with the group's information

12. What does the teacher imply about helping the singing group?

(A) She needs to talk to the school principal first.

(B) She's never helped a student group as a teacher.

(C) She isn't willing to help until she knows more about it.

(D) She wants to meet the other members of the singing group.

13. Why does the girl mention that the teacher doesn't have to come to all the meetings?

(A) To prove that the teacher is too busy to help

(B) To explain that the teacher won't have to do a lot of work

(C) To show that helping the singing group takes a lot of time

(D) To give an example of something the group wants from the teacher

Answer Key pp. 6~7

TOEFL Junior

Chapter

Announcement / Talk Question Types

Introduction

At the start of the TOEFL Junior Listening test, there are 10 questions based on short announcements / talks. These announcements / talks are smaller versions (55 ~ 65 words vs. 210 ~ 360 words) of the full length conversations / lectures found on the rest of the test. The short announcements / talks are based only on the first five TOEFL Junior question types (main idea, details, inference, prediction, and speaker's purpose). The shorter nature of announcement / talk prevents them from containing any prosody or rhetorical device questions. The announcements are more similar in structure to lectures than they are to conversations.

Unit 1 Main Idea Questions

All announcement / talk type questions are based on a class announcement or an informational speech by a school staff member (teacher, coach, principal etc.). Main Idea questions test **your ability to find the central and most important idea of the listening material**. The main idea of a passage is usually found near the beginning of the passage.

Main Idea questions ask about the main topic of the material. **Your job is to know what the main topic is**. Use the following helpful hints to answer the example questions.

「Announcement / Talk Main Idea」 questions start like this:

- What is the teacher mainly explaining?
- What is the teacher mainly talking about?
- What is the librarian talking about?
- What is the subject of the announcement?
- What is the guidance counselor talking about?

Strategy 1 Listen Carefully to the First Sentence

The first sentence in an announcement / talk almost always contains the main topic. Announcements / talks are short, so almost all of the main idea is stated early in the passage.

Strategy 2 Listen for Repetition

The key words from the main topic are repeated many times in an announcement / talk. Listen for recurring key words and phrases.

MTJ-I-LC-11
MP3

The following example illustrates main idea strategies and provides you with one main idea example question.

Track 15

Example Announcement / Talk Excerpt

N **Listen to an English teacher speaking to his class.**

M Now that we've finished reading "Romeo and Juliet," **our class will be having a speaking contest**. I'd like you all to memorize a 10-line passage you'd like to read from the play. You'll perform it in class on Wednesday. The winner of the **speaking contest** will get two tickets to the Norwich Theater's production of "A Midsummer Night's Dream." This is another play written by Shakespeare.

Question

What is the teacher mainly talking about?

(A) Wednesday's class

(B) Reading "Romeo and Juliet"

(C) Going to the Norwich Theater

(D) Performing in a speaking contest

Explanation

Choice (D) is correct. As **Strategy 1** mentions, the main idea of the passage is in the first sentence. **Strategy 2** is illustrated by the number of times that "speaking contest" is mentioned.

Main Idea Announcement / Talk Example

 Track 16

N **Listen to a teacher making an announcement in class.**

W We're expected to get a large amount of rain tonight and tomorrow, so it's possible that school will be closed. When it rains a lot, the parking lot floods with water. A flooded parking lot makes it impossible for traffic to drive through. If school is canceled tomorrow, then I want you to read Chapter 2 and Chapter 3 at home.

Question

What is the subject of the announcement?

(A) Reading Chapter 2 and 3

(B) A possible school cancellation

(C) A rain storm ruining the buses

(D) The flooding of the school parking lot

Explanation

The right answer is (B). Using **Strategy 1** and **2**, answer (B) is correct, as the speaker begins by saying it is possible school will be closed. She ends by mentioning the cancellation again. (A) and (D) are details. Choice (C) is not supported by the passage.

Main Idea

Dictation

Track 17

N **Listen to a music teacher talking to a group of students.**

W Wow, I was so ① ______________________. You all did a spectacular job playing your instruments. I think you proved to your parents and teachers how ② ______________________. Congratulations, everybody. I hope you're ready ③ ______________________. It will be in the spring.

1. What is the teacher mainly talking about?

(A) The upcoming spring concert

(B) The advanced skill level of each student

(C) Congratulating the students' parents and teachers

(D) The students' impressive performance at their concert

Track 18

N **Listen to an announcement on the school intercom.**

M Hello, students, teachers, and staff. This is a reminder that ① ______________________ this week as students ② ______________________. If you have a drama class that regularly meets in the auditorium, it will be meeting in Room 305 this week. The auditorium ③ ______________________ on Monday the 17th.

2. What is the main idea of the announcement?

(A) Buying tickets to the school musical

(B) The closing of the school auditorium

(C) The teachers and students in Room 305

(D) The drama club canceling their meetings

Answer Key pp. 8~9

Main Idea

Practice Test

Track 19~24

1. What is the teacher mainly talking about?

(A) A soccer game at recess

(B) A new student's locker combination

(C) A new student who needs some guidance

(D) The personality of a South Korean student

2. What is the main topic of the talk?

(A) The class trip to the Redwood Forest

(B) Students misbehaving at the Redwood Forest

(C) The students choosing to go on Wednesday's trip

(D) The students' behavior affecting their trip to Redwood Forest

3. What is the swimming coach mainly talking about?

(A) Students winning all their meets

(B) Which personal records need to be beaten

(C) Students writing down their goals for the season

(D) Making notes of goals that have been accomplished

4. What is the main topic of the talk?

(A) Why the essays are on World War II
(B) How he decided to choose Tuesday for a due date
(C) When he expects to give back the paper copy of the essay
(D) Why he wants students to e-mail and print their essays for him

5. What is the volunteer mainly talking about?

(A) Greek mythology
(B) The exhibition room
(C) A Greek God display
(D) The roles of Greek Gods

6. What is the main topic of the talk?

(A) How to use a USB key
(B) Important computer tips
(C) Learning how to type faster
(D) Saving work on the computer

Answer Key pp. 9~12

Unit 2 Details Questions

「**Details**」 are specific facts and information found in the listening material. Your job is to show that **you can recognize and understand specific key information from a passage**. Use the following helpful hints to answer the example questions.

「Announcement / Talk Details」 questions start like this:

- What does the teacher instruct the students to do?
- What does the teacher (principal / volunteer etc.) say about ~?

Strategy 1 Take Notes

Write down any facts, definitions and examples you hear. Also, write down any activities a speaker discusses. The information found in an announcement / talk is almost 100% relevant to the main idea. The difficult part is remembering all the facts to answer a specific detail question. Writing down key information provides you with a quick reminder of any details you may have forgotten.

Strategy 2 Paraphrase

While taking notes, it is important to NOT try and write everything you hear word for word. Write down the key information in short form. You may write down anything that helps you remember; your notes do not need to be neat, organized, or even grammatically correct. See the note taking section for more information.

MTJ-I-LC-12
MP3

The following example illustrates details strategies and provides you with one details example question.

Track 25

Example Announcement / Talk Excerpt

N **Listen to an art teacher speaking to her class.**

W Today we'll be starting our unit on self-portraits. Many, if not most, artists have created a self-portrait. Often they try to incorporate some elements of their personality, feelings, or identity into their work. In class today we'll look at self-portraits done by famous artists. For homework, I'd like you to try to draw your own.

Question

What does the teacher instruct the students to do?

(A) Draw a self-portrait for homework

(B) Create a portrait of a famous artist

(C) Research a self-portrait of a famous artist

(D) Think about their personalities and identities

Notes
- unit on self-portraits
- artists make them
- feelings, personality
- for homework, draw one

Explanation

Choice (A) is correct. The notes taken above (**Strategy 1**) show what the students are asked to do. Using **Strategy 2**, the phrase "For homework, I'd like you to draw your own" can be paraphrased into "Draw a self-portrait for homework," which is a direct instruction.

Details

Announcement / Talk Example

Track 26

N **Listen to a museum volunteer talking to a group of students.**

W Over here you'll see our exhibit on cells. Scientists have taken pictures of all different kinds of cells to display in the exhibit. You may find the photos of cancer cells interesting, as they look different from healthy cells. You'll also be able to see how the various cells in the body look different from one another. For example, blood cells look different from brain cells.

Question

What does the volunteer say about cancer cells?

(A) There are many photos of them.

(B) They were difficult to photograph.

(C) They look different from blood cells.

(D) They are different from healthy cells.

Explanation

The correct answer is (D). The speaker states that the photos of cancer cells are interesting because they look different from healthy cells. There is no evidence for (A) and (B). And the speaker never mentions cancer cells in relation to blood cells, making (C) incorrect.

Details

Dictation

Track 27

N **Listen to a teacher talking to students in a class.**

M I hope the reading on bats showed you ① ______________________________. They're not evil creatures with diseases, ② ______________________________ on Halloween. If you have time tonight, then please ③ ______________________ at twilight. See if you can find any bats. They're especially ④ __________________ at this time of year.

1. What does the teacher instruct the students to do?

(A) Realize that bats are interesting creatures

(B) Be active in their area at this time of year

(C) Think about how bats are portrayed on Halloween

(D) Go into their backyards at twilight to look for bats

Track 28

N **Listen to a drama teacher talking to students.**

W This year ① ______________________ a play called "Carousel." It's a famous American musical and love story ② __________________ Maine. Tryouts for the play will be ③ ____________________. You'll be required to ④ ______________ __________________ and sing a song. If there are a lot of people trying out, we might have another tryout session on Monday.

2. What does the teacher say about the tryouts?

(A) They will be on Friday at 3:00.

(B) They'll be taking place in Maine.

(C) They might not happen until Monday.

(D) They'll require students to have a partner.

Answer Key p. 13

Details

Practice Test

Track 29~34

1. What does the teacher say about smoking just one cigarette?

(A) It is not very harmful.

(B) It could lead to smoking more.

(C) It will make you get heart disease.

(D) It might make your body very weak.

2. What are over 90% of Stephen students doing?

(A) Recycling bottles, cans, and papers

(B) Dedicating themselves to the principal

(C) Campaigning for a healthier environment

(D) Working for the Healthy Environment Program

3. What does the teacher instruct the students to do?

(A) Find a partner to study with

(B) Write sentences about all the members of the class

(C) Review all the material since the last test with the teacher

(D) Make a list of the things they've studied with their partner

4. What does the teacher say about girls' skirts?

(A) They need to be clean.

(B) They can be worn on Fridays.

(C) They need to be long enough.

(D) They need to be black or gray.

5. What does the teacher say about the purpose of the assignment?

(A) It's to help students develop plots.

(B) It's to promote non-violent games.

(C) It's to make students think creatively.

(D) It's to write about something that students like.

6. What does the teacher want the students to do?

(A) Work with a boy if they're a girl

(B) Pick their best friend as a partner

(C) Choose a partner who has different interests

(D) Choose someone they don't usually work with

Answer Key pp. 14~16

Unit 3 Inference Questions

「**Inference」 questions** are based on the idea that information **can be inferred or implied without directly being said**. To answer inference questions, you need to make a good guess about what is true. Use the following helpful hints to answer the example questions.

「Announcement / Talk Inference」 questions start like this:

- What is probably true about ~?
- What is the class probably doing?
- What are the students probably doing?
- What can be inferred about the last field trip?
- What does the teacher suggest about the play?

Strategy 1 **Use Logic**

Inference questions ask you to think logically in order to reasonably guess the meaning behind a speaker's words. Think about what is possible and not possible based on what you heard. If you cannot give a good reason for your choice, you may have chosen the wrong answer.

Strategy 2 **Avoid Trap Answers**

The correct answer to an inference question will not be something that is directly said in the announcement/ talk. Inference questions want you to understand what is implied, rather than what was said. Do not choose an answer choice that is the same as a phrase in the listening.

MTJ-I-LC-13
MP3

The following example illustrates inference strategies and provides you with one inference example question.

Example Announcement / Talk Excerpt

N **Listen to a teacher making an announcement in class.**

W The school's final soccer game is set for this Friday at 2:00, which is usually when we have class. Because this is such a big game, I'm going to cancel class and allow you to watch it. Don't think you won't have work to do though. I've prepared an extra project for you to do over the weekend to make up for Friday's missed time.

Question

What does the teacher suggest about the soccer game?

(A) It isn't interesting to her.

(B) It is on Friday at 2:00 p.m.

(C) It is very important to the student.

(D) It isn't very important to the students.

Explanation

Choice (C) is correct. The teacher implies that the game is important to the students when she says she is going to *allow them to watch it*. There is no evidence for choice (A). Choice (B) is a trap answer (**Strategy 2**). It is a quote from the dialogue. Using logic (**Strategy 1**), choice (D) is incorrect. Logically, the teacher would not cancel class if the game wasn't important.

Inference

Announcement / Talk Example

Track 36

N **Listen to a teacher making an announcement in class.**

W I've gotten word from the school principal that there have been some problems with the afternoon school buses. The buses have been waiting for students and leaving far after they are scheduled to. This is resulting in blocked traffic in the school parking lot. From now on, the buses will leave at 3:10. If you are not on your bus at 3:10, it will leave without you.

Question

What is probably true about the students?

(A) They are often late for their buses.

(B) They usually walk home from school.

(C) They have become friends with the bus drivers.

(D) They don't have a good relationship with the principal.

Explanation

Choice (A) is correct. The announcement says that the buses have been waiting for students. Using logic (**Strategy 1**), it's obvious that the buses have been waiting because *the students are often late*. There is no evidence for choices (B), (C), or (D).

Inference **Dictation**

Track 37

N **Listen to a volleyball coach talking to her players.**

W I hope you're not nervous for the game, even though Hazel Hill ① ____________ last month. We've been practicing a lot and I'm sure you girls can beat them. Please think carefully ② ________________ . Every person on this team can ③ __________________________ . Good teamwork will be ④ ____________ ________ Hazel.

1. What can be inferred about the Hazel Hill team?

(A) They are a strong team.

(B) They are loyal to their coach.

(C) They don't practice very much.

(D) They haven't beaten the girls before.

Track 38

N **Listen to a science teacher talking to his class.**

M The safety equipment is over here—you'll find gloves, goggles, and masks. You ① ________________ when we do experiments. There are ② ____________ . I don't want anyone to get hurt because of ③ ____________________ . When you walk into the lab, walk straight over to the safety equipment. Please use the equipment ④ _______________ .

2. What does the teacher suggest about the safety equipment?

(A) It's in a far away closet.

(B) It is necessary for every experiment.

(C) It should include socks and sneakers.

(D) It's responsible for avoidable mistakes.

Answer Key pp. 17~18

Inference

Practice Test

Track 39~44

1. What does the principal suggest about the class trip?

(A) It will be in May.

(B) It will be very hot.

(C) It will be a lot of fun.

(D) The teachers are excited about it.

2. What can be inferred about Monet's blindness?

(A) It prevented him from painting.

(B) It began when Monet turned 50.

(C) It changed the way his work looked.

(D) It was not a big problem for Monet.

3. What does the teacher suggest about Memorial Day?

(A) It is mostly celebrated by soldiers.

(B) It is a great day for a family picnic.

(C) It is only celebrated by those who have lost loved ones.

(D) It is a serious holiday that should be observed in a serious way.

4. What is probably true about the seventh grade students?

(A) They won't go to the bake sale.
(B) Their hiking trip is near a bakery.
(C) They need some money for their trip.
(D) They are only selling treats to parents.

5. What does the teacher suggest about the storybooks?

(A) The due date is flexible for each student.
(B) They get more and more impressive every year.
(C) A good storybook will take a long time to complete.
(D) Two weeks isn't enough time to complete the storybooks.

6. What does the teacher suggest about female writers?

(A) They weren't very talented.
(B) They felt freer with a pen name.
(C) They always had to use pen names.
(D) They could write about their husbands.

Answer Key pp. 18~21

Unit 4 Prediction Questions

Predicting is the ability to guess something will happen before it actually does. On 「Prediction」 questions, your job is to predict what the speaker will talk about or do next. Use the following helpful hints to answer the example questions.

「Announcement / Talk Prediction」 questions start like this:

- What will the teacher probably do next?
- What is the teacher probably going to do next?
- What will the class probably do next?
- What will the students probably do next?
- What will the students probably do this evening?

Strategy **Focus on the Ending**

Prediction questions often refer to the last sentence of the passage. A prediction question asks what will happen once the announcement / talk is over, so it's helpful to listen to the ending. For example, if the last thing a speaker says is, "please choose a topic for your essay," then the next thing the students will probably do is to choose their topics.

MTJ-I-LC-14
MP3

The following example illustrates the prediction strategy and provides you with one prediction example question.

Track 45

Example Announcement / Talk Excerpt

N **Listen to a basketball coach talking to her team.**

W Girls, this is a big game today. You know this team well as we've played them a few times before. You'll remember that their best player is number 21. I think her name is Sally. When she's on the court, we need to make sure she's covered. I've developed a plan to make sure this happens.

Question

What will the coach probably do next?

(A) Find out if Sally's number is 21

(B) Explain her plan for covering Sally

(C) Ask the girls to go out onto the court

(D) Decide which girls are as good as Sally

Explanation

Choice (B) is correct. The basketball coach talks about needing to make sure that Sally is covered. Using **Strategy** and listening to the ending, we know that the coach has a plan. She will probably explain her plan next. Choices (A), (C), and (D) are possible but do not have any evidence.

Prediction

Announcement / Talk Example

Track 46

N **Listen to an English teacher speaking to his class.**

M For tonight's homework, I'd like you to interview a member of your family. Ask them about their best childhood memories. It doesn't matter if their memory is a full story or just a single moment. Record the memories on a piece of paper and bring it to class tomorrow. Don't forget to do the interview tonight!

Question

What will the students probably do this evening?

(A) Bring a list of memories to the teacher

(B) Ask a family member about their memories

(C) Try to remember their best childhood memories

(D) Start a creative writing piece about a family member

Explanation

The correct choice is (B). The teacher begins the talk by saying that interviewing a family member is "tonight's homework." He also says that this needs to be brought "to class tomorrow." He ends his talk by reminding the students to do the interview tonight. Choices (A), (C), and (D) are incorrect.

Prediction Dictation

Track 47

N Listen to a science teacher talking to students in class.

M I know we didn't have a lot of time to talk about the lab report after we ① ______________________ . Still, I hope it wasn't too difficult for you to write. If you used Chapter 4 when writing your reports, I'm sure you'll be fine. Chapter 4 has ② ____________________ the project. Okay, now ③ ______________________ __________ your lab reports.

1. What will the class probably do next?

(A) Write their reports on last week's lab

(B) Give their lab reports to their teacher

(C) Explain why they didn't read Chapter 4

(D) Decide whether or not they deserve a good grade

Track 48

N Listen to a teacher talking to her class.

W Today I'm going to teach you ① ______________________________ . You'll make the cranes from folded pieces of paper. Folding paper ② _________________________ is known as origami. This is a Japanese art. Anyway, ③ _______________ that if one person folds 1,000 paper cranes ④ ______________________________ by a crane. I doubt anyone will have time to make 1,000 today, but we can try!

2. What will the class probably do next?

(A) Make 1,000 paper cranes

(B) Learn about Japanese art

(C) Learn to fold paper cranes

(D) Make wishes to the paper cranes

Answer Key p. 22

Prediction

Practice Test

Track 49~54

1. What will the students probably do next?

(A) Send a mural design to City Hall

(B) Try to meet with their groups at home

(C) Participate in the citywide mural contest

(D) Stay to speak with the principal or leave

2. What will the students probably do as they're leaving school?

(A) Add their names to the honor list

(B) Call their parents for a ride home

(C) Post their report cards on the bulletin board

(D) Check the honor roll list on the bulletin board

3. What will the teacher probably do next?

(A) Show students how to plant their seeds

(B) Try to eat the beans the class has grown

(C) Make sure the plants grow big and strong

(D) Give students a picture of a healthy bean plant

4. What will the teacher probably do next?

(A) Look up the play in an encyclopedia

(B) Find the name of the play on her ticket

(C) Ask the students to wait until tomorrow

(D) Use the Internet to find out about the play

5. What will the students probably do next?

(A) Try to find the monkeys hiding in the bushes

(B) Feed the monkeys with bread from the basket

(C) Pet the monkeys while the zoo keeper watches

(D) Ask the zoo keeper why the monkeys are excited

6. What will the teacher probably do next?

(A) Explain the Revolutionary War

(B) Tell students what group they're in

(C) Assign each student with a different topic

(D) Ask the students to form their own groups

Answer Key pp. 23~25

Unit 5 Speaker's Purpose Questions

「Speaker's Purpose」 questions ask **if you understand the main reason the speaker is talking**. When giving an announcement/talk, the speaker always has a reason or goal for speaking. When a speaker talks, they always have a purpose. It is important to understand why a speaker is talking or making an announcement/talk. Use the following helpful hints to answer the example questions.

「Announcement / Talk Speaker's Purpose」 questions start like this:

- What is the purpose of the announcement/talk?
- What is the speaker's purpose?
- Why is the teacher talking about the assignment?
- Why is the principal talking to the students?
- Why is the principal talking about spitting on school grounds?

Strategy 1 Listen to the Start

Since the announcements/talks are so short, the speaker usually states his/her general reason for speaking at the beginning. Focus on the beginning of a passage, much like you would for a main idea, to find the answer to speaker's purpose questions.

Strategy 2 Listen to the Tone of Voice

This strategy does not provide a 100% guaranteed correct answer. Still, knowing the general mood of a speaker increases your chances of answering correctly. If a speaker sounds happy and excited, the correct answer choice should reflect that mood. If they sound upset, the answer should reflect that.

MTJ-I-LC-15
MP3

Strategy 3 Use Main Idea Strategies

Main idea and speaker's purpose questions are almost the same. The difference is that a speaker's purpose question will ask you for the reason *WHY* a speaker is talking, while a main idea question will ask you *WHAT* they're saying. These two things are closely related, so using main idea strategies will help you answer speaker's purpose questions.

Chapter 1

The following example illustrates the speaker's purpose strategies and provides you with one speaker's purpose example question.

Example Announcement / Talk Excerpt

N **Listen to a teacher speaking to her class.**

W Class, I'm sure you remember that tomorrow is our class picnic. **I'd like to remind you that you've all volunteered to bring different items**. I'll be bringing all the plates and cups, but it's your responsibility to bring the food. If you can't remember what you agreed to bring, check the list in the front of the class.

Question

What is the purpose of the talk?

(A) To describe tomorrow's schedule to the class

(B) To explain who will bring the plates and cups

(C) To remind students to bring food to the picnic

(D) To inform students about the time of the picnic

Explanation

The correct choice is (C). Listening to the beginning (**Strategy 1**), we know that the teacher is reminding students about the picnic. She talks about this further and says the students have all agreed to bring different items. Using **Strategy 2**, we might find her tone insistent, showing that it is an important reminder. With **Strategy 3**, we'll find that "students bringing food to the picnic" is the main idea of the talk, making it obvious that the teacher is reminding students of this.

Speaker's Purpose

Announcement / Talk Example

Track 56

N **Listen to a music teacher talking to his class.**

M The Beatles was one of the greatest bands to come out of the 1960s. You've probably heard of John, Paul, George, and Ringo. Their first hit was called "I want to hold your hand," and they were one of the first bands to play on live television. They were an incredibly popular band, and were loved by many young people in the 60s.

Question

What is the speaker's purpose?

(A) To introduce a band called The Beatles

(B) To identify John, Paul, George, and Ringo

(C) To explain what band played music on TV in the 60s

(D) To inform students that The Beatles are his favorite band

Explanation

The correct answer is (A). Using **Strategy 1**, we see that The Beatles are mentioned in the very beginning in a general statement. The speaker goes on to give a general description of the band. There is no evidence for (B), (C), and (D).

Speaker's Purpose

Dictation

Track 57

N **Listen to a math team coach talking to his team.**

M I know this team is older than you, but it doesn't mean that they're smarter. Remember that you have ① ________________ in your school. You can beat anyone ② ________________ math. You are a strong team and ③ ________________. Let's work together and ④ ________________!

1. Why is the coach talking to the students?

(A) To scare the other team

(B) To make the students afraid

(C) To help the students with their studies

(D) To encourage the students to be confident

Track 58

N **Listen to an English teacher speaking to her class.**

W This month is National Poetry Month, so ① ________________ by studying poetry. Poetry is ② ________________ that has helped people ③ ________________ ________________ on Earth. Some poems are long, and some poems are short. Some are funny, and others are serious and sad. We'll be studying ④ ________________ in English class this month.

2. What is the purpose of this talk?

(A) To ask students to write poetry

(B) To explain the meaning of a poem

(C) To decide who will be in the poetry contest

(D) To introduce the study of poetry during National Poetry Month

Answer Key pp. 26~27

Speaker's Purpose

Practice Test

1. What is the purpose of the talk?

(A) To find out who is the best speller
(B) To remind the students to read books
(C) To explain the rules of the Spelling Bee
(D) To ask the students to return to their seats

2. Why does the principal talk about sending text messages during a performance?

(A) To give an example of bad behavior
(B) To explain why the students were loud
(C) To show that he received the messages
(D) To prove that cell phones are a problem

3. Why does the secretary talk about report cards?

(A) To scare students about their bad grades
(B) To ask students if their parents are interested
(C) To explain what will happen without the health forms
(D) To warn students that the report cards are not finished

4. What is the purpose of the talk?

(A) To celebrate Betsy's election

(B) To ask if anyone else is proud of Betsy

(C) To explain to Betsy why she was elected

(D) To thank the students for voting for Betsy

5. Why is the librarian talking about late fees?

(A) To prove that students are always late

(B) To introduce students to their library cards

(C) To explain what happens if books aren't returned

(D) To give an example of a thing disliked by students

6. What is the purpose of the talk?

(A) To get students excited

(B) To explain the 19th century

(C) To introduce an assignment

(D) To warn about difficult homework

Answer Key pp. 27~30

TOEFL Junior

Chapter

Conversation Question Types

Introduction

During the second section of the TOEFL Junior Listening test there are 16 questions based on conversations, usually between two students, or a conversation between a student and a school staff member. These scripts are 210~360 words in length. They are based on all TOEFL Junior Listening question types (main idea, details, inference, prediction, rhetorical device, and prosody). For each question type, there will be a set of "strategies" that will help you answer correctly. All questions are accompanied by a full explanation of each correct answer.

Unit 1 Main Idea Questions

「Conversation Main Idea」 questions ask you **what two speakers are mainly talking about**. Two students or a student and a school staff member will have a conversation. Your job is to know the conversation topic. Choose an answer choice that matches the common idea of the entire conversation. Be careful! Do not choose details! Use the following helpful hints to answer the example questions.

「Conversation Main Idea」 questions start like this:

- What are the speakers talking about?
- What are the students mainly talking about?
- What is the main topic of conversation?

Strategy 1 Listen Carefully after Greetings

Speakers always greet each other in a conversation before talking about important information. If you know that the speaker's questions and key phrases come after a greeting, you can prepare to focus on the main idea.

MTJ-I-LC-21
MP3

The following example illustrates main idea strategies and provides you with one main idea example question.

Track 65

Example Dialogue Excerpt

(B: boy, G: girl)

N **Listen to a conversation between two friends.**

B Hey, Sally. How have you been?

G I've been okay, Paul, how about you?

B Pretty good, actually. **The fall fair is in town next week. Are you going**?

G I don't know. None of my friends want to go and I don't want to go alone.

B You want to come with me and my friends? We are going to go next Saturday.

G That would be great! What time should I meet you?

B Meet us at the fair's main gate at 7:00 p.m. We want to be there early so we don't need to wait in any lines to get in.

Question

What are the speakers mainly talking about?

(A) When the fair is in town

(B) If the girl wants to go to the fair

(C) Why they want to go to the fair early

(D) What time they should meet next Saturday

Explanation

The right answer is (B). If **Strategy 1** is used, you'll find the main idea right after the greetings. The boy mentions the fair and then asks if the girl is going so that he can invite her. Choice (A), (C), and (D) are details relating to her decision.

Strategy 2 Listen for Important Phrases

When two friends talk, one friend asks the other friend a question about doing an activity or helping with a problem. This question is usually the main idea.

Listen for the important phrases below. The main idea comes after sentences like these.

***Conversation Between Two Friends**

Important Phrases	Examples
Do you want to …?	**Do you want to** go to the school dance with me?
Would you like to …?	**Would you like to** work together on the project?
Are you going …?	**Are you going to** meet us in the library?
How do I …?	**How do I** do this math homework?
Do you know how …?	**Do you know how** to get to English class?

***Conversation Between a School Staff Member and a Student**

Important Phrases (Staff)	Responses (Student)
How can I help you today?	Can you help me choose my classes?
What can I do for you?	I'd like to borrow this library book.
What's the problem?	I don't have enough lunch money today.
Is there something I can help you with?	Yes, I need more time to finish the assignment.
Do you need some help?	Yes, please. Where is the science lab?

Strategy 3 Listen for Repeated Phrases

If you missed the main idea at the beginning of the conversation, listen for any phrases which are repeated. Speakers usually need to refer to main idea again in the conversation to discuss details. When a specific phrase is used repeatedly it is most likely related to the main topic of the conversation.

The following example illustrates main idea strategies and provides you with one main idea example question.

Example Dialogue Excerpt

(S: student, L: librarian)

N **Listen to a conversation between a school librarian and a student.**

S Good afternoon.

L Hello, what can I do for you, young man?

S I'm new to this school and I need to know **how to borrow books** from the library.

L I can help you with that. Do you have a student card?

S Yes, I do. Do you want to see it?

L Yes, please. **To borrow a book**, all I need to do is scan your student card and the book you want **to borrow**. When you return the book I will scan it again and remove it from your account.

S Well, that is easy. Thanks!

L No problem. Come find me if you need anything else.

Question

What is the main topic of the conversation?

(A) How to use a student card

(B) How to return a library book

(C) How to borrow library books

(D) How to use a student account

Explanation

The right answer is (C). Using **Strategy 2**, we hear the important phrase "What can I do for you?" The boy answers this question by saying he needs to borrow books. Using **Strategy 3**, book borrowing is mentioned three times (once in the main idea sentence and two more times when the librarian explains how to borrow books). Choices (A) and (B) are incorrect because they are the result of (C). Choice (D) is incorrect because there are no directions on how to use the student account.

Main Idea

Conversation Example

Track 67

(B: boy, G: girl)

N **Listen to a conversation between two friends.**

B Hey, Joanie. How are you?

G Hi, Rex! I'm okay, and you?

B I'm fine. I wanted to ask you, what elective should I do this winter?

G Well, I think I am going to do the skiing elective. You should do it, too.

B Wow. That would be fun. I wanted to do that, but it is too expensive. Which elective do you think is second best?

G Maybe the hockey elective. If you have your own equipment, it is only $10 a week.

B Great. I would love to play hockey every Friday for a month. It is also affordable.

G It is too bad you can't do skiing but I think you will have lots of fun playing hockey!

B Me too. Thanks for the help, Joanie. See you later.

Question

What are the students mainly talking about?

(A) What elective to choose

(B) How much the electives cost

(C) Why the boy cannot go skiing

(D) When the boy will play hockey

Explanation

The right choice is (A). The boy asks the girl for advice on what elective to choose. Using **Strategy 1**, we hear the boy ask "What elective should I do?" as his first question. This comes right after the greetings. Using **Strategy 3**, we hear elective choices repeated more than once. The other answer choices are details.

Main Idea

Dictation

Track 68

(S: student, T: teacher)

N **Listen to a conversation between a teacher and a student.**

S Hello, Mr. Wilson. Can I talk to you for a minute?
T Sure, Genie. What can I do for you?
S Well, sir, I wanted to know ① ______________________________ .
T Really! Excellent. First, you need to have good grades. Do you have an 80% average?
S I have a 92% average. ② ____________________ ?
T You need to officially apply to run for presidency. ③ ______________________ ________ . Return it to me when you are finished.
S OK. Is that all?
T No. You need ④ ______________________________ , so you'll need to run a campaign. If you win the vote, you'll be school president.
S Great! Thanks for your help, Mr. Wilson. Bye!
T See you soon, Genie.

Q. What are the speakers mainly talking about?

(A) Presidential campaigns
(B) Running for school president
(C) The school president's grades
(D) Applying to be school principal

Answer Key p. 32~33

Main Idea

Practice Test

Track 69~76

1. What is Jackie's problem?

(A) She caught lice from Dylan.

(B) Her mother is concerned about her.

(C) She might have lice because of Dylan.

(D) She doesn't visit the school nurse often.

2. What does Jackie say about Dylan?

(A) He's now at school.

(B) He visited the nurse last week.

(C) He caught lice from his best friend.

(D) He's been scratching his head a lot.

3. What does the nurse mean when she says "have you shared any brushes or hats with Dylan?"?

(A) She has seen the girl and the boy sharing hats.

(B) She knows the girl could catch lice from these things.

(C) She doesn't believe the girl knows anything about lice.

(D) She is worried about the girl bringing brushes and hats to school.

4. Why does the nurse mention being careful at home?

(A) Jackie can't miss any more school.

(B) There are eggs on Dylan's pillowcase.

(C) Dylan can still spread the lice to Jackie.

(D) Jackie's mother can't take care of both children.

5. What are the two speakers mainly discussing?

(A) Mr. Jackson's science class
(B) Growing a vegetable garden
(C) An idea for the school science fair
(D) How competitive the science fair will be

6. What idea does the boy give to the girl?

(A) She should find a partner.
(B) She should grow vegetables.
(C) She should taste the vegetables.
(D) She should change the plants' soil.

7. What does the girl mean when she says that the boy's vegetable idea is awesome?

(A) He's smarter than she is.
(B) He will be a very helpful partner.
(C) He's never had an awesome idea.
(D) He knows a lot about vegetables.

8. What can be inferred about the boy?

(A) He'll come up with an idea for his own project.
(B) He'll agree to work with the girl on the project.
(C) He'll think of other projects involving vegetables.
(D) He'll ask Mr. Jackson about the science fair's rules.

Answer Key pp. 33~35

Unit 2 Details Questions

Details are specific facts and information found in the listening material you hear between two friends or a student and a school staff member. Your job is to understand the specific details of their conversation.

Details questions start with question words such as *why, where, who, when, which*, or *what*. They are the most common question type on TOEFL Junior. Choose answer choices that match the detailed information best. Details questions are very exact. Use the following helpful hints to answer the example questions.

「Conversation Details」 questions start like this:

- What point do the students make about ~?
- What does the boy / girl say about ~?
- Where does the boy / girl say ~?
- What does the boy / girl want ~?
- What does the girl ask the boy to do?
- What is the boy's main complaint about the teacher?
- Why can't the boy work on the assignment with the girl tonight?

Strategy 1 **Verbatim Answer Choices**

A "verbatim" answer choice is an answer choice that uses the exact same words as the listening material. Answer choices for details questions are often direct facts taken from the conversation. You should only choose an answer choice that repeats almost exactly what a speaker said.

MTJ-I-LC-22
MP3

The following example illustrates details strategies and provides you with one details example question.

Track 77

Example Dialogue Excerpt

(B: boy, G: girl)

N **Listen to a conversation between two friends.**

B Good afternoon, Jessie.

G Afternoon, Joe. How is everything going?

B Pretty good. How about you?

G I'm great. I'm excited for the field trip to the aquarium. **Did you pay for your ticket yet**?

B **Yeah, I did**. I was happy it only cost $10. The regular price is $19.99!

G The school got a good deal because so many students are going.

B How many kids decided to go?

G About fifty out of the seventy five who were old enough to go. It is going to be a lot of fun.

B I know. I can't wait!

Question

What did the students have to pay for?

(A) Their lunch

(B) Their tickets

(C) The bus ride

(D) The souvenirs

Explanation

The right answer is (B). The students had to pay $10 for their tickets. **Strategy 1** says to listen for the same words that are in the conversation. The girl asks the boy "Did you pay for your ticket yet?" The other answer choices are not mentioned in the conversation.

Strategy 2 Note Taking

It is important to take notes because it is difficult to remember all the details you hear in one conversation. Write down any names, dates, places and key phrases you hear from the topic sentence. The notes you take will help you remember details that may later be verbatim answer choices.

The following example illustrates details strategies and provides you with one details example question.

Track 78

Example Dialogue Excerpt

(B: boy, G: girl)

N **Listen to a conversation between two friends.**

B Brianna, hey!

G Hi, Brandon. You look confused. Are you OK?

B I am fine, but I need some help. What rows in the auditorium will the grade nine students sit in during the school play?

G **Your class will be in the back, rows G to I**. Some of your classmates should be there now.

B Really? Okay, great. I will go find them. Thanks, Bri.

G Happy to help. Bye.

Question

Where will the boy sit during the school play?

(A) In rows A to C

(B) In rows D to F

(C) In rows G to I

(D) In rows J to L

Notes
B – confused
grade nine →
school play seats?
G – "Your class in back"
"Rows G-I"

Explanation

The right answer is (C). Using **Strategy 2**, the listener will take notes while listening to the conversation. If the listener takes notes, it will be easier to recall the information.

Strategy 3 **The Details "Zone"**

TOEFL Junior listening has shorter class lessons and conversations. This means most details are in a specific part of a dialogue. A dialogue has greetings, a main idea sentence, the details and the "goodbye." Focus on listening and note taking on the details section.

The following example illustrates details strategies and provides you with one details example question.

Example Dialogue Excerpt

(S: student, T: teacher)

N **Listen to a conversation between a student and a teacher.**

S Morning, Mrs. Jameson. How are you?

T I'm fine, Allen. What can I do for you today?

S I came to ask you what days our art projects are due.

T **The oil paint project is due first on April 7th** and the clay statue is due on the 14th.

S Okay, thanks.

T Happy to help. I'll see you in art class later.

S Yup! Bye, Mrs. Jameson.

Question

What day is the oil paint project due?

(A) April 7th

(B) April 14th

(C) April 21st

(D) April 28th

Explanation

The right answer is (A). The oil paint project is due on the 7th. There is only one sentence that has the detail information. All the other information in the dialogue is either part of the greeting, main idea, or "goodbye." Choice (B) is for the clay project and the other dates, choices (C) and (D), are not mentioned in the conversation.

Details

Conversation Example

Track 80

(T: teacher, S: student)

N **Listen to a conversation between a student and a teacher.**

S Good afternoon, Mr. Smith. Can I talk to you for a minute?

T Sure, Laura. What seems to be the problem?

S I am scared I might have to go to summer school for math.

T Ah, yes. Your grade is only 55% right now. That is a big problem.

S I know. I don't want to go to summer school. I have band camp to go to! I practiced playing the flute all year so I could go and show off my skills.

T Well, I don't want you to miss band camp. I can give you extra practice homework to help you. I will also help you at lunch time if you want.

S Really? That would be a great help. I don't want you to miss your lunch time for me though.

T Well, I want you to become a great flutist. Missing a lunch or two won't hurt.

S OK. I'll come in at lunch and explain what I need help with. Thank you, Mr. Smith!

T Glad to help. See you then, Laura.

Question

How will the teacher help his student with math?

(A) Teach her in summer school

(B) Give her extra practice tests

(C) Pay attention to her in class

(D) Help her during the lunch period

Explanation

The right answer is (D). Mr. Smith says he will give her more practice homework and help her during lunch time. Choices (A) and (C) are incorrect because they are not mentioned in the passage and choice (B) is wrong because the detail is extra homework, not tests.

Details

Dictation

Track 81

(B: boy, G: girl)

N **Listen to a conversation between two friends.**

B Hello, Jenny.

G Hey, Paul. What's up?

B Not much. I am ① ______________________ for our English class. What do you think of it?

G I really don't like it. The story is ② ______________________. What about you?

B I guess that is why I enjoy it. I understand ③ ______________________ ______________.

G I heard the book is very popular with male readers.

B It is about a teenage boy growing up, so I guess it is hard for a girl ④ __________ ______________ a boy does.

G True. That's OK. I've already read next month's book. It's great. Oh, I'm late for my next class. Bye, Paul.

B Cool, see you later.

Q. How does the boy feel about the novel?

(A) He enjoys it.

(B) He doesn't like it.

(C) He thinks it's uninteresting.

(D) He assumes it's not good for a boy.

Answer Key pp. 37~38

Practice Test

Track 82~89

1. Why does the student go to speak to the teacher?

(A) To see when the lab report for the experiment is due

(B) To find out if any other students missed the experiment

(C) To say that she has a stomach problem and can no longer come to class

(D) To explain why she missed the lab experiment and ask if there's another lab session

2. Why did the girl miss the science lab?

(A) She was at the hospital.

(B) She was taking a lunch break.

(C) She was sick with a stomach bug.

(D) She was with Tina, Tara, Ben, and James.

3. Why does Mr. Clemmons talk about Tina, Tara, Ben, and James?

(A) To give an example of students who wrote good reports

(B) To make sure the girl is comfortable with those students

(C) To explain to the girl that many other students had stomach bugs

(D) To tell the girl about the other students who will be at the extra lab

4. What is probably true about the girl?

(A) She's tired of experiments.

(B) She likes science experiments.

(C) She doesn't like Mr. Clemmons.

(D) She writes lab reports every week.

5. Why does the student go to speak with the teacher?

(A) He is concerned about the final exam.
(B) He wants to retake the midterm exam.
(C) He doesn't understand the homework.
(D) He wants to join the Wednesday review sessions.

6. Why can't the teacher let the boy retake the midterm?

(A) She thinks it was easy.
(B) She thinks it is against her class rules.
(C) She already allowed the boy to retake it.
(D) She knows it was given by another teacher.

7. What does the teacher say about the final exam?

(A) It will be easier and shorter than the midterm exam.
(B) It won't be taken by as many students as the midterm exam.
(C) It will be created during the Wednesday review sessions by the students.
(D) The boy can do well if he comes to review sessions and does his homework.

8. What can be inferred about the Wednesday review sessions?

(A) The boy always attends them.
(B) They will be helpful to the boy.
(C) They occur once every other week.
(D) Mrs. LeClaire wants to advertise them.

Answer Key pp. 38~41

Unit 3 Inference Questions

「Inference」 is using known information to come to a conclusion. Using the information that is given, test takers make a good guess about what is true. Test takers decide on an answer using the facts given by a speaker. The answer to an inference question is not always obvious and is never stated directly.

Example (A) All snakes are reptiles.
(B) The King Cobra is a snake. → **The king cobra is a reptile.**
(If king cobras are snakes, and all snakes are reptiles, the king cobra must be a reptile).

This is a very easy example of inference. There are two facts—(A) and (B). From these two facts, it can be concluded that king cobras are reptiles.

Inference questions ask you to use inference to make conclusions about a conversation between two people. They will discuss a school related activity or problem. **Your job is to choose a conclusion that fits best with the information from the listening.** Use the following helpful hints to answer the example questions.

「Conversation Inference」 questions start like this:

- What does boy / girl imply about ~?
- What can be inferred about ~?
- What is probably true about ~?

Strategy 1 Do Not Choose an Answer Quoted from the Listening

If an answer choice is a quote from the listening, do not choose it. The inference you make about the listening is not *in* the listening, so any answer choice quoting the listening is wrong.

This hint is true for both talk and class listening material.

MTJ-I-LC-23
MP3

The following example illustrates inference strategies and provides you with one inference example question.

Track 90

Example Dialogue Excerpt

(B: boy, G: girl)

N **Listen to a conversation between two friends.**

G Evening, Devin. How are you doing?

B I'm pretty good. How about you?

G I'm a little upset. Mr. Azzano wants me to play the flute for the school musical.

B Why is that bad? You are a great flutist. You should do it!

G I want to, but the practices are on the same night as my church youth group.

B I see. Maybe you can stop going to youth group for a few weeks.

G **I could, but I don't really want to**. It is a lot of fun.

B Well, I'm not sure! I need to go to math class, but I can help you later. Bye!

Question

What can be inferred about the girl?

(A) She is a great flutist.

(B) She will talk with Mr. Azzano.

(C) She really likes her youth group.

(D) She will stop going to youth group.

Explanation

The right answer is (C). She could stop going to youth group, but she doesn't want to. She says "it's a lot of fun." Using **Strategy 1**, you'll find that answer (A) is a direct quote from the listening, making it incorrect. There is no evidence for choice (B) or (D).

Strategy 2 Find Evidence

All conversations hold evidence to support one of the answer choices. Use the details, key phrases, solution responses and your notes to choose the correct answer. Every correct inference question answer can be supported by evidence from the dialogue.

The following example illustrates inference strategies and provides you with one inference example question.

Track 91

Example Dialogue Excerpt

(B: boy, G: girl)

N **Listen to a conversation between two friends.**

G James, how are you?

B Hey, Lacey, I'm good. You?

G I couldn't be better. It's almost summer break. What are you doing for it?

B I wanted to go to a summer camp, but my father wants us to travel around the country.

G Traveling the U.S. will be a great experience. Why would you rather go to the camp?

B Most of my friends are going. **I want to do the same thing as them**!

Question

What is probably true about the boy?

(A) He doesn't like traveling.

(B) He is close with his friends.

(C) He will go to summer camp.

(D) He wants to spend time with Lacey.

Explanation

The right answer is (B). Using **Strategy 2**, it can be guessed that the boy is close with his friends based on the idea that he "wants to do the same thing as them." There is no evidence for answers (A), (C), or (D).

Strategy 3 Focus on the Speaker with a Problem

Problem and solution conversations are often followed by inference questions. When you hear this type of conversation, focus on the speaker with a problem. Inference questions usually ask about the problem, speaker's attitudes, feelings, or opinions. Lots of evidence can be found to support a conclusion if you listen to how they respond to the solutions given.

The following example illustrates inference strategies and provides you with one inference example question.

Track 92

Example Dialogue Excerpt

(T: teacher, S: student)

N **Listen to a conversation between a student and teacher.**

T Hi, Madison. How are you doing?

S Not that great. What about you, Mr. Welsh?

T I'm good, but what's wrong? Can I help you in any way?

S **I'm stressed out about exams.** I don't feel like I'm ready to take them.

T That's not good. Have you asked someone to quiz you on important material?

S Yes. **My mother has been testing me every night** after school.

T Well, keep working with your mom. Your grades are high and you work hard. I think you'll be fine.

S Okay. Thanks, Mr. Welsh. See you in class.

Question

What can be inferred about the girl?

(A) She is outgoing.

(B) She is unmotivated.

(C) She is not confident.

(D) She is a bad student.

Explanation

The right answer is (C). Her study habits and grades indicate that she is a strong student, but she is still stressed about the exams. All the evidence that supports choice (C) can be found in the girl's responses.

Conversation Example

Track 93

(T: teacher, S: student)

N **Listen to a conversation between a student and a teacher.**

T Morning, Suzie, how are you?

S Pretty good, but I need help with something, Mr. Wayne.

T How can I help?

S I want to know what theme you think we should choose for the school dance.

T What choices did the student council suggest?

S The two most popular are "Under the Sea" and "Secret Agents."

T "Under the sea" sounds like a beach party. It's January and a little cold out. Also, I think wearing swim suits will break the school dress code.

S You make a good point, but the beach balls would have been fun to play with.

T That is true, but I think everyone will have fun dressing up as spies, too.

S I think you are right. I guess we know which theme we're using now.

T Yeah. I'm just happy it's not "Ancient Rome" themed again.

Question

What can be inferred about the school dance's theme?

(A) It will be "Secret Agent" themed.

(B) It will be "School Dance" themed.

(C) It will be "Ancient Rome" themed.

(D) It will be "Under the Sea" themed.

Explanation

The right answer is (A). They discuss choosing between choice (A) (*Secret Agent*) and choice (D) (*Under the Sea*). They decide that "Under the Sea" is a bad idea, suggesting that they will use the "Secret Agent" theme. They also mention that it will be fun to dress up as spies. Choice (B) is not considered and choice (C) was last year's theme.

Inference

Dictation

Track 94

(ST: student, SE: secretary)

N **Listen to a conversation between a student and a school secretary.**

ST Hi, Mrs. Scott.

SE Hello, Alf. What can I help you with today?

ST Mr. Pierce sent me here ① ______________ .

SE Again? This is the third time this week. What did you do this time?

ST I ② ______________ Kathy West's chair. The class thought it was funny, but Mr. Pierce didn't.

SE No, that is ③ ______________ . Did you say sorry to Kathy?

ST No. I was sent straight here.

SE Well, you ④ ______________ and say sorry. Then come right back here to do your detention.

ST Oh man! Okay, Mrs. Scott. I'll be back in five minutes.

Q. What is probably true about the boy?

(A) He likes Mrs. Scott.

(B) He is in trouble a lot.

(C) He likes to put gum on chairs.

(D) He did something to surprise his parents.

Answer Key p. 43

Inference

Practice Test

Track 95~102

1. What is the guidance counselor explaining to the boy?

(A) Why printmaking is interesting

(B) Why electives are educationally important

(C) What changes can be made to his schedule

(D) How to choose between Mr. Viggers and Mr. Cohan

2. What does the counselor imply about printmaking?

(A) It's less fun than a music class.

(B) It has a very passionate teacher.

(C) It isn't as desirable as a regular art class.

(D) It doesn't have any of Toby's friends in it.

3. What will the speakers probably do next?

(A) Go to printmaking

(B) Change Toby's schedule

(C) Say goodbye to each other

(D) Sign up for next semester's classes

4. Why does the boy need to sign up for next semester's art elective as soon as possible?

(A) It will be taught by Mr. Viggers.

(B) The art elective may fill up quickly.

(C) He's not qualified for the art elective.

(D) He will have to take printmaking again.

5. Why were the speakers awake last night?

(A) They were watching TV.

(B) They were playing a storm game.

(C) They were surprised by bad weather.

(D) They were doing their research about storm.

6. What does the girl suggest about the storm?

(A) She liked it a lot.

(B) It lasted a long time.

(C) There was lots of rain.

(D) She was afraid of it.

7. What happened to the girl's father's truck?

(A) It got crushed by a tree.

(B) It caused a lot of problems.

(C) It hit a car during the storm.

(D) It broke down because of its engine.

8. What will the girl probably do in English class?

(A) Borrow a pen or pencil from the boy

(B) Ask to go home early to help her father

(C) Write about the tree hitting the truck in her journal

(D) Tell Mrs. Williams that she couldn't do her homework

Answer Key pp. 44~46

Unit 4 Prediction Questions

「**Prediction**」 questions ask you to make **an educated guess about what a speaker will say or do in the future**. For example, you can predict a plant will die if it is not watered. Here are more examples:

Action		Prediction
• You put water in the freezer.	→	It will turn to ice.
• You do not do your homework.	→	Your teacher will scold you.

On prediction questions, your job is to choose the correct prediction from the answer choices. A correct prediction is supported by facts from the listening material. Use the following helpful hints to answer the example questions.

「Conversation Prediction」 questions start with sentences like these:

- What will probably happen ~?
- What will the speaker do next?
- What will the speaker say next?

Strategy 1 **General Opinion (Tone and Responses)**

By listening for a speaker's tone and their responses to questions or solutions you can learn how the speaker feels generally about a topic. So, even if a speaker does not directly share their opinion (For example: "I really don't like Mr. Irving's class") you can still make a good prediction based on these other factors.

MTJ-I-LC-24
MP3

The following example illustrates prediction strategies and provides you with one prediction example question.

Track 103

Example Dialogue Excerpt

(B: boy, G: girl)

N **Listen to a conversation between two friends.**

G Hi, John. Nice to see you again!

B Hey, Mary. It has been a while, hasn't it?

G I was going to call you and ask if you are going to take family studies next semester. I want to have a friend in the class.

B Well... that class is mostly girls. **I might not fit in**.

G You have lots of girl friends. It won't be too bad.

B Maybe not, but **I am not very interested in cooking or sewing** either. I also **signed up to take computer science** at that time.

G I see. Maybe Natalie will want to come.

B You should ask her. I just saw her in the library.

G OK. I'll go find her. See you later.

Question

What will probably happen next semester?

(A) The boy will take both classes.

(B) The boy will take neither class.

(C) The boy will take family studies.

(D) The boy will take computer science.

Explanation

The right answer is (D). The boy does not want to be in a class full of girls; he has no interest in the subject, and he has computer class at the same time. These same reasons make (A), (B) and (C) incorrect. Also the speaker's tone (*uncertainty*) and his excuses to not take the class indicate his opinion of family studies is poor.

Chapter 2

Strategy 2 Listen Closely to the Ending

It is important to listen to the last exchange of a conversation because when answering a prediction question, the final exchange is usually the strongest clue to what one of the speakers will do next.

Last exchange example:

G "Well, I have a note from the teacher but why are you here?"

B "Oops! I lost track of time! My math class started five minutes ago!"

With only this last sentence, you can predict the correct answer relates to the boy going to math class.

The following example illustrates prediction strategies and provides you with one prediction example question.

 Track 104

Example Dialogue Excerpt

(B: boy, G: girl)

N **Listen to a conversation between two friends.**

B Hey, Emily.

G Hi, Jordon, how are you?

B Good! I came to find you because I wanted to know if you want to sign up for the school spelling bee with me.

G Me? Spell? I'm a terrible speller.

B You are not that bad. I want someone to go with me. Please come!

G Hmm... I have a piano class on the same day.

B I think you can cancel one piano class.

G I think so, too. I'll just cancel it. Do I need to do anything else to join the competition?

B Yes. **You need to sign up today**. There are **sign-up sheets in any English class**.

G Okay, cool. I have English next period. I think **I'll head to class now**, actually. Bye!

B Yup. See you later.

Question

What will the girl probably do next?

(A) Go to her piano class

(B) Go to class with her friend

(C) Sign up for the spelling bee

(D) Practice for the spelling bee

Explanation

The right answer is (C). She is going to sign up next because she is already going to English class and the due date is today. Choice (A) is wrong because the girl is planning on canceling it. Choice (B) is incorrect because the girl says goodbye at the end of the dialogue. They are not going to English class together. Lastly there are no details to support (D).

Prediction

Conversation Example

(B: boy, G: girl)

N **Listen to a conversation between two friends.**

G Hey, Mark. I didn't know you were in this class!

B I changed class times. How is your day going?

G It's going well. Do you have a partner for the science lab experiments yet?

B No, do you?

G No. We haven't done any group work yet, but next week is the first lab.

B Aren't we supposed to choose partners in class today?

G Yes, we are. That will be good. That way we can start our experiments.

B Yes, I agree. I can't wait.

Question

What will the speakers probably do in their class?

(A) Decide to work alone

(B) Change their class times

(C) Plan to do their homework

(D) Find partners for their experiments

Explanation

The right answer is (D). The students are talking about the fact they will pick partners that day, making answer (D) correct. There is no evidence for answers (A), (B), or (C).

Prediction

Dictation

Track 106

(S: student, C: cook)

N **Listen to a conversation between a student and school cafeteria cook.**

S Hi, Mr. Webb. I've got a question for you.

C Sure, Kelly. What is it? Are you wondering about the menu?

S No, it's not that. I've noticed that many students are throwing away their cans and bottles ① ________________________. That upsets me. Anyway, I'm wondering if you can get the students to start recycling.

C Well, Kelly, the staff at this school has been trying to get the kids to recycle for many years. At this point, we believe ② ________________________.

S Well, I'm a student. Don't you think I can do something?

C Sure! I'm sure if you talk to your friends and classmates ③ __________________, they'll listen to you.

S Hmm... okay... maybe there are other students who feel the same way.

C Exactly. You can work together ④ ________________________________.

S Okay, great idea! Thanks, Mr. Webb.

Q. What will probably happen next?

(A) The cook will try to recycle himself.

(B) The girl will talk to her friends about recycling.

(C) All the students at the school will start recycling.

(D) The cook will come up with a new recycling plan.

Answer Key p. 48

Prediction

Practice Test

Track 107~114

1. What is Amy's problem?

(A) She can't find her bus pass.

(B) Her friend has her bus pass.

(C) The bus pass is too expensive.

(D) She doesn't know the receptionist.

2. What does the bus driver ask Amy to do?

(A) Ask her friend what to do

(B) Always ride the bus without a pass

(C) Get a bus pass from the office by Friday

(D) Put her information in the school computer

3. What is probably true about the bus driver?

(A) He only drives in the morning.

(B) He wants to lend money to Amy.

(C) He has never met the school receptionist.

(D) He has seen students lose their passes before.

4. What is the girl probably going to do after getting to school?

(A) Find $5.00 in her pocket

(B) Call her mother for a ride home

(C) Go to the office to get a new bus pass

(D) Find someone else using her bus pass

5. What are the two students mainly talking about?

(A) The boy's important tennis match

(B) The boy and girl's interest in tennis

(C) The best place to play sports in their town

(D) The amount of time the girl has been playing tennis

6. What does the boy say about playing tennis?

(A) He has never played before.

(B) He used to be part of a team.

(C) He sometimes plays with his brother.

(D) His brother plays tennis for his school.

7. What does the girl mean when she says "Hey, are you doing anything this afternoon?"?

(A) She hopes the boy is busy.

(B) She wants him to come and watch her match.

(C) She expects him to try out for the team today.

(D) She knows the boy has tennis lessons on Tuesday.

8. What will the boy probably do this afternoon?

(A) Join the tennis team

(B) Go to tennis try-outs

(C) Play tennis with his brother

(D) Go to the girl's tennis match

Answer Key pp. 49~51

Unit 5 Rhetorical Device Questions

Rhetoric is the art of speaking with a goal of persuading the listener to think of the topic in a different way.

「Rhetorical Device」 questions ask you why a specific phrase or statement is made and how it was used as rhetoric. **Think about why the speaker is saying what they are saying**. Use the following helpful hints to answer the example questions.

「Conversation Rhetorical Device」 questions start with sentences like this:

- Why does the speaker mention... ?
- Why does the speaker talk about... ?

Strategy 1 **Tone of Voice**

Tone of voice is the most important thing to remember when answering a rhetorical device question. A speaker's tone of voice is the biggest clue to their opinion on a topic. On a rhetorical device question, an answer choice should match the tone of the specific phrase the question is about.

Tone of Voice	Correct Answer Choice
Excited / Interested / Happy	Positive / Agreeable answer
Unsure / Upset / Questioning	Negative / Disagreeable answer

MTJ-I-LC-25
MP3

The following example illustrates rhetorical device strategies and provides you with one rhetorical device example question.

Example Dialogue Excerpt

(B: boy, G: girl)

N **Listen to a conversation between two friends.**

B Hey, Miki.

G Hey, Adam. Where have you been? You're really late.

B I know. Today has been ridiculous.

G Why? What happened?

B Well first, I forgot to set my alarm clock. Then, I missed the bus.

G Is that why you are so late?

B No. My mom said she would drive me to school, but on the way to the car I slipped and fell into a puddle. I was soaked, so I had to go change.

G Wow. You're not having any luck today.

B (*Sarcastically*) **Oh, it gets better**. It looks like I forgot my homework at home too!

G Oh no, and here comes Ms. June to do the homework check!

Question

Why does the boy mention his day getting better?

(A) To show it is an average day

(B) To imply his day is going great

(C) To point out his day is improving

(D) To indicate his day is getting worse

Explanation

The right answer is (D). The boy is already having a difficult day and it becomes worse because he forgot his homework. If the phrase "Oh, it gets better" is used in a positive tone, it really means the day doing very well. A negative tone like Adam's implies the day is going badly.

Strategy 2 **Agreement**

The purpose of a rhetorical device can be found by how often a speaker agrees with the other speaker. If they agree with the ideas and thoughts of the other speaker, then their attitude is positive. If a speaker always disagrees, it is likely their attitude is negative. Choose a correct rhetorical device answer by choosing an answer that fits with the speaker's general attitude.

The following example illustrates rhetorical device strategies and provides you with one rhetorical device example question.

Track 116

Example Dialogue Excerpt

(B: boy, G: girl)

N **Listen to a conversation between two friends.**

G Hi, Peter. Why are you so happy?

B Friday is pizza day! It's the best day of the week.

G I guess you're having pizza for lunch then?

B I sure am. My mom gave me five dollars for lunch. I can buy three pieces of pizza.

G **That's a bit expensive**. You can get a full pizza for $6.99 at the pizza parlor.

B I know, but I can't leave school property.

G You could go after school. **The school pizza slices are small and greasy**. I'd wait and get it after school.

B Thanks for the advice, but I think I will just go eat pizza with everyone else.

Question

Why does the girl mention the size and greasiness of the school pizza?

(A) To indicate it is cheap
(B) To explain why she likes it
(C) To point out how bad it is
(D) To prove it is a healthy lunch

Hint
The girl has a negative attitude towards the school pizza throughout the conversation. Eliminate the answer choices that do not match her negative opinion.

Explanation

The right answer is (C). Calling something small and greasy does not indicate that it is well-liked or healthy, so choices (B) and (D) are poor choices. Secondly, small and greasy do not relate to price, making choice (A) a wrong answer.

Strategy 3 Self References

When a speaker talks about their personal feelings or opinions during a conversation (Example: I think ~, I feel~, I like ~, etc.), note them down. Using personal feelings and opinions is a great way to convince someone to feel the same way you do about a topic (rhetoric). Match their tone (**Strategy 1**) to choose the correct answer choice and their opinions / feelings to their agreeableness (**Strategy 2**).

Example ***Yes*, I also think** it is a good idea we go camping during summer vacation.

→ The speaker agrees (*yes*) and shares his / her opinion (*I also think*) using a positive tone.

The following example illustrates rhetorical device strategies and provides you with one rhetorical device example question.

 Track 117

Example Dialogue Excerpt

(S: student, T: teacher)

N **Listen to a conversation between a student and a teacher.**

T Good afternoon, Joe. Welcome.

S Hi, Mrs. Wells. How are you?

T Fine, thank you. I wanted to know what you thought of the math final.

S I felt there were too many questions. <u>I didn't have time to do them all</u>.

T Really? **I think most students finished early**.

S Maybe they are better at math than I am. I didn't even recognize some of the formulas.

T I'm sorry to hear that. All the formulas were given before the test.

Question

Why does the teacher talk about students finishing the test early?

(A) To tell the boy that he worked quickly

(B) To point out that the boy studied hard

(C) To hint the test was easier for most students

(D) To demonstrate that the test was very difficult

Explanation

The right answer is (C). If the other children finished quickly the test was probably easy for them. The teacher mentions her thoughts about the test. When she does this, she shares important information—to most students, the test was fast and easy.

Rhetorical Device

Conversation Example

Track 118

(T: teacher, S: student)

N **Listen to a conversation between a student and a teacher.**

S Nice to see you again, Mr. Robins.

T You too, Jane. Did you have a good first day of school?

S It was okay, but I was pretty shocked by the student fees when I paid them this morning.

T Yes, the price went up from last year.

S Why did the school do that?

T It wasn't the school's choice. The company that the school uses to print notebooks, planners, and folders raised the prices.

S Well, it's really expensive.

T Well, next time you can get your school supplies from a store.

S I might do that, but I like having supplies with the Fillmore School logo.

T Yes, I understand. It's too bad the prices went up.

S It sure is!

Question

Why does the girl ask about the school's decision to raise student fees?

(A) To understand why the student fees went up

(B) To show how happy she is with the new planners

(C) To argue that the student fee prices shouldn't be raised

(D) To get information about this year's class from the teacher

Explanation

The right answer is (A). The girl asks the teacher ("Why did the school do that?") so that she can understand the rise in price. The teacher goes on to explain why the prices were raised. There is no evidence for answers (B), (C), and (D).

Rhetorical Device

Dictation

Track 119

(B: boy, G: girl)

N **Listen to a conversation between two friends.**

G Morning, Jason.

B Hey, Brittany, how was your morning?

G Good, ① ____________________ I got from the school.

B What does it say?

G It is about the changes to the school dress code. The girls ② ______________ ____________, while the boys can wear whatever they want.

B Really? What are ③ ____________________ ?

G Girls can no longer wear short skirts or shirts that show our shoulders.

B That isn't too bad. What's the big deal?

G I feel like I should wear what I want to.

B ④ ____________________. At least we do not need to wear uniforms to school.

G I guess that is true, but I got to get to gym. See you.

B Bye, Brit.

Q. Why does the girl mention that the boys can wear whatever they want?

(A) To explain why the boys are angry

(B) To argue the dress code is a positive change

(C) To suggest the new dress code is unfair to girls

(D) To explain why girls don't need school uniforms

Answer Key pp. 53~54

Practice Test

Track 120~127

1. What is the teacher explaining to the girl?

(A) When to go see a doctor
(B) Why colds are dangerous
(C) How to avoid getting a cold
(D) Why some people get more colds than others

2. Why does the girl mention that she gets a cold every fall?

(A) To get sympathy from the nurse
(B) To see if she's the only one with the problem
(C) To ask if colds only come during specific seasons
(D) To explain why she wants to protect herself from colds

3. What does the teacher imply about a person's hands?

(A) They should not be placed in pockets.
(B) They are in contact with a lot of germs.
(C) They need to be washed only once a day.
(D) They are the first part of the body to get sick.

4. What does the girl say about her parents?

(A) They often get sick with colds.
(B) They have a close relationship with the school nurse.
(C) They don't take her to the doctor when she has a cold.
(D) They drink a lot of tea and eat healthy foods to cure a cold.

5. Why does the boy go to speak with the girl?

(A) To see if she has roller-skates

(B) To ask her to buy a ticket from him

(C) To ask her to come to the roller-skate night

(D) To ask her to donate money to the eighth grade class

6. Why is the eighth grade hosting a roller-skate night?

(A) To try the new roller-skates

(B) To raise money for their class trip

(C) To give students a good deal on tickets

(D) To have fun with other middle school students

7. What does the girl imply when she asks the boy if the roller-skate rental is expensive?

(A) Her parents will pay for it.

(B) She doesn't have her own skates.

(C) She would rather borrow from a friend.

(D) She's worried the price will prevent her from going.

8. Why does the girl ask about the other seventh graders who are going?

(A) She doesn't want to go with some of them.

(B) She doesn't want to be the only seventh grader.

(C) She doesn't have any friends in the eighth grade.

(D) She doesn't get along with the students in her class.

Answer Key pp. 54~56

Unit 6

Prosody Questions

Prosody is the tone, emphasis, stress and rhythm in speech. Prosody tells us a speaker's emotions when their vocabulary or grammar might not. Prosody is found in any type of spoken sentence. It is also used to express irony and sarcasm. Prosody questions ask you **what a speaker means when they use a specific prosodic phrase**.

On 「**Prosody**」 questions, your job is to show you understand the intended meaning of a prosodic phrase. Use the following helpful hints to answer the example questions.

「Conversation Prosody」 questions start with sentences like this:

- What does the speaker mean when he / she says ~?
- What does the speaker imply when he / she says ~?

Strategy 1 Tone of Voice

Like 「Rhetorical Device」 questions, tone of voice is the most important thing you should think back to when doing prosody questions. A speaker's tone of voice when saying a prosodic phrase is your biggest clue to the correct answer. Their tone lets you eliminate any answer choice that does not match the tone of the phrase.

Tone of Voice	Correct Answer Choice
Excited / Enthusiastic / Happy	Positive / Agreeable answer
Unsure / Worried / Disappointed	Negative / Disagreeable answer

MTJ-I-LC-26
MP3

The following example illustrates prosody strategies and provides you with one prosody example question.

Track 128

Example Dialogue Excerpt

(T: teacher, S: student)

N **Listen to a conversation between a teacher and a student.**

S Hi, Mrs. Biggs. Can I talk to you?

T Of course. What can I help you with?

S I've not finished my English paper. I want to know if I can have an extension.

T It is due tomorrow, Zach. Sorry.

S But, Mrs. Biggs, I had hockey last weekend.

T (*Strictly*) **You had a month to finish**. Have the paper on my desk tomorrow. Goodbye, Zach.

Question

What does the teacher mean when she says "You had a month to finish."?

(A) She thinks the boy plays too much hockey.

(B) She doesn't think the boy's excuse is good.

(C) She will consider giving the boy an extension.

(D) She won't give any more month-long assignments.

Explanation

The right answer is (B). When the teacher says "you had a month to finish," she is saying that having hockey last weekend is not a good excuse. Using **Strategy 1**, the listener should pay attention to the teacher's tone, which is stern and strict. This shows that the correct answer choice will not be a positive one for the boy, making answer (C) incorrect. There isn't any evidence for answers (A) and (D).

Strategy 2 Think about Context

Context is the situation a prosodic phrase is used in. Find the context by asking yourself. Is the topic positive (*good exam score*) or negative (*late for class*)? What is the tone of each speaker (*Positive or negative*)? Use your notes to find other details that support your answer choice.

The following example illustrates prosody strategies and provides you with one prosody example question.

Track 129

Example Dialogue Excerpt

(B: boy, G: girl)

N **Listen to a conversation between two friends.**

B Hi, Selena. What's new?

G Nothing really. You?

B I need a partner for gym today. Do you want to work with me?

G I don't know, Dave; I think Jennifer wants to be on my team. Maybe you should be partners with Nathan.

B That's not a bad idea. Nathan is very good at gym and I like playing basketball with him because he is so tall.

G I would like to play with you, but Jen did ask me first.

B **No big deal**. I'll go see if Nate has a teammate yet.

G Good luck. See you next period.

Question

What does the boy mean when he says "No big deal"?

(A) He's OK not partnering with the girl.

(B) He's sad the girl can't be his partner.

(C) He's happy the girl can't be his partner.

(D) He thinks the girl doesn't want to be his partner.

Explanation

The right answer is (A). "No big deal" means "It's not important." The details suggest he is OK partnering with Nathan. The topic and tones are all positive.

Strategy 3 Watch out for Sarcasm

Sarcasm is saying one thing but meaning the opposite. It is usually used with a negative tone; the tone sounds opposite to the tone usually used with the phrase. When listening, if the tone does not match the normal tone you hear the phrase in, you may be hearing sarcasm.

Example **Normal Tone** *Fantastic! You got an A⁺.*

Sarcastic *Fantastic! I missed the bus.*

The following example illustrates prosody strategies and provides you with one prosody example question.

 Track 130

Example Dialogue Excerpt

(T: teacher, S: student)

N **Listen to a conversation between a teacher and a student.**

T Nicole!

S Yes, Mrs. Ranger?

T (*Yelling*) **What do you think you're doing**?

S Nothing, Mrs. Ranger! Sorry!

T Good. Now, pay attention please.

Question

What does the teacher imply when she says "What do you think you are doing?"?

(A) The student is listening carefully.

(B) The student is doing her class work.

(C) The student is doing something bad.

(D) The student doesn't know what to do.

Explanation

The right answer is (C). The teacher is yelling at the student to stop her bad behavior. The teacher is using sarcasm. She knows what the student is doing (*not listening*). So she asks the student what she is doing sarcastically.

Chapter 2

Prosody

Conversation Example

(S: student, C: school counselor)

N **Listen to a conversation between a student and a school guidance counselor.**

C Welcome, Ray. Have a seat.

S Hi, Ms. Clancy. Am I in trouble?

C No, Ray, you are not. I wanted to ask you if you want to tutor some other students in math.

S I like helping people and it would be a good experience. How many hours a week should I help?

C It's up to you. E-mail any student on this list. If they need help, the two of you can meet.

S Great. So if I get too busy, I can just take on fewer hours?

C Yup. That's right. Any time you spend tutoring will count as your community service hours. You'll need those to graduate.

S Thanks for letting me know about this, Ms. Clancy.

C No problem, Ray. Have a good day.

S Bye!

Question

What does the counselor mean when she says "It's up to you."?

(A) The boy decides who to tutor.

(B) The boy must sign up to tutor.

(C) The boy should tutor up to ten hours.

(D) The boy can choose how much he tutors.

Explanation

The right answer is (D). The expression "It's up to you" means "you can choose." Using **Strategy 2**, we hear the boy ask if he can work fewer hours if he gets too busy. In this context, the boy is choosing how much time he spends tutoring.

Prosody

Dictation

Track 132

(T: teacher, S: student)

N **Listen to a conversation between a teacher and a student.**

S Hi, Mr. Irving. How is your day going?

T Good, Stacey. What can I do for you?

S I wanted to ask you about the score you gave me ① ____________________ .

T Okay, what is your question?

S Well, I think I got this question right, but ② ______________________________ .

T Let me take a look. ③ _________________ ! The answer is right. Sorry about that, Stacey.

S It's OK, Mr. Irving, but ④ ______________________________ please?

T Of course. I'm giving you ⑤ _________________________ for proving me wrong, too!

Q. What does the teacher imply when he says "Look at that!"?

(A) He thinks he was right.

(B) He knows she is wrong.

(C) He is surprised she is correct.

(D) He is angry she saw his mistake.

Answer Key pp. 58~59

Prosody

Practice Test

Track 133~140

1. What is the girl's problem?

(A) She isn't prepared to play against Portland.

(B) She has to miss the game on Friday because of a meeting.

(C) She can't come to today's practice because of her schedule.

(D) She has a dentist appointment at the same time as the big game.

2. What does the girl imply when she says "I thought it was on Monday."?

(A) She confused the day of the game.

(B) She only wants to play on Monday.

(C) She isn't prepared to play on Friday.

(D) She doesn't want to have a game this week.

3. What does the coach mean when he says "I think it's important that you try to make it."?

(A) It is necessary that the girl come to the game.

(B) The team needs the girl for her defensive skills.

(C) The other girls already cancelled their appointments.

(D) He will understand if the girl needs to go to the dentist.

4. What does the girl say about her dentist appointment?

(A) She can't miss it.

(B) She wants to go to it.

(C) She's going to cancel it.

(D) She will move it to Thursday.

5. What are the students mainly discussing?

(A) The Middle Ages

(B) Giving a good presentation

(C) The approval of Mrs. Edwards

(D) The topic for their history project

6. What does the girl mean when she says "Is there anything else we could do it on?"?

(A) She always disagrees with the boy over his ideas.

(B) She's not interested in any part of the Middle Ages.

(C) She wants to find another topic besides knights and armor.

(D) She is willing to do a project on something she isn't interested in.

7. What does the girl want to research?

(A) Why the plague was so deadly

(B) Why knights used such heavy armor

(C) How the plague killed so many children

(D) Why the plague happened only in Europe

8. What does the girl mean when she says "I don't see why not."?

(A) She considers Mrs. Edwards to be easy to please.

(B) She thinks Mrs. Edwards will support their project.

(C) She doesn't think Mrs. Edwards will agree to help them.

(D) She doesn't see why the Middle Ages is a good project idea.

Answer Key pp. 59~61

TOEFL Junior

Actual Test

Actual Test

Track 141~183

Listening Comprehension

The listening section has 42 questions. Follow along as you listen to the directions to the listening section.

Directions

In this section of the test, you will hear a teacher or other school staff member talking to students. Each talk is followed by one question. Choose the best answer to each question and mark the letter of the correct answer on your answer sheet. You will hear each talk only one time.

Here is an example: 

What does the teacher want the students to do?

(A) Choose buddies

(B) Make new friends

(C) Behave on the bus

(D) Empty their backpacks

The correct answer is (A), "Choose buddies."

Here is another example: 

What will the students probably do next?

(A) Find lab partners

(B) Use the microscopes

(C) Explore the supplies

(D) Choose a pair of safety goggles

The correct answer is (D), "Choose a pair of safety goggles."

Go on to the next page, and the test will begin with question number one.

GO ON TO THE NEXT PAGE

PART 1

1. **What is probably true about the teacher?**
   (A) She wants to stay after school to clean the desks.
   (B) She wants students to stop writing on their desks.
   (C) She has tried to destroy the classroom's desks before.
   (D) She would like it if students wrote on their desks with pencil.

2. **What does the principal instruct the students to do?**
   (A) Buy lunch in the cafeteria
   (B) Clean up after they eat lunch
   (C) Talk with the cafeteria workers
   (D) Eat lunch outside on the playground

3. **What is the speaker's purpose?**
   (A) To create a box for the Lost and Found box
   (B) To tell the students to check their backpacks
   (C) To ask students to check the Lost and Found box
   (D) To convince their parents to buy them new clothes

4. **What is the subject of the announcement?**
   (A) The dangers of flu season
   (B) Bringing an insurance card
   (C) Flu shots given by the school
   (D) Where to sign up for flu shots

5. **What is the teacher probably going to do next?**
   (A) Show the students drawings of faces
   (B) Explain how to accurately draw a face
   (C) Show the students a variety of photographs
   (D) Use a student to show measurements of a face

6. **Why does the teacher talk about helping the students?**
   (A) To give students a topic
   (B) To tell students not to worry
   (C) To prove that the library is big
   (D) To warn students about getting lost

GO ON TO THE NEXT PAGE

PART 1

7. What is the teacher mainly talking about?

(A) Good musicians

(B) Trying out for the band

(C) Trumpet and trombone players

(D) How fun it is to play in the band

8. What is probably true about the teacher?

(A) He never gives bad scores.

(B) He is proud of the students.

(C) He hasn't finished correcting tests.

(D) He expected the students to do better.

9. What does the principal instruct the students to do?

(A) Buy pizza

(B) Eat lunch outside

(C) Plant flowers and trees

(D) Bring snacks to the party

10. What are the students probably going to do next?

(A) Talk about fruit

(B) Draw pictures of fruit

(C) Hang up their pictures

(D) Ask the teacher questions

GO ON TO THE NEXT PAGE

Answer Key pp. 62~66

PART 1

Now you will hear some conversations. Each conversation is followed by three or more questions. Choose the best answer to each question and mark the letter of the correct answer on your answer sheet. You will hear each conversation only one time.

11. Why does the student go to speak with the librarian?

(A) He needs help with a paper.

(B) He left his books in the library.

(C) He needs help with the computer.

(D) The librarian knows about the Civil War.

12. What does the librarian imply when she says "You're lucky that these books weren't put back on the shelf."?

(A) Jesse is generally a lucky student.

(B) Books left in the library are usually put away.

(C) She doesn't think Jesse is an organized student.

(D) Books on the Civil War are not often loaned from the library.

13. Why does the boy talk about what his books looked like?

(A) To help the librarian find his books

(B) To complain about Mr. Anderson's library skills

(C) To tell the librarian that his books were interesting

(D) To discuss the reasons why he doesn't usually study

14. What does the librarian ask the boy to do?

(A) Leave the books on the desk

(B) Return the books in three weeks

(C) Remember to take his books with him

(D) Wait a few days before speaking with Mr. Anderson

GO ON TO THE NEXT PAGE

PART 1

15. What are the speakers mainly talking about?

(A) Making videos for contests

(B) The biology of the animals in Hawaii

(C) The video cameras owned by the school

(D) The boy entering a junior biology contest

16. What does the teacher say about the contest's prize?

(A) It is a new video camera.

(B) It will be given to many students.

(C) It includes a one-week trip to Hawaii.

(D) It will change depending on the video.

17. What does the boy imply when he says "Okay, I think I can handle it."?

(A) He's never used a camera before.

(B) He will borrow a camera from a friend.

(C) He believes he can take care of a camera.

(D) He always borrows cameras from the school.

18. What will the speakers probably do next?

(A) Plan a trip to Hawaii

(B) Write a script for the boy's movie

(C) Discuss how to use a video camera

(D) Talk more about the contest and its rules

GO ON TO THE NEXT PAGE

Answer Key pp. 66~69

PART 1

19. What are the students mainly talking about?

(A) Mr. Brooklyn's unfair system of grading

(B) A difficult test that may lead to bad grades

(C) How much they study for Mr. Brooklyn's class

(D) Asking their friends from class about the difficulty of the exam

20. What does the boy say about the test?

(A) It was taken in the cafeteria.

(B) It was easier than he expected.

(C) It probably wasn't written by Mr. Brooklyn.

(D) It was full of things that weren't studied in class.

21. What will the students probably do next?

(A) Talk with Mr. Brooklyn

(B) Say goodbye to each other

(C) Take the test in the cafeteria

(D) Talk to their friends about the test

22. Why does the girl talk about the last test being easy?

(A) To show that she doesn't like the class

(B) To explain why Mr. Brooklyn's test was hard

(C) To prove that she studied more than the boy

(D) To give an example of a time when she got an A^+

GO ON TO THE NEXT PAGE

PART 1

23. What is the boy's problem?

(A) He is afraid to take the test.

(B) He can't meet on Tuesday after school.

(C) He wants to tell other students about the test.

(D) He has a doctor's appointment during the test.

24. What does the teacher say about taking the test early?

(A) The boy should study hard.

(B) The test will be more difficult.

(C) The classmates will take it early too.

(D) The boy can't tell his classmates about it.

25. What is probably true about the boy?

(A) He is trusted by the teacher.

(B) He is lying about his appointment.

(C) He isn't friends with his classmates.

(D) He hurt himself while playing sports.

26. What will the boy probably do after school?

(A) Send an e-mail to Mr. Jordan

(B) Cheat on the test with his friends

(C) Change his doctor's appointment

(D) Study for the test that he'll take on Tuesday

GO ON TO THE NEXT PAGE

Answer Key pp. 69~71

PART 1

Now you will hear some talks and discussions about academic topics. Each talk or discussion is followed by four or more questions. Choose the best answer to each question and mark the letter of the correct answer on your answer sheet. You will hear each talk or discussion only one time.

27. What are the teacher and student mainly talking about?

(A) A growing American middle-class

(B) How the Industrial Revolution changed America

(C) The growth and development of America throughout history

(D) How and why Americans moved from the country to the city

28. Why does the teacher mention the American middle class?

(A) To explain why it moved all over the country

(B) To prove that it started the Industrial Revolution

(C) To show that the Industrial Revolution affected it

(D) To suggest that it was not affected by this change

29. According to the teacher, what was an effect of the Industrial Revolution?

(A) Americans became more like Europeans.

(B) People didn't use many electrical appliances.

(C) People moved from the countryside to the cities.

(D) Goods were machine-made and therefore more expensive.

30. What can be inferred about the development of cars and trains?

(A) It isn't something the girl has studied before.

(B) It happened in a unique and new way in America.

(C) It would have occurred without the use of machines.

(D) It wouldn't have been possible without the Industrial Revolution.

GO ON TO THE NEXT PAGE

PART 1

31. What is the speaker mainly talking about?

(A) Huckleberry Finn's friendship with a slave named Jim

(B) The background of Mark Twain's *Adventures of Huckleberry Finn*

(C) The Mississippi River's influence on *Adventures of Huckleberry Finn*

(D) The characters in Mark Twain's *Adventures of Huckleberry Finn*

32. According to the teacher, what is special about *Adventures of Huckleberry Finn?*

(A) It was published in 1885.

(B) It uses vernacular language.

(C) It was written by Mark Twain.

(D) It was written after slavery ended.

33. Why does the teacher talk about the Mississippi River?

(A) To explain where the book takes place

(B) To show how the boys get into trouble

(C) To help students understand why Huck runs away

(D) To prove that traveling on the river is an adventure

34. What does the speaker want the students to think about as they read?

(A) Why Mark Twain wrote this book

(B) What Huckleberry Finn's overall goal is

(C) Why Huckleberry Finn becomes friends with Jim

(D) How Mark Twain deals with slavery and racism

GO ON TO THE NEXT PAGE

Answer Key pp. 71~74

PART 1

35. What are the teacher and student mainly talking about?

(A) The story of Pythagoras' life

(B) How to use the Pythagorean Theorem

(C) Pythagoras' ideas and his religious followers

(D) Why Pythagoras is important to their math class

36. Which of the following is true about Pythagoras?

(A) He didn't have many followers.

(B) He lived in Ancient Rome in the 6th century.

(C) He came up with a way to measure triangles.

(D) Historians and mathematicians know a lot about his life.

37. What does the teacher say about Pythagoras' life?

(A) It was very long.

(B) There's a lot of information about it.

(C) It was filled with many important discoveries.

(D) It wasn't written about while he was alive.

38. What does the teacher imply about the Pythagoras theorem?

(A) It has changed over the years.

(B) It is only helpful when measuring triangles.

(C) It is not usually taught in geometry classes.

(D) It won't be too difficult for the students to learn.

GO ON TO THE NEXT PAGE

PART 1

39. What is the main topic of the talk?

(A) Places where squirrels live

(B) How squirrels survive in winter

(C) Surprising information about common squirrels

(D) Why squirrels are related to chipmunks and woodchucks

40. What false belief about squirrels does the teacher correct?

(A) That they live in trees

(B) That they are great climbers

(C) That they are very closely related to mice

(D) That they are unique creatures who eat seeds

41. What can be inferred from the talk about squirrels?

(A) They usually live in suburban streets.

(B) They are closely related to mice and rats.

(C) They compete with rabbits to eat green leaves.

(D) They are willing to eat unusual foods to survive.

42. According to the teacher, why are squirrels great climbers?

(A) They are very fast.

(B) They have useful thumbs.

(C) They have strong legs and claws.

(D) They have 4 or 5 toes on each foot.

Answer Key pp. 74~78

Improving Skills and Knowledge for the TOEFL Junior Test

Master TOEFL Junior

Intermediate

1

Transcripts and Answer Key
정답 및 해설

Listening Comprehension

Each book in the *Master TOEFL Junior* series includes a carefully researched and detailed guide to each part of the TOEFL Junior Test. This series was designed to give test-takers the skills and knowledge needed to obtain a high score on the TOEFL Junior Test administered by ETS.

Master TOEFL Junior

Intermediate

1

Transcripts and Answer Key

정답 및 해설

Listening Comprehension

Sample

Listen to a teacher speaking to her students.

W Good morning, class. I hope you're all excited for today's trip to the Hunting Park Zoo. The school bus will be arriving in 20 minutes, so I'd like you all to choose a buddy while we wait. You and your buddy need to stay together all day so that you can look out for each other. We wouldn't want anyone getting lost!

번역 **선생님이 학생들에게 하는 얘기를 들으세요.**

여 안녕하세요 여러분. 여러분 모두 오늘 헌팅턴 공원 동물원으로의 현장 학습에 대해 기대하고 있기를 바랍니다. 학교 버스는 20분 안에 도착할 텐데요, 기다리는 동안 짝을 고르세요. 서로 잘 챙길 수 있도록 하루 동안 여러분과 여러분의 짝이 함께 지낼 겁니다. 길을 잃는 학생이 나오길 바라지 않으니까요.

선생님은 학생들에게 무엇을 하기를 원하나요?

(A) 짝을 골라라.

(B) 새로운 친구를 사귀어라.

(C) 버스 안에서 바르게 행동해라.

(D) 가방을 비워라.

Listen to a science teacher talking to his students.

M Okay, this section of the lab is where we keep our supplies. On the right you'll see the microscopes and scales, which we'll use fairly often. This table is where we keep the safety goggles, which are perhaps the most important things in the lab. Please take a pair. You'll need to use them today.

번역 **과학 선생님이 학생들에게 하는 얘기를 들으세요.**

남 좋아요, 실험실에서 이곳은 우리 장비를 보관해 두는 곳입니다. 오른쪽에는 현미경과 큰 저울이 있는데, 우리가 꽤 자주 사용하게 될 겁니다. 이 탁자에는 안전 보호 안경을 놔두는데, 아마도 실험실에서 가장 중요한 장비일 겁니다. 하나씩 가지세요. 오늘 여러분들은 이것들을 사용하게 될 겁니다.

학생들은 다음에 무엇을 할까요?

(A) 실험실 파트너를 구한다.

(B) 현미경을 사용한다.

(C) 장비를 살펴본다.

(D) 안전 보호 안경을 고른다.

Diagnostic Test

1. (A) 2. (B) 3. (D) 4. (D) 5. (C) 6. (D) 7. (C) 8. (D) 9. (D) 10. (D) 11. (D) 12. (C) 13. (B)

1 Listen to a teacher talking to a science class.

M Class, please come to the school science fair this Thursday. The science fair is put on by the eighth grade students every year. The eighth graders work on their projects for three or four months. The fair will be open during recess, lunchtime, and after school. There are always fascinating projects. Stop by and take a look.

번역 선생님이 과학반 학생들에게 하는 말을 들으세요.

남 여러분, 이번 주 목요일에 교내 과학 전시회에 오세요. 과학 전시회는 매년 8학년 학생들이 수행합니다. 8학년 학생들은 3~4개월 간 프로젝트 작업을 합니다. 전시회는 쉬는 시간, 점심 시간, 그리고 방과 후에 개방됩니다. (전시회에는) 늘 멋진 프로젝트들이 나오니까, 잠시 들러서 구경하도록 하세요.

1. 선생님은 학생들에게 무엇을 하라고 지시하나요?

(A) 과학 전시회에 와라.

(B) 8학년 학생들과 얘기하라.

(C) 3~4개월 간 일하라.

(D) 과학 프로젝트 작업에 공들여 일하라.

fair 전시회, 박람회 **put on** (연극, 쇼 등을) 무대에 올리다 **recess** 휴식 시간 **fascinating** 대단히 흥미로운, 매력적인 **stop by** ~에 잠시 들르다

정답 및 해설 **[세부사항을 묻는 문제]** 선생님이 학생들에게 이번 주 목요일에 있을 과학 전시회에 대해 안내하는 내용이다. 전시회에 대해 소개한 후, 마지막에 "잠시 들러서 구경해 보라(Stop by and take a look.)"면서 학생들에게 '과학 전시회에 올 것'을 지시하고 있다. 따라서 정답은 (A)이다.

2 Listen to a hockey coach talking to his team.

M Boys, don't get upset. I know we're losing by 2, but we can beat Brooksly. I think you're playing lazily. You're not trying hard. Maybe this is because we beat this team the last time we played them. You are a better team than Brooksly, so you can win this game. Be excited! This is our game.

번역 하키 코치가 팀 선수들에게 하는 말을 들으세요.

남 선수들, 실망하지 마라. 우리 팀이 지금 2점 뒤지긴 했지만, 우리는 Brooksly 팀을 이길 수 있다. 내 생각엔 여러분들이 지금 너무 태만하게 경기를 하는 것 같다. 열심히 하고 있지 않아. 아마도 지난번 경기에서 우리가 이 팀을 이겼기 때문이겠지. 너희들은 Brooksly보다 더 뛰어난 팀이니까, 우리가 이길 수 있다. 힘내도록! 이건 우리 경기이다.

2. 지난번 Brooksly와의 경기에 대해 무엇을 추론할 수 있나요?

(A) 경기에 졌다.

(B) 쉽게 이겼다.

(C) 재미있는 경기가 아니었다.

(D) 반칙이 많았다.

beat (게임, 시합에서) 이기다 **lazily** 게을리, 태만하게

정답 및 해설 **[추론 문제]** 하키 코치가 경기 중 2점 차로 지고 있는 팀을 격려하고 있다. 코치는 태만하게 경기하고 있다고 말하면서 "아마 지난번 시합에서 우리가 Brooksly 팀을 이겼기 때문인 것 같다(Maybe this is because we beat this team the last time we played them.)"고 한다. 이를 볼 때 Brooksly 팀과의 지난 시합에서 '쉽게 이겼음'을 추론할 수 있다. 따라서 정답은 (B)이다. (A)는 정답과 반대되는 내용이므로 오답이고, (C)와 (D)는 언급되지 않았다.

3 Listen to a teacher talking to her class.

W During next week's trip to the public library, we're going to go to the history section so that you can find some books for your research project. The history section is divided into many different parts: there's American history, European history, Asian history, and all sorts of other histories. You should be able to find the sources that you're looking for.

번역 선생님이 반 학생들에게 하는 말을 들으세요.

여 다음 주 공공 도서관 견학을 가게 되면 여러분들 연구 프로젝트에 필요한 책을 찾을 수 있도록 역사 서적 코너로 가게 될 거예요. 역사 서적 코너는 미국 역사, 유럽 역사, 아시아 역사, 그리고 기타 모든 역사를 다루는 다양한 부분들로 나뉘어져 있습니다. 여러분들이 원하는 자료들을 찾을 수 있을 겁니다.

3. 이야기의 목적은 무엇인가요?
(A) 도서관이 크다는 것을 증명하는 것
(B) 학생들이 길을 잃어버리지 않도록 경고하는 것
(C) 학생들에게 쓰기에 관한 방법을 알려 주는 것
(D) 학생들이 어디에서 책을 찾을 수 있는지 설명하는 것

public library 공공 도서관 be divided into ~로 나뉘어지다 source 자료, 자료의 출처

정답 및 해설 **[화자의 의도를 묻는 문제]** 선생님이 학생들에게 다음 주에 있을 도서관 견학에 대해 말하고 있다. "역사 서적 코너로 가서 여러분들의 연구 프로젝트를 위한 책을 찾을 수 있을 것(~ you can find some books for your research project.)"이라고 했고, 마지막에 "여러분이 찾고자 하는 자료를 찾을 수 있을 것(You should be able to find the sources that you're looking for.)"이라고 다시 한번 말하고 있다. 따라서 정답은 (D)이다. (A), (B), (C)는 언급되지 않았다.

4 Listen to a museum volunteer talking to students.

W If you've enjoyed today's presentation at our planets and stars exhibit, then I think you should come to our sky viewing nights on Fridays. On these nights, we use the museum's telescopes to get a good look at stars, planets, and the moon. The viewing nights happen every Friday and they take place on the roof. You can't get there by yourself though. You'll have to go with a staff member.

번역 박물관 자원봉사자가 학생들에게 하는 말을 들으세요.

여 여러분들이 오늘 우리 행성과 별 전시에서의 프레젠테이션을 재미있게 봤다면 금요일 밤마다 열리는 밤하늘 관측의 밤에도 와보라고 권하고 싶군요. 금요일 밤마다 박물관 망원경을 사용해 별과 행성, 그리고 달을 관측합니다. 매주 금요일 밤, 지붕 위에서 열립니다. 물론 여러분 혼자서는 갈 수 없습니다. 직원 한 명과 동행해야 합니다.

4. 박물관 자원봉사자는 다음에 무엇을 하게 될까요?
(A) 학생들과 함께 별을 본다.
(B) 학생들에게 어디서 점심을 살 수 있는지 말한다.
(C) 학생들에게 새 천체 투영관을 보여 준다.
(D) 학생들이 왜 직원과 함께 가야 하는지 설명한다.

presentation 프레젠테이션, (작품 등에 관한) 발표; 공연, 상연 planet 행성 exhibit 전시품 telescope 망원경

정답 및 해설 **[예측 문제]** 박물관 자원봉사자가 학생들에게 금요일 밤 밤하늘 관측 행사에 올 것을 권장하면서 마지막에 "직원과 함께 가야 한다(You'll have to go with a staff member.)"고 말하고 있다. 때문에 이어서 '왜 그들이 직원과 함께 가야만 하는지를 설명할 것'임을 예측할 수 있다. 따라서 정답은 (D)이다. (A)의 '학생들과 함께 별을 본다'는 이미 소개한 내용이고, (B)와 (C)는 언급되지 않았으므로 오답이다.

5 Listen to a music teacher talking to a group of students.

M You've all shown interest in playing music and I know that it's important to all of you. That's why I want you to try out for the Salem Junior Orchestra next month. The orchestra is for middle school students. It meets twice a week during the school year. The orchestra has three or four performances a year and offers a great opportunity for young musicians like you.

번역 음악 선생님이 몇몇 학생들에게 하는 얘기를 들으세요.

남 여러분들 모두 음악 연주에 흥미를 보였고 저 역시 이게 여러분 모두에게 중요하다는 걸 압니다. 그래서 여러분들이 다음 달에 있는 Salem Junior 오케스트라에 한번 응시해보기를 원하는 겁니다. 이 오케스트라는 중학생들에게 해당하며, 학기 중에 일주일에 두 번씩 모입니다. 한 해에 서너 차례 공연을 하며 여러분 같은 어린 음악가들에게 아주 좋은 기회를 제공해 줍니다.

5. 선생님은 주로 무엇에 대해 얘기하고 있나요?
(A) 음악 애호가가 되기
(B) 일주일에 두 번씩 연습하기
(C) 오케스트라에 응시해보기
(D) 공연에 관심을 가지기

try out (팀원 선발 등을 위한 시험에) 응시하다, 지원하다 performance 공연 offer an opportunity 기회를 제공하다

정답 및 해설 [주제를 묻는 문제] 음악 선생님이 학생들에게 "너희들 모두 음악 연주에 흥미를 보여왔다(You've all shown interest in playing music ~)"고 말한 뒤 "다음 달에 있을 Salem Junior 오케스트라에 한번 응시해보길 원한다(~ I want you to try out for the Salem Junior Orchestra next month.)"고 한다. 이어서 오케스트라에 대해 자세히 설명하고 있다. 따라서 정답은 (C)이다.

[6-9] Listen to a conversation between two students as they leave a classroom. (B: boy, G: girl)

B Hi, Abby. How are you?
G I'm great, John. How are you doing?
B I'm fine. I was wondering what you thought about the field trip to Tuck's Point that Mr. Horowitz mentioned today.
G I think it sounds like a great trip. Why? What do you think?
B Well, I think it sounds like a great trip, too, but Mr. Horowitz said there are a limited number of spots. I'm worried that I might not get to go.
G That's true, but he also said that the spots will go to the students who write the best essays on why they want to go. You're one of the best writers in our class. I'm sure you'll get a spot.
B Maybe, but there are a lot of other good writers.
G Listen, John, I really don't think you need to worry. It's true there are other writers, but some of them might not want to go on the field trip.
B I think everyone will want to go. It sounds like such a good trip.
G I'm not so sure. Mr. Horowitz said that the trip would require a lot of additional work. I think many students are busy and don't want to work on extra assignments.
B Okay, I guess you're right. Maybe I do have a good chance of getting a spot on the trip.
G Of course you do! Now start writing your essay!

번역 두 학생이 교실을 나서며 나누는 대화를 들으세요.

남 안녕 Abby. 잘 지내니?
여 잘 지내 John. 너는 어때?
남 좋아. 오늘 Horowitz 선생님이 말씀하신 Tuck's Point로 견학 여행 가는 거에 대해 넌 어떻게 생각해?
여 멋진 여행이 될 것 같아. 왜? 너는 어떻게 생각하는데?
남 음, 나도 멋진 학습이 될 것 같긴 한데, Horowitz 선생님이 자리가 한정될 거라고 하셨잖아. 내가 못 갈까 봐 걱정 돼.
여 그렇긴 해. 하지만 선생님께서 왜 가고 싶은지에 대한 에세이를 제일 잘 쓴 학생들한테 자리가 갈 거라고도 하셨잖아. 너는 우리 반에서 글을 제일 잘 쓰는 애들 중 하나니까 너한테 틀림없이 자리가 날 거야.
남 그럴지도. 하지만 글을 잘 쓰는 애들은 많아.
여 있잖아, John. 난 정말이지 네가 걱정할 필요가 없다고 생각해. 다른 애들도 글을 잘 쓰는 건 사실이지만 그 중에 어떤 애들은 현장 학습에 가고 싶어 하지 않을 수도 있잖아.
남 내 생각엔 다들 가고 싶어 할 것 같아. 재미있는 학습이 될 것 같으니까 말이야.
여 난 잘 모르겠어. Horowitz 선생님께서 현장 학습에 여러 가지 별도의 작업들이 필요할 거라고 하셨잖아. 내 생각엔 바쁜 애들도 많고 추가 과제를 하기 싫어하는 애들도 많을 거야.
남 알겠어, 네 말이 맞아. 아마도 내가 견학 여행에 한 자리를 차지할 가능성이 높을 것 같아.
여 당연하지! 자 이제 작문 쓰기를 시작해!

field trip 견학 여행, 현장 학습 limited 한정된, 제한된 require 요구하다 additional 추가의 extra 추가의, 가외의
have a good chance 가능성이 있다, 좋은 기회를 갖다

6. 학생들은 주로 무엇에 관해 얘기하고 있나요?

(A) Horowitz 선생님의 어려운 숙제
(B) 여학생의 여행 참여 결정
(C) 학급에서 가장 재능 있는 작가인 남학생
(D) Tuck's Point로 가는 여행에 대해 걱정하는 남학생

정답 및 해설 **[주제를 묻는 문제]** 두 학생이 Tuck's Point로의 견학에 대해 나누는 대화이다. 남학생은 견학에 가고 싶으나 "자리가 한정되어 있어서 못 갈 것 같아 걱정이 된다(~ there are a limited number of spots. I'm worried that I might not get to go.)"고 말하자, 여학생은 남학생이 갈 수 있을 것이라고 격려해주고 있다. 따라서 핵심어인 'Tuck's Point 견학'과 '남학생의 걱정'을 포함한 (D)가 정답이다.

7. 남학생은 여행에 관해 무슨 말을 하나요?

(A) 아무도 가려고 하지 않을 것이다.
(B) Horowitz 선생님은 가지 않을 것이다.
(C) 자리가 많지 않다.
(D) 여학생이 함께 가지 않는다면 별로 좋지 않을 것이다.

정답 및 해설 **[세부사항을 묻는 문제]** 남학생은 "나도 멋진 견학일 것이라고 생각한다. 하지만 Horowitz 선생님이 자리가 한정되어 있다고 했다(I think it sounds like a great trip, too, but, Mr. Horowitz said there are a limited number of spots.)"고 말한다. 따라서 정답은 (C)이다. (A), (B), (D)는 내용과 다르거나 언급되지 않았으므로 오답이다.

8. 남학생의 다음 말은 무엇을 의미하나요? *(Maybe, but there are a lot of other good writers.)*

(A) 자신이 글을 무척 잘 쓰는지 잘 모르겠다.
(B) 여학생이 자신보다 글을 더 잘 쓴다고 생각한다.
(C) 다른 학생들이 긴장할 거라고 생각하지 않는다.
(D) 다른 학생들이 더 좋은 에세이를 쓸 거라고 생각한다.

정답 및 해설 **[화자의 어조를 묻는 문제]** 이 말은, 여학생이 남학생에게 "너는 우리 반에서 글을 제일 잘 쓰는 애들 중 하나니까 분명 자리를 얻을 것이다(You're one of the best writers in our class. I'm sure you'll get a spot.)"라고 격려한 말에 대한 답이다. 이런 상황에서 볼 때 '남학생은 다른 학생들이 더 좋은 에세이를 쓸 것이라고 믿는다'고 추론할 수 있다. 따라서 정답은 (D)이다.

9. 남학생은 방과 후에 무엇을 하게 될까요?

(A) 부모님과 함께 Tuck's Point를 방문한다.
(B) 여학생에게 에세이 쓰는 것을 도와달라고 부탁한다.
(C) Horowitz 선생님께 자신이 걱정하는 일에 관해 이메일을 보낸다.
(D) 자신이 Tuck's Point에 가고 싶은 이유에 대한 에세이를 쓰기 시작한다.

정답 및 해설 **[예측 문제]** 여학생은 남학생에게 "너는 우리 반에서 에세이를 가장 잘 쓰는 학생 중 하나(You're one of the best writers in our class.)"이고, "많은 학생들이 바빠서 추가 과제를 하고 싶지 않을 것이다(~ don't want to work on extra assignments.)"고 말한다. 남학생은 이 말을 듣고 자신이 견학에 갈 수 있을 것 같다고 생각하게 된다. 마지막에 여학생이 "이제 에세이 쓰기를 시작하라(Now start writing your essay!)"라고 말한 것을 볼 때 남학생은 'Tuck's Point에 가고 싶은 이유에 대한 에세이를 쓰기 시작할 것'이라고 예측할 수 있다. 따라서 정답은 (D)이다.

[10-13] Listen to a conversation between a student and a teacher. (S: student, T: teacher)

S Hi, Miss Jenkins.
T Hi, Eliza. How can I help you today?
S Well, I wanted to ask if you'd be interested in helping with a new singing group I'm starting.
T Okay, what kind of help do you need?
S Since it's a student club, we need a teacher to sponsor us. That means a teacher has to make sure we're doing good things. You don't have to come to all our meetings... I know you're busy... but you're welcome to come if you want.

번역 **학생과 선생님과의 대화를 들으세요.**

학생 안녕하세요, Jenkins 선생님.
교사 안녕, Eliza. 오늘은 뭘 도와줄까?
학생 저, 선생님께서 제가 시작하는 새로운 노래 동아리 일에 도움을 주실 수 있는지 여쭤보려고요.
교사 좋아, 어떤 도움이 필요하니?
학생 이게 학생 동아리라서 저희를 후원해주실 선생님이 필요해요. 그러니까 선생님께서 저희가 일을 제대로 하고 있는지 확인해 주시면 됩니다. 저희 모임에 매번 참석하실 필요는 없어요. 선생님께서 바쁘신 걸 아니까요. 하지만 오시고 싶으면 언제든 환영이에요.

T Hmm... well, I'd love to help you out, but I want more information about your singing group. Do you think you could write me an e-mail with all the details?
S Sure, of course I can.
T If I have all the details about the group, then I'll feel more comfortable sponsoring you.
S That's fair. I'll send you an e-mail tonight.
T Thanks, Eliza.

교사 음, 글쎄다. 선생님이 도와주고 싶다만, 그러려면 너희 노래 동아리에 관해 좀더 정보가 필요하구나. 구체적인 내용을 담은 이메일을 써서 보내줄 수 있겠니?
학생 네, 그럼요.
교사 너희 동아리에 대한 세부사항을 알게 되면 너희를 도와주는 게 좀더 편할 것 같구나.
학생 맞는 말씀이세요. 오늘밤에 이메일을 보내겠습니다.
교사 고맙다, Eliza.

singing group 노래 동아리 **sponsor** 후원하다, 지원하다; 후원자 **details** 세부 사항 **fair** 타당한; 공평한, 올바른

10. 여학생의 문제는 무엇인가요?
(A) 이메일 계정이 없다.
(B) 노래 동아리에 음악 선생님이 필요하다.
(C) 친구들이 노래 동아리에 들어오고 싶어 하지 않는다.
(D) 자신의 노래 동아리를 후원해 줄 선생님이 필요하다.

정답 및 해설 **[주제를 묻는 문제]** 학생이 선생님께 노래 동아리 후원자가 되어 줄 것을 부탁하는 대화이다. 대화의 앞부분에 학생이 "선생님께서 새로 시작하는 노래 동아리를 돕는 일에 흥미가 있는지 여쭤보러 왔다(**I wanted to ask if you'd be interested in helping with a new singing group I'm starting.**)"라고 말한다. 또한 "학생 동아리이기 때문에 후원해 줄 선생님이 있어야 한다(**Since it's a student club, we need a teacher to sponsor us.**)"고 했다. 따라서 정답은 (D)이다.

11. 선생님은 여학생에게 무엇을 하라고 하나요?
(A) 다른 선생님에게 노래 동아리를 후원해달라고 부탁해라.
(B) 노래 동아리에 가입할 다른 회원들을 좀더 찾아봐라.
(C) 선생님에게 미리 콘서트 날짜를 알려달라.
(D) 이메일로 노래 동아리에 관한 정보를 보내라.

정답 및 해설 **[세부사항을 묻는 문제]** 선생님은 학생의 부탁에 "노래 동아리에 대한 더 자세한 정보를 원한다(**~ I want more information about your singing group.**)"고 말하면서 "모든 세부사항에 대한 이메일을 보내줄 수 있겠냐(**Do you think you could write me an e-mail with all the details?**)"고 물었다. 그러므로 정답은 (D)이다. (A), (B), (C)는 대화에서 언급되지 않았다.

12. 선생님은 노래 동아리를 돕는 일에 관해 무엇을 암시하나요?
(A) 먼저 교장 선생님에게 얘기할 필요가 있다.
(B) 자신은 교사로서 학생 동아리를 도와 준 적이 없다.
(C) 노래 동아리에 대해 더 알게 되기 전에는 도우려고 하지 않을 것이다.
(D) 노래 동아리의 다른 회원들을 만나 보기를 원한다.

정답 및 해설 **[추론 문제]** 선생님은 세부사항에 대한 이메일을 보내 줄 것을 요청한 후 "동아리에 대한 모든 세부사항을 알게 되면 너희를 후원하는 일이 좀더 편할 것 같다(**If I have all the details about the group, then I'll feel more comfortable sponsoring you.**)"라고 말한다. 이를 볼 때 선생님은 '동아리에 대해 더 자세히 알기까지는 기꺼이 도와주려고 하지 않을 것'이라고 추론할 수 있다. 따라서 정답은 (C)이다.

13. 여학생이 선생님에게 모든 모임에 참여할 필요는 없다고 말한 이유는 무엇인가요?
(A) 선생님이 너무 바빠서 도움을 줄 수 없다는 것을 증명하려고
(B) 선생님이 해야 할 일이 많지 않다는 점을 설명하려고
(C) 노래 동아리를 돕는 데 시간이 많이 든다는 것을 보여주려고
(D) 노래 동아리에서 선생님으로부터 무엇을 얻고자 하는지 예를 하나 들려고

정답 및 해설 **[수사학적 구조를 묻는 문제]** 학생은 선생님께 "모든 모임에 올 필요는 없다. 바쁘다는 걸 안다(**You don't have to come to all our meetings. I know you're busy.**)"라고 말한다. 즉, 바쁜 선생님께 '많은 일을 안 해도 된다는 것을 설명하기 위해' 모든 모임에 오시지 않아도 된다고 말한 것임을 알 수 있다. 그러므로 정답은 (B)이다.

Unit 1 Main Idea Questions

□ Example Announcement / Talk Excerpt

영어 선생님이 반 학생들에게 하는 얘기를 들으세요.

남 〈로미오와 줄리엣〉 읽기를 끝냈기 때문에 이제 말하기 대회를 열 겁니다. 여러분들 모두 연극에서 읽고 싶은 부분을 골라 10줄짜리 단락을 암기하기 바랍니다. 수요일 수업 시간에 암기한 것을 보여주게 될 겁니다. 말하기 대회 우승자는 Norwich Theater가 제작한 〈한여름 밤의 꿈〉의 티켓 2장을 받게 될 텐데요, 이 역시 셰익스피어의 작품입니다.

Q. 선생님은 주로 무엇에 대해 얘기하나요?

(A) 수요일 수업
(B) 〈로미오와 줄리엣〉 읽기
(C) Norwich Theater에 가기
(D) 말하기 대회에서의 실연

memorize 암기하다 winner 우승자 production (영화, 연극 등의) 제작 written by ~가 쓴, ~에 의해 쓰여진

□ Announcement / Talk Example

선생님이 수업 시간에 전달하는 공지 내용을 들으세요.

여 오늘과 내일 많은 양의 비가 내릴 것으로 예상되기 때문에 휴교할 가능성이 있습니다. 비가 많이 내리면 주차장이 물에 잠기게 됩니다. 주차장이 물에 잠기면 차들이 다닐 수가 없게 되거든요. 만약 내일 휴교를 하게 되면 집에서 2장과 3장을 읽어오도록 하세요.

Q. 공지 사항의 주제는 무엇인가요?

(A) (교과서) 2장과 3장 읽기
(B) 휴교 가능성
(C) 버스에 피해를 입히는 폭우
(D) 학교 주차장 홍수

an amount of 상당한 ~, 상당한 양의 ~ flood 물에 잠기다, 침수되다 traffic 차량들, 교통(량) cancel 취소하다

□ Dictation

1 Listen to a music teacher talking to a group of students.

W Wow, I was so ① impressed at the concert last night. You all did a spectacular job playing your instruments. I think you proved to your parents and teachers how ② invested you are in music. Congratulations, everybody. I hope you're ready ③ to start practicing for the next concert. It will be in the spring.

번역 **음악 선생님이 몇몇 학생들에게 하는 얘기를 들으세요.**

여 와, 선생님은 어젯밤 콘서트에 무척 감명을 받았습니다. 여러분 모두 악기 연주를 굉장히 잘 했어요. 여러분 부모님이나 다른 선생님들께 여러분이 음악에 얼마나 많은 공을 들였는지를 잘 보여주었다고 생각해요. 모두들 축하해요. 이제 다음 콘서트를 연습할 준비가 되어 있길 바랍니다. 다음 콘서트는 봄에 있을 겁니다.

1. 선생님은 주로 무슨 얘기를 하나요?
(A) 곧 다가오는 봄 콘서트
(B) 학생 개개인의 성급 기량
(C) 학부모와 교사들을 축하하기
(D) 콘서트에서 보인 학생들의 인상적인 공연

impressed 감명/감동 받은, 인상 깊게 생각하는 spectacular 장관을 이루는 instrument 악기 prove 증명하다, 입증하다
invest (시간이나 노력을) 투자하다 congratulations 축하합니다 (감탄사)

정답 및 해설 [주제를 묻는 문제] 음악 선생님이 학생들에게 "어젯밤 콘서트에 정말 감명받았다(I was so impressed at the concert last night.)"고 말하면서 모두 악기 연주를 굉장히 잘 했다고 칭찬한다. 따라서 정답은 (D)이다. (A)는 언급되었으나 세부사항이므로 주제로 볼 수 없고, (C)는 학부모나 선생님이 아닌 학생들을 축하하는 내용이었으므로 오답이다.

2 Listen to an announcement on the school intercom.

M Hello, students, teachers, and staff. This is a reminder that ① the school auditorium will be closed this week as students ② prepare for the school musical. If you have a drama class that regularly meets in the auditorium, it will be meeting in Room 305 this week. The auditorium ③ will open again on Monday the 17th.

번역 **학교 안내 방송을 들으세요.**

남 학생 여러분, 선생님, 그리고 직원 여러분, 안녕하십니까. 학생들의 교내 뮤지컬 준비 관계로 이번 주에는 학교 강당이 문을 닫게 됨을 다시 한번 알려드립니다. 강당에서 정기적인 모임을 가졌던 드라마 수업은 이번 주에는 305호 강의실에서 모임을 갖게 됩니다. 강당은 17일 월요일에 다시 개방할 것입니다.

2. 안내 방송의 주제는 무엇인가요?
(A) 교내 뮤지컬 티켓 구입
(B) 교내 강당 (임시) 폐쇄
(C) 305호 강의실의 교사와 학생들
(D) 드라마 클럽의 모임 취소

reminder (잊고 있던 것을)상기시키는 것 auditorium 강당 prepare 준비하다, 준비시키다 regularly 정기적으로; 자주

정답 및 해설 [주제를 묻는 문제] 이번 주 학생들의 뮤지컬 준비로 강당 문을 닫을 것을 공지하는 내용이다. 인사와 더불어 "학교 강당이 문을 닫을 것이다(~ school auditorium will be closed.)"라고 했기 때문에 정답은 (B)이다. (A)와 관련된 내용은 언급되지 않았고, (C), (D)의 경우 강당에서 하던 드라마 수업을 이번 주에는 305호 강의실에서 한다는 내용에 일치하지 않으므로 오답이다.

□ Practice Test

1. (C)	2. (D)	3. (C)	4. (D)	5. (C)	6. (B)

1 Listen to a teacher talking to her class.

W Class, this is Ellie. She just moved here from South Korea, so please help her adjust to our school. I'd like you to show her where the reading books are and help her with her locker. She told me that she loves playing soccer, so I hope that some of you will include her in a game during recess.

번역 **선생님이 학생들에게 하는 얘기를 들으세요.**

여 여러분, 여기 Ellie를 소개합니다. Ellie는 한국에서 방금 전학을 왔으니까 우리 학교에 적응할 수 있도록 도와 주세요. 읽기 도서들이 어디에 있는지 보여 주고 사물함 사용법도 가르쳐 주도록 해요. Ellie는 축구를 좋아한다고 하니까 휴식 시간에는 경기에 끼워주면 좋겠네요.

1. 선생님은 주로 어떤 얘기를 하나요?
(A) 쉬는 시간의 축구 경기
(B) 새로 온 학생의 사물함 비밀 번호
(C) 안내를 필요로 하는 새로 온 학생
(D) 한국 학생의 성격

adjust to ~에 적응하다 locker 개인 물품 보관함, 로커 include 포함시키다; 포함하다

정답 및 해설 [주제를 묻는 문제] 선생님이 반 학생들에게 새로 전학 온 Ellie를 소개하고 있다. 선생님이 Ellie는 한국에서 전학을 왔으니 "우리 학교에 적응할 수 있도록 도와주라(~ so please help her adjust to our school.)"고 당부하고 있다. 즉 '안내가 필요한 새로운 학생'을 소개하고 있기 때문에 정답은 (C)이다. (A)는 세부적인 내용이고, (B), (D)는 언급되지 않았으므로 오답이다.

2 Listen to a principal talking to a group of students.

M I need to tell you again that your behavior on Wednesday's field trip will determine whether or not you can go to the Redwood Forest. If you behave on Wednesday, you will be able to go to the Redwood Forest in June with the rest of your classmates. If not, you'll be staying at school with me.

번역 **교장 선생님이 몇몇 학생들에게 하는 얘기를 들으세요.**

남 다시 한번 말하겠습니다. 수요일 현장 학습에서 여러분이 어떻게 행동하느냐에 따라 여러분들을 Redwood Forest로 가게 할지 말지를 결정할 겁니다. 수요일에 태도가 좋으면 여러분 학급 친구들과 마찬가지로 6월에 Redwood Forest에 갈 수 있을 겁니다. 만약 그렇지 못할 경우엔 나와 함께 학교에 남게 될 겁니다.

2. 교장 선생님 말씀의 주제는 무엇인가요?
(A) Redwood Forest로의 학급 여행
(B) Redwood Forest에서 행실이 바르지 못한 학생들
(C) 수요일 여행에 가기로 한 학생들
(D) Redwood Forest 학습 여행에 영향을 미칠 학생들의 태도

behavior 행동, 행실, 태도 determine 결정하다 whether (or not) ~인지 아닌지 the rest of ~의 나머지

정답 및 해설 **[주제를 묻는 문제]** 교장 선생님이 학생들에게 "수요일 현장 학습에서의 태도를 보고 Redwood Forest로 가게 할지 말지를 결정한다(~ your behavior on Wednesday's field trip will determine whether or not you can go to the Redwood Forest.)"고 말하고 있다. 이어서 "수요일에 태도가 좋으면 6월에 Redwood Forest에 갈 수 있을 것(If you behave on Wednesday, ~)"이라고 말한다. 따라서 정답은 (D)이다.

3 Listen to a swimming coach talking to her team.

W Since it's the start of the season, I want you to think about what you want to accomplish. Do you want to break any personal records? Are there any meets you feel determined to win? I want you to write down your feelings so that I can give them back to you at the end of the season. That way you'll be able to see if you accomplished your goals.

번역 **수영 코치가 팀 선수들에게 하는 얘기를 들으세요.**

여 이제 시즌 초반이니까 여러분들이 어떤 걸 이루고 싶은지 생각해 보기를 바란다. 자기 개인 기록을 깨고 싶은가? 아니면 우승을 목표로 하는 경기가 있는가? 나중에 시즌이 끝날 때 여러분들에게 다시 돌려주도록 할 테니, 여러분들 각자의 마음을 써 내길 바란다. 그렇게 하면 (나중에 시즌이 끝난 후) 여러분들이 자신의 목표를 달성했는지 확인할 수 있을 것이다.

3. 수영 코치는 주로 무슨 얘기를 하나요?
(A) 시합에서 모두 우승한 학생들
(B) 어떤 개인 기록을 갱신해야 하는지
(C) 이번 시즌에 대해 학생들이 각자의 목표를 쓰는 것
(D) (학생들이 각자) 달성한 목표를 적는 것

accomplish 성취하다, 해내다 break a record 기록을 경신하다, 기록을 깨다 meet (운동) 경기/대회 goal 목표

정답 및 해설 **[주제를 묻는 문제]** 수영 코치가 학생들에게 "시즌 초반이니까 여러분들이 어떤 것을 이루고 싶은지 생각해 보기 바란다(Since it's the start of the season, I want you to think about what you want to accomplish.)"고 말한다. 그리고 "여러분들 각자의 마음을 써 내면 시즌이 끝날 때 돌려주겠다(I want you to write down your feelings ~)"라고 덧붙인다. 그러므로 정답은 (C)이다. (D)는 '(지금껏) 성취한 목표를 적는 것'인데, 코치가 말한 것은 앞으로의 성취 목표이므로 시제가 맞지 않는다.

4 Listen to a teacher talking to students in class.

M Let me remind you that your essays on World War II are due next Tuesday. After you finish your essay, I'd like you to both e-mail and print out a copy. I'd like to have both so that I can refer to your essays on the computer after I've given the paper copy back to you. Both the paper copy and the e-mail are due by class on Tuesday.

번역 **선생님이 반 학생들에게 하는 얘기를 들으세요.**

남 제 2차 세계대전에 관한 에세이는 다음 주 화요일까지라는 걸 다시 한번 말합니다. 에세이를 다 쓰면 이메일로도 보내고 종이로도 출력해서 제출하도록 하세요. 여러분들에게 프린트한 에세이를 돌려주고 난 후에도 컴퓨터 상에서 여러분 에세이를 참조할 수 있도록 두 가지 모두 필요합니다. 인쇄물과 이메일 모두 화요일 수업 시간까지입니다.

4. 선생님 말씀의 요지는 무엇인가요?

(A) 왜 2차 세계대전을 에세이 주제로 했는지

(B) 어떻게 (에세이)마감일을 화요일로 선택했는지

(C) 언제 에세이 인쇄물을 돌려줄 것으로 예상되는지

(D) 왜 학생들이 이메일과 인쇄물 두 가지로 냈으면 좋겠는지

due ~하기로 되어 있는, ~로 예정된 print out (프린터로) 출력하다 copy 복사(본) give something back to ~을 …에게 돌려주다

정답 및 해설 **[주제를 묻는 문제]** 선생님이 학생들에게 다음 주 화요일에 제출할 제 2차 세계대전에 대한 보고서에 대해 공지한다. "에세이를 쓴 후 이메일로도 보내고, 종이로도 출력해서 제출해야 한다(After you finish your essay, I'd like you to both e-mail and print out a copy.)"고 말하고 있다. 따라서 정답은 (D)이다. (A), (B), (C)는 언급되지 않았다.

5 Listen to a museum volunteer talking to students on a tour.

M Welcome to the Megacity Museum, children. This month, the museum has an excellent Greek God display in our exhibition hall. There are statues, portraits, and also interesting information about each God's role in Greek mythology. Anyone who wants to listen to an audio tape can rent one in the exhibition hall.

번역 **박물관 자원봉사자가 관람 중인 학생들에게 하는 얘기를 들으세요.**

남 Megacity 박물관에 온 여러분들, 환영합니다. 이번 달에는 박물관 전시실에서 굉장히 멋진 그리스 신 전시를 합니다. 조각상과 초상화들이 있으며, 이들 신들이 그리스 신화에서 각자 어떤 역할을 했는지에 관한 흥미로운 정보도 함께 나와 있습니다. 오디오 테이프를 듣고 싶은 사람들은 전시실에서 빌릴 수 있습니다.

5. 자원봉사자는 주로 어떤 얘기를 하나요?

(A) 그리스 신화

(B) 전시실

(C) 그리스 신 전시

(D) 그리스 신들의 역할

display 전시, 진열 exhibition hall 전시회장 statue 조각상 portrait 조상화, 인물 사진(*보통 이께 윗부분까지 나옴) mythology 신화 rent (사용료를 내고)빌리다

정답 및 해설 **[주제를 묻는 문제]** 박물관 견학을 온 학생들에게 전시물을 소개하고 있다. "이번 달에는 박물관 전시실에서 굉장히 멋진 그리스 신에 대한 전시를 하고 있다(This month, the museum has an excellent Greek God display in our exhibition hall.)"라고 말하면서 전시물에 대한 개략적인 설명과 오디오 테이프 대여에 대해 소개한다. 따라서 정답은 (C)이다.

6 Listen to a teacher talking to students in a class.

W Class, today I want to give you some important tips when using a computer. First, always remember to save your work. Save it on the computer often but also save it to a USB in case the computer dies. Also don't look at the keyboard when you type. It might be difficult to type now, but if you always look at the keys, you will never get any faster.

번역 **선생님이 반 학생들에게 하는 얘기를 들으세요.**

여 여러분, 오늘은 여러분들에게 컴퓨터 사용 시 몇 가지 중요한 정보를 알려 줄게요. 첫째, 항상 여러분이 작업한 것들을 잊지 말고 저장하도록 하세요. 컴퓨터에 수시로 저장을 해야 하지만 컴퓨터가 고장 날 경우에 대비해서 USB에도 저장해야 합니다. 그리고 타이핑을 할 때는 자판을 보지 않도록 하세요. 지금은 (보지 않고)타이핑을 하는 게 어렵겠지만 (타이핑 때마다)자판을 보고 하면 절대 속도가 빨라지지 않습니다.

6. 이야기의 주제는 무엇인가요?
(A) USB 키를 사용하는 방법
(B) 중요 컴퓨터 (사용)정보
(C) 더 빠르게 타이핑 하는 방법 배우기
(D) 컴퓨터에 작업물 저장하기

save 저장하다 USB(=Universal Serial Bus) 유에스비(*컴퓨터와 주변 기기를 연결하는 데 쓰이는 입출력 표준의 하나) in case ~할 경우에 대비해서 keyboard (컴퓨터) 키보드/자판 type (컴퓨터로)타자 치다, 입력하다

정답 및 해설 [주제를 묻는 문제] 선생님이 학생들에게 "오늘은 컴퓨터 사용 시 몇 가지 중요한 정보에 대해 가르쳐 주겠다(~ I want to give you some important tips when using a computer.)"고 말한 후 몇 가지 정보를 세부적으로 설명한다. 그러므로 정답은 (B)이다. (A)는 언급되지 않았고, (C)와 (D)는 각각의 정보에 해당하는 내용이므로 전체 주제가 될 수 없다.

Unit 2 Details Questions

□ Example Announcement / Talk Excerpt

미술 선생님이 학생들에게 하는 얘기를 들으세요.

여 오늘부터 자화상에 관련한 과를 시작하겠습니다. 대다수는 아닐지라도 예술가들 중에는 자화상을 그린 화가들이 많습니다. 이들은 종종 작품 속에 자신의 성격, 감정, 그리고 자신을 드러낼만한 요소들을 집어넣었습니다. 오늘 수업 시간에는 유명 화가들이 그린 자화상을 살펴보겠습니다. 여러분은 과제로 자신의 자화상을 그려오도록 하세요.

Q. 선생님은 학생들에게 무엇을 하라고 지시하나요?
(A) 과제로 자신의 자화상을 그려라.
(B) 유명 화가의 초상화를 그려라.
(C) 유명 화가의 자화상에 대해 조사하라.
(D) 자신의 성격과 자신만의 독자성에 대해 생각해 봐라.

self-portrait 자화상 incorporate (일부로)포함하다 element 요소, 성분 personality 성격, 인격 identity 독자성; 신분, 정체

□ Announcement / Talk Example

박물관 자원봉사자가 몇몇 학생들에게 하는 얘기를 들으세요.

여 여기 이곳에서는 세포에 관한 전시물을 보게 될 겁니다. 과학자들이 여러 다양한 세포를 사진으로 찍어서 전시실에 전시했습니다. 특히 암세포 사진은 건강한 세포와는 다르게 보여 무척 흥미로울 겁니다. 또한 몸 속에 있는 다양한 세포들이 서로 어떻게 달리 보이는지도 알 수 있습니다. 예를 들어, 혈액 세포와 뇌 세포는 다르게 보입니다.

Q. 자원봉사자는 암세포에 관해 뭐라고 하나요?
(A) 여러 가지 다양한 사진이 찍혀 있다.
(B) 사진을 찍기가 어렵다.
(C) 혈액 세포와 다르게 보인다.
(D) 건강한 세포와 다르다.

cell 세포 cancer 암 blood cell 혈액 세포 brain cell 뇌세포

□ Dictation

1 Listen to a teacher talking to students in a class.

M I hope the reading on bats showed you ① how interesting these creatures are. They're not evil creatures with diseases, ② even though they seem this way on Halloween. If you have time tonight, then please ③ go into your backyard at twilight. See if you can find any bats. They're especially ④ active in our area at this time of year.

번역 선생님이 반 학생들에게 하는 얘기를 들으세요.

남 박쥐에 관한 읽기 자료가 이 생물체가 얼마나 흥미로운지를 보여줬기를 바랍니다. 박쥐는 병균을 지닌 해로운 생물체가 아닙니다. 할로윈 때는 그렇게 보일지도 모르지만요. 오늘밤에 시간이 된다면 해질녘에 뒷마당으로 나가서 박쥐가 보이는지 살펴보도록 하세요. 해마다 이맘때면 우리 지역에 박쥐가 무척 활발하게 활동하니까요.

1. 선생님은 학생들에게 무엇을 하라고 지시하나요?
(A) 박쥐가 흥미로운 생물체임을 인정하라.
(B) 이 지역에서는 이맘때에 가장 활발히 움직여라.
(C) 할로윈에 박쥐가 어떻게 묘사되는지 생각해 봐라.
(D) 해질녘에 뒷마당으로 나가서 박쥐를 찾아봐라.

creature 생물 evil 사악한, 유해한 twilight 해질녘, 땅거미 active 활동적인

정답 및 해설 [세부사항을 묻는 문제] 선생님이 학생들에게 박쥐에 대한 얘기를 하면서 "만약 오늘밤 시간이 있다면 해질 무렵 뒷마당으로 가서 박쥐를 찾아보라(If you have time tonight, then please go into your backyard at twilight. See if you can find any bats.)"고 말한다. 따라서 정답은 (D)이다. (B)는 학생이 아니라 박쥐를 대상으로 한 내용이다.

2 Listen to a drama teacher talking to students.

W This year ① we'll be putting on a play called "Carousel." It's a famous American musical and love story ② that takes place in Maine. Tryouts for the play will be ③ on Friday at 3:00. You'll be required to ④ read a portion of the script and sing a song. If there are a lot of people trying out, we might have another tryout session on Monday.

번역 연극 선생님이 학생들에게 하는 얘기를 들으세요.

여 올해 우리는 〈회전목마〉라는 연극을 상연할 겁니다. 미국의 유명한 뮤지컬이며 메인(*미국 동북부의 주)에서 일어나는 러브스토리입니다. 연극 선발 시험은 금요일 3시에 있습니다. 대본의 한 부분을 읽어보고 노래를 한 곡 불러야 합니다. 응시자가 많으면 월요일에 한 차례 더 선발 시험이 있을 겁니다.

2. 선생님은 연극 선발 시험에 대해 뭐라고 하나요?
(A) 금요일 3시에 있을 것이다.
(B) 메인에서 열릴 것이다.
(C) 월요일까지는 열리지 않을 것이다.
(D) 학생들에게 파트너를 구하라고 요구할 것이다.

carousel 회전목마 musical 뮤지컬 take place (사건, 일 등이) 일어나다, 발생하다 tryout 시험해보기, 테스트하기 require 요구하다, 필요로 하다 a portion of ~의 부분/일부 session (특정 활동의) 시간/기간

정답 및 해설 [세부사항을 묻는 문제] 연극 선생님이 학생들에게 올해에는 〈회전목마〉라는 연극을 공연할 것이라고 하면서 "연극 선발 시험은 금요일 3시에 있을 것(Tryouts for the play will be on Friday at 3:00)"이라고 말한다. 그러므로 정답은 (A)이다. (B)의 Maine은 선발 시험 장소가 아닌 연극의 배경이기 때문에 오답이 된다.

□ Practice Test

1. (B)	2. (A)	3. (D)	4. (C)	5. (C)	6. (D)

1 Listen to a health teacher talking to students.

W There's no way around it. Smoking is terrible for your health. It can lead to cancer and heart disease. Although it may seem harmless to smoke just one cigarette, smoking one can lead to smoking many more. Cigarettes are filled with special chemicals that make you want to smoke. Once you start smoking, it could be difficult to stop.

번역 양호 선생님이 학생들에게 하는 얘기를 들으세요.

여 다른 방법은 없습니다. 흡연은 건강에 대단히 나쁩니다. (담배를 피면) 암이나 심장 질환이 발생할 수 있습니다. 겨우 담배 한 개피 정도 피는 건 해롭지 않아 보일지도 모르지만, 담배 한 개피는 담배 여러 대 피는 것으로 이어집니다. 담배는 흡연 욕구를 생성하는 특별한 화학물질로 가득 차 있습니다. 따라서 한번 흡연을 시작하면 끊기가 어렵습니다.

1. 선생님은 겨우 담배 한 개피 피는 것에 대해 뭐라고 하나요?
(A) 그다지 위험하지 않다.
(B) 더 많은 흡연으로 이어질 수 있다.
(C) 심장 질환에 걸리게 할 것이다.
(D) 몸을 무척 약하게 만들 것이다.

lead to 초래하다, (결과를) 가져오다 **heart disease** 심장 질환 **harmless** 해가 없는, 무해한 **cigarette** 담배

정답 및 해설 **[세부사항을 묻는 문제]** 선생님이 학생들에게 흡연이 건강에 해롭다고 말하면서, "담배 한 개피 피는 것은 해롭지 않은 것처럼 보일 수 있으나 담배 한 개피 피는 것이 더 많은 흡연으로 이어질 수 있다(**Although it may seem harmless to smoke just one cigarette, smoking one can lead to smoking many more**)"고 한다. 이어서 담배는 "흡연하고 싶게 만드는 특별한 화학 물질들로 가득 차 있다(**~ filled with special chemicals that make you want to smoke.**)"고 덧붙인다. 따라서 정답은 (B)이다. (C)는 담배 한 개피가 아닌 일반적인 흡연에 관련된 내용이므로 정답이 될 수 없다.

2 Listen to a principal talking to a group of students.

W Your work to start a recycling program at our school is impressive and admirable. Since your group started the Healthy Environment Program, over 90% of Stephen students report that they recycle their bottles, cans, and papers. All this is because of your campaign. Thank you very much for your dedication.

번역 교장 선생님이 몇몇 학생들에게 하는 얘기를 들으세요.

여 여러분들이 우리 학교 재활용 프로그램을 시작한 일은 무척 인상적이고 칭찬받을만한 일이에요. 여러분들이 〈건강한 환경 프로그램〉을 시작한 이후로 우리 Stephen 학교 학생들의 90퍼센트 이상이 병이나 캔, 종이를 재활용한다고 합니다. 이 모든 게 다 여러분들의 캠페인 덕분이에요. 여러분들 노고를 무척 고맙게 생각합니다.

2. Stephen 학생들의 90% 이상은 무엇을 하나요?
(A) 병, 캔, 종이를 재활용한다.
(B) 교장 선생님에게 헌신한다.
(C) 보다 건강한 환경을 위한 캠페인을 한다.
(D) 〈건강한 환경 프로그램〉에서 일한다.

recycling 재활용, 재생 이용 **admirable** 감탄할만한, 존경스러운 **campaign** 캠페인 **dedication** 헌신, 전념

정답 및 해설 **[세부사항을 묻는 문제]** 교장 선생님이 학생들이 하고 있는 재활용 캠페인에 대해 칭찬하는 내용이다. 재활용 프로그램 시작 이후, "90% 이상의 학생들이 병, 깡통, 신문 등을 재활용했다고 보고했다(**~ over 90% of Stephen students report that they recycle their bottles, cans, and papers.**)"고 말한다. 따라서 정답은 (A)이다.

3 Listen to a history teacher talking to a class.

M As a way to study for the exam, I've divided the class into pairs. You and your partner will work together to create a list of all the things we've studied since our last test. Then you will write 2-3 sentences about each date, person, or important event. Working this way will be a good review for you.

번역 역사 선생님이 학생들에게 하는 얘기를 들으세요.

남 시험 대비 공부를 위해서 선생님이 여러분들을 짝지어 나누었습니다. 여러분과 여러분 짝이 함께 작업해서 지난 시험 이후로 공부한 내용들을 모두 목록으로 만들 거예요. 그런 다음 각각의 날짜나 인물, 중요 사건들에 관해 2~3줄의 문장을 씁니다. 이렇게 작업하면 복습하는 데 큰 도움이 될 겁니다.

3. 선생님은 학생들에게 무엇을 하라고 지시하나요?
(A) 함께 공부할 짝을 구하라.
(B) 반 친구들 모두에 대한 문장을 써라.
(C) 지난 시험 이후로 배운 내용들에 관해 선생님과 복습하라.
(D) 각자 짝과 함께 학습한 내용들에 관한 목록을 만들어라.

divide 나누다, 가르다 pair 짝, 쌍, 두 사람 review 복습, 시험 공부

정답 및 해설 **[세부사항을 묻는 문제]** 역사 선생님이 학생들의 시험 공부를 위해 학생들을 짝지어 나누었다고 말한다. 그러면서 "짝과 함께 지난 시험 이후 배웠던 것들 모두에 대한 목록을 작성하라(**You and your partner will work together to create a list of all the things we've studied since our last test.**)"고 지시하고 있다. 따라서 정답은 (D)이나. 이미 선생님이 짝을 정해놓은 상황이므로 (A)는 오답이고, (B)와 (C)는 일부 내용만 맞는 Trap Answer의 한 유형이다.

4 Listen to a teacher making an announcement in class.

W Earlier this week, Principal Burgess decided to change the dress code. You will still have to wear school uniforms on Monday through Thursday, but you can wear whatever you like on Friday. I'd like to remind you that you still need to wear appropriate clothing. Girls, your skirts need to be long enough. Boys, please make sure your clothes are clean.

번역 선생님이 반에 전하는 공지 내용을 들으세요.

여 이번 주 초에 Burgess 교장 선생님께서는 복장 규정을 바꾸기로 결정하셨습니다. 월요일부터 목요일까지는 여전히 교복을 입어야 하지만 금요일에는 여러분들이 원하는 대로 입을 수 있습니다. 그렇지만 물론 제대로 된 옷을 입어야 한다는 점을 상기시켜 주고 싶군요. 여학생들은 치마 길이가 충분히 길어야 합니다. 남학생들은 특히 깨끗한 차림이 되도록 하세요.

4. 선생님은 여학생들의 치마에 대해 뭐라고 하나요?
(A) 깨끗해야 한다.
(B) 금요일마다 입을 수 있다.
(C) 길이가 충분히 길어야 한다.
(D) 검은색이나 회색이이야 한다.

dress code 복장 규정 appropriate 적절한, 알맞은

정답 및 해설 **[세부사항을 묻는 문제]** 선생님은 학생들에게 교장 선생님이 변경한 복장 규정에 대해 공지하고 있다. 월요일부터 목요일까지는 평상시와 마찬가지로 교복을 입어야 하지만, 금요일에는 자유 복장을 할 수 있다고 한다. 다만 옷차림이 적절해야 한다고 하면서 일례로 "여학생들의 치마는 충분히 길어야 한다(**Girls, your skirts need to be long enough.**)"고 했다. 따라서 정답은 (C)이다. (A)는 남학생들의 옷에 해당하는 내용이므로 오답이고, (B)와 (D)는 구체적으로 언급되지 않았다.

5 Listen to an English teacher talking to students.

M I realize that many of you like to play video games, so I want you to think about what would make the best game. Then I want you to create your own game in a writing piece, complete with a story, characters, and setting. The purpose of this assignment is to make you think creatively. There's one rule: your game cannot be violent.

번역 영어 선생님이 학생들에게 하는 얘기를 들으세요.

남 여러분 중 상당수가 비디오 게임을 좋아한다고 알고 있습니다. 그래서 여러분들이 어떤 게임이 최고의 게임이 될지 생각해봤으면 해요. 그런 다음 종이에 여러분 자신만의 게임을 하나 만들어서 이야기와 등장 인물 그리고 배경을 만들어 보는 겁니다. 이번 과제의 목적은 여러분들이 창의적으로 생각해보도록 하는 것입니다. 한 가지 규칙이 있는데, 게임이 폭력적이면 안 됩니다.

5. 선생님은 과제의 목적에 대해 뭐라고 말하나요?
(A) 학생들이 줄거리를 만드는 데 도움이 된다.
(B) 비폭력적인 게임을 홍보한다.
(C) 학생들이 창조적으로 생각하도록 한다.
(D) 학생들이 좋아하는 것에 관해 쓰는 것이다.

complete 완료하다, 끝마치다 **character** 등장 인물 **setting** 배경, 배경이 되는 무대, 설정 **creatively** 창조적으로, 독창적으로
violent 폭력적인, 난폭한

정답 및 해설 **[세부사항을 묻는 문제]** 선생님이 학생들에게 직접 자신만의 게임을 만들 것을 지시하면서, "이 과제의 목적은 여러분이 창의적으로 생각하도록 하는 것(The purpose of this assignment is to make you think creatively.)"이라고 직접적인 과제의 목적을 밝히고 있다. 따라서 정답은 (C)이다.

6 Listen to a history teacher talking to a class.

W Please choose a partner for your next presentation. The presentation will be on a topic that you choose. I'd like you to work with someone you don't usually work with. If you pick your best friend, I'm just going to separate you. Everyone has been talking about their interests in class, so choose someone who shares your interests.

번역 역사 선생님이 반 학생들에게 하는 얘기를 들으세요.

여 다음 번 발표를 위해 각자 파트너를 고르도록 하세요. 다음 발표는 여러분들이 선택하는 주제로 할 것입니다. 여러분들이 평상시 함께 하지 않던 사람을 파트너로 하길 바랍니다. 가장 친한 친구와 파트너가 되면 선생님이 따로 떼놓을 겁니다. 여러분 모두 반에서 각자의 관심사에 대해 얘기했었으니까 여러분들과 공통의 관심사를 가진 친구들을 고르도록 하세요.

6. 선생님은 학생들이 무엇을 하기를 원하나요?
(A) 여학생인 경우 남학생과 함께 작업해라.
(B) 파트너로 가장 친한 친구를 선택해라.
(C) 자신과 다른 관심사를 가진 친구를 선택해라.
(D) 평상시 함께 작업하지 않던 친구를 골라라.

presentation 발표, 프레젠테이션 **separate** 떼어놓다, 갈라지게 하다 **share** (생각 등을)공유하다, 같은 ~을 갖다
interest 관심, 흥미

정답 및 해설 **[세부사항을 묻는 문제]** 선생님이 학생들에게 다음 발표를 위한 파트너를 정할 것을 지시하면서 "평상시 같이 하지 않았던 친구와 함께 하기를 원한다(I'd like you to work with someone you don't usually work with.)"고 한다. 또한 "친한 친구를 선택할 경우 갈라놓겠다(If you pick your best friend, I'm just going to separate you.)"라고 덧붙인다. 따라서 정답은 (D)이다. (A)는 언급되지 않았고, (B)와 (C)는 선생님의 지시 사항과 상반되는 내용이므로 오답이다.

Unit 3 Inference Questions

□ Example Announcement / Talk Excerpt

선생님이 반에 전달하는 공지 내용을 들으세요.

여 학교 축구 결승 경기가 이번 주 금요일 2시로 예정되었는데, 이때는 보통 수업이 있죠. 이번 경기는 무척 중요한 경기이기 때문에 수업을 취소하고 경기 관람을 허락하겠습니다. 그렇다고 공부를 하지 않아도 된다고 생각하면 안 됩니다. 금요일에 빠진 수업을 보충할 수 있도록 여러분들이 주말 동안 해야 할 추가 과제를 준비해 두었습니다.

Q. 선생님은 축구 경기에 관해 무엇을 암시하나요?

(A) 자신은 축구 경기가 재미없다.
(B) 금요일 오후 2시에 치러진다.
(C) 학생들에게 무척 중요한 경기이다.
(D) 학생들에게 별로 중요하지 않다.

be set (날짜, 장소 등이) 잡히다, 정해지다 allow 허락하다, 허용하다 make up for 벌충하다, 만회하다 missed 놓친, 손실된

□ Announcement / Talk Example

선생님이 반에 전달하는 공지 내용을 들으세요.

여 선생님이 교장 선생님으로부터 오후 스쿨 버스(운행)에 문제가 좀 있다는 말씀을 들었습니다. 학생들을 기다리느라 버스가 예정된 시간보다 훨씬 늦게 출발한다고 하는군요. 이 때문에 학교 주차장에 교통 체증이 발생되고 있습니다. 이제부터 버스는 3시 10분에 (정확히) 출발할 겁니다. 3시 10분까지 버스에 타지 않으면 (여러분이 다 못 타더라도) 그냥 출발할 겁니다.

Q. 학생들에 관해 사실은 무엇일까요?

(A) 학교 버스 타는 시간에 종종 늦는다.
(B) 보통 학교에서 집까지 걸어간다.
(C) 버스 운전 기사들과 친구가 되었다.
(D) 교장 선생님과의 관계가 좋지 않다.

be scheduled to ~할 예정이다 result in (결과적으로) ~을 야기하다 parking lot 주차장, 주차 지역

□ Dictation

1 Listen to a volleyball coach talking to her players.

W I hope you're not nervous for the game, even though Hazel Hill ① beat us last month. We've been practicing a lot and I'm sure you girls can beat them. Please think carefully ② about teamwork. Every person on this team can ③ contribute to winning the game. Good teamwork will be ④ our advantage over Hazel.

번역 **배구 코치가 선수들에게 하는 말을 들으세요.**

여 비록 우리가 지난 달에 Hazel Hill 팀에 졌지만, 그렇다고 해서 이번 시합에 두려움을 갖는 일은 없기를 바란다. 우리는 지금껏 많이 연습해왔고, 그래서 여러분들이 이 팀을 이길 수 있다고 확신한다. 팀워크에 대해서 잘 생각해 보도록 해라. 우리 팀 선수들은 모두 경기에서 승리하는 데 기여할 수 있다. 팀워크가 좋다면 우리가 Hazel 팀에 우위를 점할 수 있을 것이다.

1. Hazel Hill 팀에 대해 무엇을 추론할 수 있나요?

(A) 그들은 강팀이다.
(B) 그들은 감독에게 매우 충성스럽다.
(C) 그들은 연습을 많이 하지 않는다.
(D) 그들은 이전에 이 팀을 이겨본 적이 없다.

practice 연습하다, 실습하다; 연습, 실습 teamwork 팀워크, 협동 작업 contribute to ~에 공헌하다, ~에 기여하다 advantage 유리한 점, 이점, 장점

정답 및 해설 **[추론 문제]** 배구 코치가 Hazel Hill 팀과의 경기를 앞두고 선수들을 격려하는 내용이다. 코치가 처음에 "비록 지난달에는 Hazel Hill 팀에게 졌지만 시합을 두려워하지 않기를 바란다(I hope you're not nervous for the game, even though Hazel Hill beat us last month.)"고 말하고, "팀워크가 좋으면 우위를 점할 수도 있다(Good teamwork will be our advantage over Hazel.)"고 한 것 등을 볼 때 Hazel Hill 팀이 강팀이라는 것을 알 수 있다. 따라서 정답은 (A)이다. (B), (C)와 관련된 내용은 언급되지 않았고, 지난달 시합에서 Hazel Hill 팀에 졌다고 했으므로 (D)는 오답이다.

2 Listen to a science teacher talking to his class.

M The safety equipment is over here—you'll find gloves, goggles, and masks. You ① must use these items when we do experiments. There are ② no exceptions. I don't want anyone to get hurt because of ③ an avoidable mistake. When you walk into the lab, walk straight over to the safety equipment. Please use the equipment ④ to stay safe.

번역 **과학 선생님이 반 학생들에게 하는 말을 들으세요.**

남 안전 장비는 여기 이쪽에 있어요. 장갑, 고글, 그리고 마스크가 보일 거예요. 실험을 할 때는 이 장비들을 반드시 착용해야 합니다. 예외는 없습니다. 여러분들이 미리 피할 수 있는데도 불구하고 부주의 때문에 다치는 건 원치 않습니다. 실험실에 들어올 때는 안전 장비가 있는 곳으로 곧장 가도록 하세요. 안전을 위해 꼭 장비를 사용하도록 합니다.

2. 선생님은 안전 장비에 대해 무엇을 암시하나요?
(A) 멀리 떨어진 벽장 안에 있다.
(B) 모든 실험에 반드시 필요하다.
(C) 양말과 스니커즈를 포함해야 한다.
(D) 피할 수 있는 실수가 발생하는 건 이 때문이다.

safety equipment 안전 장비 **goggle** 고글(*물, 바람 등이 들어가지 않게 얼굴에 밀착되게 쓰는 안경)
exception 예외 **avoidable** 막을 수 있는, 피할 수 있는

정답 및 해설 **[추론 문제]** 과학 선생님이 학생들에게 실험을 할 때는 반드시 안전 장비를 착용하라고 지시하고 있다. 안전 장비의 위치를 가리킨 후, "실험을 할 때는 반드시 이 장비들을 사용해야 하며, 예외는 없다(You must use these items when we do experiments. There are no exceptions.)"고 말한다. 따라서 선생님은 '안전 장비가 매 실험마다 필요하다'는 것을 암시하고 있다고 볼 수 있다. 그러므로 정답은 (B)이다.

□ Practice Test

1. (B)	2. (C)	3. (D)	4. (C)	5. (C)	6. (B)

1 Listen to a principal talking to students.

W This year's class trip will take place in June at Myles Standish National Park. Make sure you bring sunscreen, a hat, a bathing suit, and a water bottle. Your teachers will bring a fair amount of water in big bottles and jugs, but I'd like you to also have a water bottle on you at all times. I don't want anyone getting sick from the heat, so please bring a bottle from home.

번역 **교장 선생님이 학생들에게 하는 말을 들으세요.**

여 올해는 6월에 Myles Standish National Park로 수학 여행을 갑니다. 선크림과 모자, 수영복, 그리고 물병을 꼭 챙겨오도록 하세요. 선생님들께서 큰 병과 주전자에 물을 충분히 담아오시긴 하지만, 그래도 여러분들 각자 항상 물병을 들고 다니세요. 더위 때문에 병이 나면 안 되니까 집에서 물병을 가져오도록 하세요.

1. 교장 선생님은 수학 여행에 대해 무엇을 암시하나요?
(A) 5월에 있을 것이다.
(B) 무척 더울 것이다.
(C) 무척 재미있을 것이다.
(D) 선생님들이 신이 나 있다.

sunscreen 자외선 차단 크림 **water bottle** 물병 **a fair amount of** 상당한 양의 **jug** (주둥이와 손잡이가 달린)주전자
at all times 항상, 언제나

정답 및 해설 **[추론 문제]** 교장 선생님은 학생들에게 수학 여행 일정을 안내하면서 "반드시 선크림, 모자, 수영복, 그리고 물병을 가져오라(Make sure you bring sunscreen, a hat, a bathing suit, and a water bottle.)"고 당부한다. 그리고 마지막에 "누구도 더위 때문에 병이 나는 건 원치 않는다(I don't want anyone getting sick from the heat ~)"고 덧붙인다. 이를 볼 때 이번 수학 여행을 가는 시기가 무척 더울 것이라고 추론할 수 있다. 따라서 정답은 (B)이다.

2 Listen to a museum volunteer talking to a group of students.

M Over here you'll see a number of paintings by Monet, the famous French artist. These works are studied around the world. If you're wondering why these paintings look so blurry, it's because they are some of the last that Monet painted. In the second half of his life, Monet was going blind.

번역 **박물관 자원봉사자가 몇몇 학생들에게 하는 말을 들으세요.**

남 여기에서는 유명한 프랑스 화가인 모네의 여러 작품들을 볼 수 있습니다. 이 작품들은 세계 여러 곳에서 연구를 했습니다. 이 그림들을 보면 왜 이렇게 흐릿한지 궁금할 텐데요, 이들은 모네가 그린 마지막 작품들 중 일부이기 때문입니다. 모네는 인생 후반부에 시력을 잃어가고 있었습니다.

2. 모네의 실명에 관해 무엇을 추론할 수 있나요?
(A) 작품 활동을 할 수 없게 되었다.
(B) 모네가 50세를 넘긴 이후에 시작되었다.
(C) 모네의 작품이 보여지는 방식에 변화를 가져 왔다.
(D) 모네에게는 그리 큰 분세가 되지 않았다.

a number of 얼마간의, 다수의 blurry 흐릿한, 모호한 go blind 실명하다, 시력을 잃다

정답 및 해설 **[추론 문제]** 박물관 자원봉사자가 학생들에게 모네의 작품들을 소개하면서 "이 작품들이 왜 흐릿하게 보이는지 궁금할 텐데 그 이유는 모네가 그린 마지막 작품들이기 때문이고, 모네는 인생 후반부에 시력을 잃어가고 있었다(If you're wondering why these paintings look so blurry, ~ Monet was going blind.)"고 설명한다. 이를 근거로 모네가 시력을 잃은 것이 '그의 작품들을 다르게 보이게 했다'는 것을 추론할 수 있다. 따라서 정답은 (C)이다.

3 Listen to a teacher talking to his students.

M You might remember that next Monday is Memorial Day, meaning that we'll have no school. Memorial Day commemorates all of the American soldiers who died for our country in numerous wars. I know you'll be tempted to simply enjoy your day off, but make sure you take a moment to think about what these soldiers gave for you and your country.

번역 **선생님이 학생들에게 하는 말을 들으세요.**

남 다음 주 월요일이 (미국)전몰 장병 추모일인 걸 기억하고 있겠죠. 그래서 이 날은 수업이 없습니다. 전몰 장병 추모일은 여러 전쟁에서 우리 나라를 위해 싸우다 죽어간 모든 미국 군인들을 추모하는 날입니다. 여러분들이야 단순히 휴일을 즐기고 싶겠지만, 잠깐이라도 시간을 내어 이들 군인들이 여러분과 여러분의 조국에 무엇을 주고 갔는지를 생각해 보길 바랍니다.

3. 선생님은 전몰 장병 추모일에 대해 무엇을 암시하나요?
(A) 주로 군인들이 기념한다.
(B) 가족 여행하기에 무척 좋은 날이다.
(C) 사랑하는 사람을 잃은 사람들만 추모하는 날이다.
(D) 진지하게 생각해야 하는 엄숙한 기념일이다.

Memorial Day (미국)전몰 장병 추모일 commemorate (중요 인물이나 사건을)기념하다 numerous 많은, 다수의
be tempted to ~하고 싶어지다 day off (학교, 직장 등의 일을)쉬는 날

정답 및 해설 **[추론 문제]** 선생님이 학생들에게 다음 주 월요일은 전몰 장병 추모일로 휴일이라고 말한다. 이 날의 의미를 설명하면서 단순히 휴일을 즐기고 싶겠지만 "군인들이 여러분과 나라를 위해서 무엇을 주었는지 잠시 생각할 시간을 꼭 갖도록 하라(~ make sure you take a moment to think about what these soldiers gave for you and your country.)"고 말한다. 이를 볼 때 선생님은 '전몰 장병 추모일을 진지하게 생각'하고 있음을 유추할 수 있다. 따라서 정답은 (D)이다.

4 Listen to a secretary making an announcement.

W Hello, students and teachers. This is a reminder that the seventh grade bake sale will be taking place today and tomorrow. Brownies, muffins, cookies, and other treats will be on sale in the main lobby. On both days, the sale will start when school finishes at 2:30 and will go until 3:30. The money from the bake sale will go to the seventh grade class's hiking trip.

번역 학교 서기가 전달하는 공지 내용을 들으세요.

여 학생 여러분, 그리고 선생님 여러분, 안녕하세요. 7학년 학생들의 빵 판매일이 오늘과 내일임을 다시 한번 알려드립니다. 메인 로비에서 브라우니, 머핀, 쿠키, 그리고 기타 다른 과자들을 판매합니다. 판매는 양일 모두 수업이 끝난 이후인 2시 30분에 시작해서 3시 30분까지 진행됩니다. 빵 판매로 얻은 수익은 7학년 학생들의 하이킹 여행에 쓰이게 됩니다.

4. 7학년 학생들에 관해 사실은 무엇일까요?
(A) 그들은 빵 판매에 참석하지 않을 것이다.
(B) 그들의 하이킹 여행은 빵집 근처에서 열린다.
(C) 그들은 여행 자금이 좀 필요하다.
(D) 그들은 오직 학부모한테만 과자를 팔고 있다.

brownie 브라우니, 초콜릿 케이크(*작게 네모로 잘라낸 모양) **muffin** 머핀 **treat** (대접하여 주는)특별한 것, 대접, 한턱
on sale 판매되는

정답 및 해설 **[추론 문제]** 학생들과 선생님들에게 오늘내일 양일간 7학년 학생들의 빵 판매가 있을 거라고 공지하고 있다. 마지막에 "빵 판매로 얻은 수익은 7학년 학생들의 여행을 위해 쓰일 것(The money from the bake sale will go to the seventh grade class's hiking trip.)"이라고 말하는 것으로 볼 때 '7학년 학생들의 여행을 위해 돈이 필요하다'고 유추할 수 있다. 따라서 정답은 (C)이다. (A), (B), (D) 모두 논리적으로 옳지 않다.

5 Listen to a teacher speaking to a class.

M Class, the due date for your storybooks is two weeks from today, on March 27th. Two weeks will give you a lot of working time so I should see some impressive storybooks. I want to see finished books with typed pages and colored illustrations. Don't wait until the night before to start your book. If you want a good grade, you'll need much more time than one night.

번역 선생님이 반 학생들에게 하는 말을 들으세요.

남 여러분, 스토리 북의 제출 기한은 오늘부터 2주 후인 3월 27일입니다. 2주면 작업 시간은 충분히 주는 거니까 스토리 북에서 뭔가 인상적인 면을 볼 수 있길 바랍니다. (컴퓨터로) 타이핑한 인쇄물에 컬러 삽화를 곁들인 완성된 책을 보여 주세요. 마지막 날까지 기다렸다가 책 작업을 시작하지 마세요. 좋은 성적을 받고 싶다면 하룻밤 이상의 훨씬 많은 시간을 들여야 할 겁니다.

5. 선생님은 스토리 북에 대해 무엇을 암시하나요?
(A) 마감일은 학생마다 다르게 융통적이다.
(B) 해마다 스토리 북이 점점 더 인상적이 돼간다.
(C) 좋은 스토리 북을 만들려면 완성하는 데 오랜 시간이 소요될 것이다.
(D) 스토리 북을 완성하기에 2주는 충분치 못하다.

due date 만기일, 마감일 **impressive** 인상적인, 인상 깊은, 감명 깊은 **illustration** 삽화

정답 및 해설 **[추론 문제]** 선생님은 학생들에게 스토리 북 제출일이 2주 후라고 공지하면서, 마지막에 "제출 전날까지 미뤘다가 시작하지 말라(Don't wait until the night before to start your book.)"고 한다. 특히 "좋은 점수를 받고 싶으면 하룻밤 이상의 시간이 필요할 것이다(If you want a good grade, you'll need much more time than one night.)"고 말하는 것을 볼 때, '좋은 스토리 북을 완성하는 데 시간이 많이 걸린다'고 유추할 수 있다. 따라서 정답은 (C)이다.

6 Listen to an English teacher talking to her class.

W Many writers in history have taken pen names. There are many cases of female writers having to write under male pen names. With a pen name, these women could write whatever they wanted. They didn't have to worry about getting in trouble for their words.

번역 영어 선생님이 반 학생들에게 하는 말을 들으세요.

여 역사적으로 많은 작가들이 필명을 사용했습니다. 남성의 필명으로 글을 써야 했던 여성 작가들의 사례도 많이 있습니다. 필명을 사용함으로써 이들 여성 작가들은 자신들이 원하는 건 무엇이든 쓸 수가 있었습니다. 자신들이 쓰는 내용 때문에 문제가 생길지도 모른다는 염려를 할 필요가 없었죠.

6. 선생님은 여성 작가들에 관해 무엇을 암시하나요?

(A) 그다지 재능이 없었다.

(B) 필명을 사용하면서 보다 자유로움을 느꼈다.

(C) 그들은 언제나 필명을 사용해야 했다.

(D) 자신들의 남편에 관한 글을 쓸 수 있었다.

pen name 필명, 펜네임 female 여자의, 여성의 male 남자의, 남성의 whatever 어떤 ~일지라도, 어떤 ~이든
get in trouble 곤경에 빠지다, 큰일나다

정답 및 해설 **[추론 문제]** 선생님은 역사적으로 볼 때 많은 작가들이 필명을 사용했다고 말하면서, 특히 여성 작가들이 남성의 이름을 딴 필명으로 글을 쓴 사례들이 있었음을 언급한다. 덧붙여 "필명을 사용함으로써 여성 작가들은 원하는 것은 무엇이든지 쓸 수 있었다(With a pen name, these women could write whatever they wanted.)"고 설명한다. 이를 근거로 '여성 작가들이 진짜 이름이 아닌 필명을 사용함으로써 글쓰기에 좀더 자유로움을 느꼈을 것'이라고 유추할 수 있다. 따라서 정답은 (B)이다.

Unit 4 Prediction Questions

□ Example Announcement / Talk Excerpt

농구 코치가 팀 선수들에게 하는 말을 들으세요.

여 선수들, 오늘 경기는 무척 중요한 경기이다. 전에 몇 차례 경기를 해봤으니까 이 팀에 대해서는 잘 알고 있을 것이다. 기억하겠지만 이 팀의 최고 선수는 21번 선수다. 아마 이름이 Sally였던 것 같다. 그 선수가 코트에 나오면 반드시 커버하도록 해야 한다. 내가 이 선수를 확실히 커버할 수 있는 전략을 세웠다.

Q. 코치는 다음에 무엇을 할까요?

(A) Sally의 번호가 21번인지 확인한다.

(B) Sally를 막을 수 있는 전략을 설명한다.

(C) 선수들에게 코트로 나가라고 지시한다.

(D) 어떤 선수가 Sally만큼 잘 하는지 결정한다.

best player 최고 선수, 가장 우수한 선수 court (농구 등의) 코트, 경기장 cover (스포츠 경기에서 상대 선수를) 마크하다, 커버하다
plan 전략, 계획, 플랜

□ Announcement / Talk Example

영어 선생님이 반 학생들에게 하는 말을 들으세요.

남 오늘밤 숙제는 여러분들 가족 중 한 명을 인터뷰하는 것입니다. 어릴 적에 가장 좋았던 기억에 대해 물어보세요. 완전한 하나의 이야기여도 좋고, 어떤 한 순간의 기억이어도 좋습니다. 종이에 그 기억들을 기록해서 내일 수업 시간에 가져오도록 해요. 오늘밤 인터뷰하는 것 잊지 마세요!

Q. 학생들은 오늘 저녁에 무엇을 할까요?

(A) 선생님에게 여러 기억들의 목록을 가져다 드린다.

(B) 가족 중 한 사람에게 그들의 기억에 관해 물어본다.

(C) 자신의 어린 시절 가운데 최고의 기억을 떠올려본다.

(D) 가족 구성원에 관한 독창적인 글을 쓰기 시작한다.

interview 인터뷰하다, 면담하다 childhood 어린 시절 single 단 하나의, 단일의 record 기록하다, 적어 놓다

□ Dictation

1 Listen to a science teacher talking to students in class.

M I know we didn't have a lot of time to talk about the lab report after we ① completed the lab. Still, I hope it wasn't too difficult for you to write. If you used Chapter 4 when writing your reports, I'm sure you'll be fine. Chapter 4 has ② all the information about the project. Okay, now ③ it's time to hand in your lab reports.

번역 과학 선생님이 반 학생들에게 하는 말을 들으세요.

남 지난번에 실험을 끝내고 난 후 실험 보고서에 관해 얘기해 볼 시간이 많지 않았다는 건 알고 있습니다. 그렇지만 여러분들이 보고서를 쓰는 게 많이 힘들지는 않았기를 바랍니다. 보고서 작성시 (교과서) 4단원을 참고했다면 별 문제가 없었을 겁니다. 4단원은 그 실험 프로젝트에 관한 모든 정보를 담고 있으니까요. 좋습니다, 이제 여러분이 쓴 보고서를 제출할 시간입니다.

1. 이 반은 다음에 무엇을 할까요?
(A) 지난 주 실험에 대한 보고서를 쓴다.
(B) 선생님에게 실험 보고서를 제출한다.
(C) 왜 4단원을 읽지 않았는지 설명한다.
(D) 자신들이 좋은 점수를 받을 자격이 있는지에 관해 결정한다.

lab report 실험 보고서 complete 완료하다, 끝마치다 it's time to ~할 시간이다 hand in (과제물 등을)제출하다, 내다

정답 및 해설 [예측 문제] 과학 선생님이 실험 보고서에 대해 말하고 있다. 보고서 작성이 너무 어렵지 않았기를 바란다면서 (교과서)4단원을 참고했다면 별 문제 없었을 거라고 한다. 그리고 마지막에 "이제 실험 보고서를 제출할 시간이다(Okay, now it's time to hand in your lab reports.)"라고 말하는데, 이 말로 미루어볼 때 학생들이 곧이어 '선생님께 실험 보고서를 제출할 것'임을 예측할 수 있다. 따라서 정답은 (B)이다.

2 Listen to a teacher talking to her class.

W Today I'm going to teach you ① how to make paper cranes. You'll make the cranes from folded pieces of paper. Folding paper ② to create beautiful artwork is known as origami. This is a Japanese art. Anyway, ③ legend says that if one person folds 1,000 paper cranes ④ they will be granted a wish by a crane. I doubt anyone will have time to make 1,000 today, but we can try!

번역 선생님이 반 학생들에게 하는 말을 들으세요.

여 오늘은 여러분들에게 종이학 접는 방법을 가르쳐 줄게요. 여러분들은 종이를 접어서 학을 만들 거예요. 종이 접기를 통해 아름다운 수공예품을 만드는 걸 '오리가미'라고 합니다. '오리가미'는 일본 예술입니다. 자, 전설에 따르면 한 사람이 1,000 개의 종이학을 접으면 학이 소원을 들어준다고 합니다. 여러분들 중에 오늘 1,000마리나 되는 종이학을 접을 사람이 있을 거라고는 생각지 않지만, 한번 시도해볼까요?

2. 반 학생들은 다음에 무엇을 할까요?
(A) 종이학 1,000 마리를 접는다.
(B) 일본 예술에 대해 배운다.
(C) 종이학 접는 방법을 배운다.
(D) 종이학에게 소원을 빈다.

crane 학, 두루미 fold (종이나 천을)접다 artwork 수공예품, 예술적 제작 활동 origami 종이 접기 legend 전설 grant a wish 소원을 하나 들어주다

정답 및 해설 [예측 문제] 선생님이 학생들에게 "오늘은 여러분들에게 종이학 접는 방법을 가르쳐 주겠다(Today I'm going to teach you how to make paper cranes.)"고 말한 후, 종이학 접기와 관련된 이야기를 한다. 마지막에 "시도는 해 볼 수 있다(~ we can try!)"며 종이 접기를 시작할 것임을 시사한다. 그러므로 학생들이 곧 '종이학 접는 방법을 배울 것이다'라고 짐작할 수 있다. 따라서 정답은 (C)이다.

□ Practice Test

1. (D)	2. (D)	3. (A)	4. (B)	5. (B)	6. (B)

1 Listen to a principal talking to a group of students.

W I wanted to tell you that the city is having a mural contest. A mural will be painted on City Hall sometime this summer. Each school in the city is sending in a mural design and I'd like you to work as a group to do it. I hope many of you are interested. If you'd like to participate, then come speak with me now. Otherwise, you can go home.

번역 교장 선생님이 몇몇 학생들에게 하는 말을 들으세요.

여 시에서 벽화 그리기 대회를 개최할 거라는 걸 알려주고 싶었습니다. 벽화는 올 여름 중에 시청에 그려지게 될 것입니다. 시 소재 학교는 각각 벽화 디자인을 제출하게 되는데, 여러분들이 그 일을 함께 했으면 합니다. 여러분들 중에 관심 있는 학생들이 많으면 좋겠군요. 참가하고 싶은 학생은 지금 나하고 얘기를 하면 됩니다. 아니면 집에 가도 좋아요.

1. 학생들은 다음에 무엇을 할까요?
(A) 시청에 벽화 디자인을 보낸다.
(B) 집에서 (자기가 속한) 모임 사람들과 만나보도록 한다.
(C) 시에서 펼쳐지는 벽화 대회에 참가한다.
(D) 남아서 교장 선생님과 얘기를 나누거나 집으로 간다.

mural 벽화 **City Hall** 시청 **send in** 제출하다; (처리될 곳으로) 발송하다 **participate** 참가하다, 참여하다
otherwise 그렇지 않으면; 그 외에는

정답 및 해설 **[예측 문제]** 교장 선생님이 학생들에게 시에서 개최하는 벽화 그리기 대회에 대해 설명하고 있다. 마지막에 "참가하고 싶으면 지금 나와 함께 얘기를 나누고, 그렇지 않으면 집에 가도 된다(If you'd like to participate, then come speak with me now. Otherwise, you can go home.)"라고 했다. 이를 볼 때 학생들은 '교장 선생님과 이야기하기 위해 남거나 집으로 가거나' 둘 중 하나를 선택한다고 예측할 수 있다. 따라서 정답은 (D)이다.

2 Listen to an announcement on the school intercom.

M Hello, everyone. All student report cards were handed out today. These report cards need to be signed by your parents and brought back to school as soon as possible. When you are leaving school, check the bulletin boards. We've posted the list for the honor roll. Many of you will be happy to see your names on the list.

번역 학교 안내 방송을 들으세요.

남 안녕하십니까, 여러분. 오늘 전교생 성적표를 배부했습니다. 이번 성적표는 부모님 서명을 받은 후 가능한 빨리 학교에 제출하여야 합니다. 하교할 때 게시판을 확인해 주세요. 우등생 명단을 게시해 두었습니다. 많은 학생들이 명단에 이름이 올라가 기쁠 것입니다.

2. 학생들은 하교길에 무엇을 할까요?
(A) 우등생 명단에 자신의 이름을 추가한다.
(B) 부모님께 전화해서 집까지 데려다 달라고 한다.
(C) 각자 성적표를 게시판에 게시한다.
(D) 게시판에 붙은 우등생 명단을 확인한다.

report card 성적표 **sign** 서명하다, 사인하다 **bulletin board** 게시판 **post** (안내문 등을) 게시하다, 공고하다
honor roll 우등생 명단

정답 및 해설 **[예측 문제]** 학생들에게 오늘 성적표가 배부되었으니까 집에 가서 서명을 받아오라고 공지한다. 또 마지막에 "우등생 명단을 게시했으니 하교할 때 게시판을 확인해 보라(When you are leaving school, check the bulletin boards. We've posted the list for the honor roll.)"고 했다. 때문에 학생들은 집에 돌아가는 길에 '게시판의 우등생 명단을 확인해 볼 것'이라고 예측할 수 있다. 따라서 정답은 (D)이다.

3 Listen to a teacher talking to a class.

W Class, we're going to start our work with bean plants. First, I'm going to show you the best way to plant your bean seeds. It's important that everyone's seeds grow big and strong so that we can work with the plants later. We'll take care of the growing plants in class together, but it's important that you plant your seeds correctly first. OK, let's go. Take your seed cup and fill it with soil.

번역 **선생님이 학생들에게 하는 말을 들으세요.**

여 여러분, 콩 나무로 수업을 시작하겠습니다. 먼저, 선생님이 콩 씨앗을 심는 가장 좋은 방법을 보여줄게요. 여러분들이 심은 씨앗이 모두 크고 건강하게 자라게 하는 게 중요합니다. 그래야 나중에 그 식물로 함께 작업할 수 있습니다. 학급 친구들이 모두 함께 성장하는 식물을 보살피겠지만, 우선은 씨앗을 제대로 심는 것이 중요합니다. 자, 시작하죠. 씨앗 컵에 흙을 채우도록 하세요.

3. 선생님은 다음에 무엇을 할까요?

(A) 학생들에게 씨앗 심는 방법을 보여준다.

(B) 반에서 재배한 콩을 먹는다.

(C) 식물이 크고 건강하게 자라도록 신경 쓴다.

(D) 학생들에게 건강한 콩 식물의 사진을 준다.

bean 콩 **plant** 식물; (나무나 씨 등을) 심다 **seed** 씨, 씨앗 **grow** (식물 등이) 자라다; (식물 등을) 재배하다 **soil** 흙, 토양

정답 및 해설 **[예측 문제]** 선생님이 학생들에게 콩 씨앗 심기를 시작할 것이라고 말하면서 "먼저, 선생님이 콩 씨앗을 가장 잘 심는 방법을 보여주겠다(**First, I'm going to show you the best way to plant your bean seeds.**)"라고 한다. 그리고 마지막에 "시작할 테니 씨앗 컵을 가져와서 흙으로 채워라(**OK, let's go. Take your seed cup and fill it with soil.**)"라고 지시한다. 이를 볼 때 선생님이 학생들에게 '씨앗을 심는 방법을 보여줄 것'을 예측할 수 있다. 따라서 정답은 (A)이다.

4 Listen to a teacher talking to students.

W If you're interested in theater, a great play is coming to town next month. It's about soldiers and their families during World War I. It starts on Friday, November 3rd and goes until the end of the month. Hmm... I can't seem to remember the name of the play. Wait a moment... I'll take a look at my ticket.

번역 **선생님이 학생들에게 하는 말을 들으세요.**

여 여러분들이 연극에 관심이 있다면, 다음 달 우리 고장에 멋진 연극 상연이 있습니다. 1차 세계대전 당시 군인과 그 가족들에 관한 이야기인데요. 11월 3일 금요일에 시작해서 11월 말까지 공연됩니다. 음… 연극 이름이 생각나지 않는군요. 잠깐만요… 선생님이 티켓을 한번 볼게요.

4. 선생님은 다음에 무엇을 할까요?

(A) 백과사전에서 연극을 찾아본다.

(B) (자신의) 티켓에서 연극 이름을 찾아본다.

(C) 학생들에게 내일까지 기다리라고 한다.

(D) 인터넷을 통해 연극에 관해 알아본다.

theater 연극, 극작품 **play** 연극; 희곡 **soldier** 군인, 병사 **the end of** ~의 끝, ~의 종말

정답 및 해설 **[예측 문제]** 선생님이 다음 달에 있을 연극에 대해 소개하고 있다. 연극의 내용과 공연 기간에 대해 알려주다가 마지막에 "연극의 제목이 기억나지 않으니 티켓을 봐야겠다(**I can't seem to remember the name of the play. ~ I'll take a look at my ticket.**)"라고 말한다. 그러므로 선생님이 자신의 티켓을 꺼내어 '연극 제목을 확인할 것'임을 예측할 수 있다. 따라서 정답은 (B)이다.

5 Listen to a zoo keeper talking to a group of students.

M I'm so glad you were able to come to the zoo today. Here we are at my favorite exhibit. Can you see the monkeys? These monkeys come from all over the world, but most are from Indonesia. If you'd like to feed the monkeys, come and take a piece of bread from this basket. They're always hungry. I'm sure they want to eat!

번역 **동물원 사육사가 몇몇 학생들에게 하는 말을 들으세요.**

남 여러분들이 오늘 동물원에 와 주어서 무척 기쁩니다. 이곳은 제가 제일 좋아하는 곳이에요. 여러분들 원숭이가 보이나요? 이 원숭이들은 세계 여러 곳에서 왔는데요, 대개는 인도네시아에서 왔습니다. 원숭이에게 먹이를 주고 싶다면 여기 와서 바구니에서 빵 한 조각을 집도록 해요. 원숭이들은 언제나 배고파 하거든요. 틀림없이 먹고 싶어 할 겁니다.

5. 학생들은 다음에 무엇을 할까요?
(A) 덤불 속에 숨은 원숭이를 찾는다.
(B) 바구니 안에 든 빵을 원숭이에게 먹인다.
(C) 동물원 사육사가 지켜보는 가운데 원숭이를 쓰다듬는다.
(D) 동물원 사육사에게 왜 원숭이가 신나 하는지 물어본다.

come from ~에서 나오다, ~ 출신이다 **Indonesia** 인도네시아(*동남아시아의 말레이 제도로 이루어진 공화국)
feed (동물에게) 먹이를 주다 **basket** 바구니

정답 및 해설 **[예측 문제]** 동물원 사육사가 동물원에 견학 온 학생들에게 원숭이를 소개하고 있다. "원숭이에게 먹이를 주고 싶으면 와서 바구니에 든 빵 조각을 가져가라(**If you'd like to feed the monkeys, come and take a piece of bread from this basket.**)"라고 말한 것을 볼 때, 학생들이 '바구니에 들어 있는 빵을 원숭이에게 먹일 것'이라고 예측할 수 있다. 따라서 정답은 (B)이다. (A), (C), (D)와 관련된 내용은 언급되지 않았다.

6 Listen to a history teacher talking to a class.

W Okay, so your next presentation will be on Monday. This presentation will be on an aspect of the Revolutionary War. You'll be working in groups of three to four and will be working on a topic that I've assigned you. I've already organized the groups and I'm sure you want to know what they are.

번역 **역사 선생님이 학생들에게 하는 말을 들으세요.**

여 자, 여러분의 다음 발표는 월요일에 있을 겁니다. 이번 발표는 독립 전쟁의 특성을 주제로 할 겁니다. 3~4명의 그룹을 만들어 하게 되는데 선생님이 각 그룹에 정해준 주제에 대해 발표하면 됩니다. 선생님이 벌써 그룹을 분류했는데요, 여러분들이 분명 궁금할 테지요.

6. 선생님은 다음에 무엇을 할까요?
(A) 독립 전쟁에 대해 설명한다.
(B) 학생들이 속한 그룹을 말해 준다.
(C) 학생 개개인에게 다른 토픽을 지정해 준다.
(D) 학생들에게 각자 그룹을 만들라고 말한다.

aspect 측면, 양상 **Revolutionary War** 독립 전쟁(*미국사: 1775~1783) **in groups** 무리를 이루어, 집단을 이루어
assign (일, 책임 등을)맡기다, 부과하다 **organize** (특정한 구조로)정리하다, 체계화하다; (어떤 일을)준비하다, 조직하다

정답 및 해설 **[예측 문제]** 역사 선생님이 월요일에 있을 다음 발표는 독립 전쟁에 대한 것이고 선생님이 정해 준 주제에 대해 3~4명씩 그룹으로 나뉘어 발표하게 될 것이라고 말한다. 마지막에 "이미 그룹을 정했는데 여러분이 어떤 그룹인지 알고 싶을 것이다(**I've already organized the groups and I'm sure you want to know what they are.**)"라고 한 것을 볼 때 선생님이 곧이어 '학생들이 어떤 그룹에 속했는지 알려줄 것'이라고 예측할 수 있다. 따라서 정답은 (B)이다. (C)는 그룹 발표 후에 할 일이고, 또한 각자가 아닌 그룹 프로젝트라고 했으므로 정답이 될 수 없다.

Unit 5 Speaker's Purpose Questions

□ Example Announcement / Talk Excerpt

선생님이 학생들에게 하는 말을 들으세요.

여 여러분, 모두들 기억하겠지만, 내일은 우리 학급 소풍날입니다. 여러분들이 자진해서 각자 다른 물품들을 가져오기로 했다는 걸 다시 한번 말합니다. 선생님은 접시와 컵을 가져올게요, 음식을 가져오는 건 여러분 몫입니다. 어떤 음식을 가져오기로 했는지 기억나지 않으면 교실 앞쪽에 있는 목록을 확인해 보도록 하세요.

Q. 선생님이 하는 말의 목적은 무엇인가요?

(A) 학생들에게 내일 일정을 설명하는 것
(B) 누가 접시와 컵을 가져오는지 설명하는 것
(C) 학생들이 소풍날 음식을 가져오도록 다시 한번 상기시키는 것
(D) 학생들에게 소풍 시간을 알려주는 것

> **volunteer** (자발적으로) 지원하다, 자진하다; 자원 봉사로 하다 **item** 물품, 품목, 항목 **plate** 접시 **responsibility** 책임, 맡은 일 **agree** 동의하다, 의견이 일치하다

□ Announcement / Talk Example

음악 선생님이 반 학생들에게 하는 말을 들으세요.

남 비틀스는 1960년대에 탄생한 가장 위대한 그룹 가운데 하나입니다. 여러분들도 아마 John, Paul, George, 그리고 Ringo라는 이름을 들어봤을 겁니다. 비틀스의 첫 번째 히트곡은 <I want to hold your hand>인데요, 이들은 TV에서 라이브로 연주한 최초의 밴드이기도 합니다. 이 그룹은 정말 대단한 인기를 끌었으며 1960년대에 많은 젊은이들의 사랑을 받았습니다.

Q. 화자의 목적은 무엇인가요?

(A) 비틀스라는 밴드 소개
(B) John, Paul, George, 그리고 Ringo에 대한 신원 확인
(C) 1960년대에 TV에서 어떤 밴드가 음악을 연주했는지에 대한 설명
(D) 비틀스가 자신이 가장 좋아하는 밴드임을 학생들에게 알림

> **The Beatles** 비틀스(*1962~1970년에 활동한 영국의 4인조 락그룹) **hit** 히트 곡, 히트 음반 **live** 라이브의, 실황인; 생방송의 **incredibly** 믿을 수 없을 정도로; 엄청나게

□ Dictation

1 Listen to a math team coach talking to his team.

M I know this team is older than you, but it doesn't mean that they're smarter. Remember that you have ① the best math skills in your school. You can beat anyone ② when it comes to math. You are a strong team and ③ haven't lost a meet. Let's work together and ④ beat this team!

번역 수학 팀 코치가 팀원들에게 하는 말을 들으세요.

남 이 팀이 여러분들보다 나이가 많다는 건 선생님도 압니다. 하지만 그 말이 곧 그들이 여러분보다 더 똑똑하다는 의미는 아니에요. 여러분들의 수학 실력이 학교에서 가장 뛰어나다는 걸 잊지 말도록 해요. 수학에 관해서라면 여러분들은 그 누구라도 이길 수 있습니다. 여러분들은 강한 팀이고, 한번도 진 적이 없습니다. 함께 힘써서 이 팀을 이겨보도록 합시다.

1. 코치가 학생들에게 말하는 이유는 무엇인가요?

(A) 다른 팀을 겁주기 위해서
(B) 학생들이 겁먹도록 하기 위해서
(C) 학생들의 학업을 도와주기 위해서
(D) 학생들에게 자신감을 심어주기 위해서

skill 기량, 솜씨; 기능, 기술	when it comes to ~에 관한 한, ~에 관해서라면	meet 대회, 경기

정답 및 해설 **[화자의 의도를 묻는 문제]** 수학 팀 코치가 대회를 앞둔 멤버들을 격려하고 있다. "너희들 수학 실력이 학교에서 가장 뛰어나다는 걸 명심하라(**Remember that you have the best math skills in your school**)"고 말하면서, "수학에 관해서라면 어느 누구라도 이길 수 있다(**You can beat anyone when it comes to math.**)"라고 덧붙인다. 이런 격려의 말들을 볼 때, 코치는 '학생들에게 자신감을 가지라고 격려'하고 있음을 알 수 있다. 따라서 정답은 (D)이다.

2 Listen to an English teacher speaking to her class.

W This month is National Poetry Month, so ① we'll be celebrating by studying poetry. Poetry is ② a timeless art that has helped people ③ to express and explain life on Earth. Some poems are long, and some poems are short. Some are funny, and others are serious and sad. We'll be studying ④ all sorts of different poems in English class this month.

번역 **영어 선생님이 반 학생들에게 하는 말을 들으세요.**

여 이번 달은 〈전국 시의 달〉이죠, 그래서 시 공부를 해서 이를 기념하려고 해요. 시는 사람들로 하여금 이 지구상에서의 삶을 표현하고 설명할 수 있게끔 하는, 세월이 흘러도 변치 않는 예술입니다. 어떤 시들은 길고, 또 어떤 시들은 짧죠. 어떤 시들은 재미있고, 또 어떤 시들은 엄숙하고 슬픕니다. 이달 영어 수업 시간에는 이런 모든 종류의 시들에 관해 공부할 겁니다.

2. 선생님이 하는 말의 목적은 무엇인가요?
(A) 학생들에게 시를 쓰라고 하는 것
(B) 시의 의미에 대해 설명하는 것
(C) 시 대회에 누가 나갈 것인지를 결정하는 것
(D) 〈전국 시의 달〉 기간 동안 시에 대한 공부를 하겠다고 소개하는 것

poetry 시	celebrate 기념하다, 축하하다	timeless 세월이 흘러도 변치 않는; 영원한	express 나타내다, 표하다

정답 및 해설 **[화자의 의도를 묻는 문제]** 영어 선생님이 학생들에게 "이번 달은 〈전국 시의 달〉이기 때문에 시 공부를 통해 이를 기념할 것(**This month is National Poetry Month, so we'll be celebrating by studying poetry.**)"이라고 한다. 이어서 시에 대한 보충 설명을 한 후 마지막에 "이번 달 영어 시간에는 모든 종류의 시들을 공부할 것(**We'll be studying all sorts of different poems in English class this month.**)"이라고 했다. 즉, 선생님은 '시 공부에 대한 소개'를 목적으로 하고 있음을 알 수 있다. 따라서 정답은 (D)이다. (B)는 세부 사항의 하나이고, (A)와 (C)는 언급되지 않았다.

□ Practice Test

1. (C)	2. (A)	3. (C)	4. (A)	5. (C)	6. (C)

1 Listen to a teacher talking to her class.

W Well, students, today is the day of the Spelling Bee. Please stand up and get in a line. I will give you a word and you'll have to spell it. You will only have one chance to spell each word. If you're incorrect, you have to return to your seat. The last person standing will win tickets to the movie theater.

번역 **선생님이 반 학생들에게 하는 말을 들으세요.**

여 자, 여러분, 오늘은 〈스펠링 비(철자 맞추기 대회)〉의 날입이다. 일어서서 한 줄로 서세요. 선생님이 여러분한테 단어를 하나 제시하면 여러분들은 철자를 대는 겁니다. 단어 당 철자를 말할 수 있는 기회는 딱 한 번입니다. 틀리게 말하면 자기 자리로 돌아가는 거예요. 가장 마지막까지 서 있는 사람은 영화 표를 받게 됩니다.

1. 선생님이 하는 말의 목적은 무엇인가요?
(A) 누가 가장 철자를 잘 맞추는지 찾아내기
(B) 학생들에게 책을 읽으라고 상기시키기
(C) 〈스펠링 비〉의 규칙을 설명하기
(D) 학생들에게 자기 자리로 돌아갈 것을 지시하기

Spelling Bee 철자법 대회 in a line 한 줄로, 일렬로 spell 철자를 말하다, (단어를)맞춤법에 따라 쓰다 incorrect 틀린, 맞지 않는 seat 자리, 좌석

정답 및 해설 **[화자의 의도를 묻는 문제]** 선생님이 학생들에게 "오늘은 〈철자 맞추기 대회〉가 있는 날이다(**Well, students, today is the day of the Spelling Bee.**)"라고 말한다. 이어서 대회의 방법과 규칙을 구체적으로 설명한다. 따라서 선생님의 주된 목적은 '〈철자 맞추기 대회〉에 관한 규칙을 설명하는 것'이라고 볼 수 있다. 그러므로 정답은 (C)이다. (A)와 (B)는 언급되지 않았고, (D)는 여러 규칙 중 하나에 해당하므로 정답이 될 수 없다.

2 Listen to a principal talking to a group of students.

M I was not impressed with your behavior during today's talent show. Those were your friends and classmates who were performing on stage. It was very rude of you to talk loudly and send text messages throughout the performance. An audience should not act that way. I'm very disappointed in you.

번역 **교장 선생님이 몇몇 학생들에게 하는 말을 들으세요.**

남 여러분들이 오늘 장기자랑에서 보여준 행동은 무척 실망스러웠습니다. 무대에서 공연한 학생들은 여러분의 친구이자 반 친구들입니다. 공연 내내 큰 소리로 떠들고 문자를 보내는 건 무척 무례한 행동입니다. 관객들은 그렇게 행동하면 안 됩니다. 여러분들에게 무척 실망했습니다.

2. 교장 선생님이 공연 중 문자 보내는 것에 대해 말한 이유는 무엇인가요?

(A) 좋지 못한 행동의 예를 들기 위해
(B) 학생들이 왜 시끄러웠는지 설명하기 위해
(C) 자신이 문자 메시지를 받았다는 것을 보여주기 위해
(D) 휴대 전화가 문제라는 것을 증명하기 위해

talent show 장기자랑 on stage 무대에 서서, 공연 중인 rude 무례한, 예의가 없는 loudly 큰 소리로; 소란하게 text message (휴대 전화로 보내는)문자 메시지 throughout ~ 동안, 죽, 내내 audience 청중, 관중 disappointed 실망한, 낙담한

정답 및 해설 **[화자의 의도를 묻는 문제]** 교장 선생님이 오늘 장기자랑에서 보였던 학생들의 태도에 실망감을 보이며 그들을 훈계하는 내용이다. 이런 상황에서 "공연 내내 큰 소리로 말하거나 문자 메시지를 보내는 것은 매우 무례하다(**It was very rude of you to talk loudly and send text messages throughout the performance.**)"라고 말한 것을 볼 때, 여기서의 '문자 메시지'는 '좋지 못한 행동에 대한 한 가지 예'라는 것을 알 수 있다. 따라서 정답은 (A)이다.

3 Listen to an announcement on the school intercom.

W Hello, students. This is Secretary Searles speaking. This is a reminder that your health forms are due to the front office by tomorrow. If we don't have your health forms, we will not give you your report cards. I imagine you and your parents would like to see your grades, so I hope to see the forms by tomorrow.

번역 **학교 안내 방송을 들으세요.**

여 학생 여러분, 안녕하세요. 저는 학교 서기 Searles입니다. 내일까지 여러분의 건강 양식을 사무실로 제출해야 함을 다시 한번 알립니다. 건강 양식을 제출하지 않으면 성적표를 주지 않을 겁니다. 여러분이나 여러분 부모님 모두 성적표가 궁금할 테니 내일까지 꼭 양식을 제출하기 바랍니다.

3. 학교 서기가 성적표에 대해 말하는 이유는 무엇인가요?

(A) 학생들 성적이 좋지 않다고 겁주려고
(B) 학부모님들이 관심을 가지고 있는지 물어보려고
(C) 건강 양식을 제출하지 않으면 어떤 일이 발생하는지 설명하려고
(D) 성적표가 마무리되지 않았음을 경고하려고

secretary 총무, 서기, 비서 form 양식; (문서의)서식

정답 및 해설 **[화자의 의도를 묻는 문제]** 학생들에게 내일까지 건강 양식을 제출하라고 공지하면서 "만약 건강 양식을 제출하지 않으면, 성적표를 주지 않을 것(**if we don't have your health forms, we will not give you your report cards.**)"이라고 말한다. 이를 볼 때 성적표를 언급한 이유는 '건강 양식을 제출하지 않으면 성적표를 내주지 않을 것'이라는 일종의 경고성 공지임을 알 수 있다. 따라서 정답은 (C)이다. (A), (B), (D)는 언급되지 않았다.

4 Listen to a teacher talking to a class.

M I'm pleased to announce that our own Betsy Phillips has been elected as the president of the eighth grade class. I'm so proud that someone from our homeroom has taken the position and I know how much work some of you put into helping Betsy. Congratulations, everybody. Betsy, I'm sure you'll do a great job.

번역 **선생님이 반 학생들에게 하는 말을 들으세요.**

남 우리 반의 Betsy Phillips가 8학년 회장으로 선출되었다는 소식을 전하게 되어 기쁘군요. 우리 반 학생이 회장직을 맡아 무척 자랑스럽습니다. 여러분들이 Betsy를 도우려고 많이 노력했다는 걸 압니다. 여러분 모두 축하합니다. Betsy, 선생님은 네가 회장직을 잘 수행할 거라고 믿는다.

4. 선생님 말씀의 목적은 무엇인가요?
(A) Betsy의 선출을 축하하는 것
(B) Betsy를 자랑스러워하는 사람이 있는지 물어보는 것
(C) Betsy에게 회장직으로 선출된 이유를 설명하는 것
(D) Betsy에게 투표한 학생들에게 감사 인사를 하는 것

announce 발표하다, 알리다 be elected as ~로 선출되다, ~로 당선되다 homeroom 홈룸(*학생들이 등교하면 모이는 교실)
position (영향력과 관련된) 위치; 직위

정답 및 해설 **[화자의 의도를 묻는 문제]** 선생님이 반 학생들에게 "우리 반의 Betsy Phillips가 8학년 회장으로 선출되었다는 소식을 전하게 되어 기쁘다(**I'm pleased to announce that our own Betsy Phillips has been elected as the president of the eighth grade class.**)"라고 말하면서 축하하고 있다. 따라서 화자의 목적은 'Betsy의 당선을 축하하기 위한 것'이고, 정답은 (A)이다.

5 Listen to a librarian talking to a group of students.

W If you take out a book, it's very important that you return the book on time. It is likely that there are many other students who'd like to read the book or use the book for a class project. If your book is over two weeks late, you will be charged a fee. The more days that go by, the bigger that fee gets.

번역 **도서관 사서가 몇몇 학생들에게 하는 말을 들으세요.**

여 책을 대출한 경우 제때에 반납하는 일은 무척 중요합니다. 학급 과제 때문에 그 책을 읽거나 사용해야 할 학생들이 많이 있을 수 있습니다. 2주가 지나도 책을 반납하지 않으면 연체료를 물어야 합니다. 날이 지날수록 연체료도 더 올라갑니다.

5. 도서관 사서가 연체료에 대해 말하는 이유는 무엇인가요?
(A) 학생들이 항상 (도서 반납을) 늦게 한다는 점을 증명하려고
(B) 학생들에게 도서관 카드를 소개하려고
(C) 책을 반납하지 않으면 어떤 일이 일어나는지를 설명하려고
(D) 학생들이 싫어하는 것 중 한 가지 예를 들려고

return 돌려주다, 반납하다; 돌아가다, 돌아오다 on time 제때에, 시간을 어기지 않고, 정각에 be likely ~할 것 같다
charge a fee 수수료를 받다

정답 및 해설 **[화자의 의도를 묻는 문제]** 도서관 사서가 학생들에게 책 대출을 했을 경우 제때에 반납할 것을 당부하고 있다. "만약 2주가 지나도 책을 반납하지 않으면, 연체료를 내야 한다(**If your book is over two weeks late, you will be charged a fee.**)"라고 말한 것으로 보아 사서가 연체료에 대해 언급한 이유는 '책이 반납되지 않을 경우 어떤 일이 발생하는지를 설명하기 위한 것'으로 파악할 수 있다. 따라서 정답은 (C)이다. (A), (B), (D)는 언급되지 않았다.

6 Listen to a history teacher talking to a class.

M For this unit, we're going to do something a little bit different. Instead of writing a paper about the time period we just discussed, we're going to put on a play about it. I'd like you to get into groups and each write one scene. This scene should show something important that happened during the 19th century.

번역 역사 선생님이 반 학생들에게 하는 말을 들으세요.

남 이번 과에서는 (평상시와는) 조금 다르게 해보겠습니다. 우리가 방금 토론한 시대에 관한 보고서를 쓰는 대신 이것과 관련한 연극을 하나 만들 겁니다. 그룹을 지어서 각 그룹에서 한 장면을 쓰는 거예요. 각 장면은 19세기에 발생했던 중요 사건을 보여주어야 합니다.

6. 선생님 말씀의 목적은 무엇인가요?

(A) 학생들을 들뜨게 만들기

(B) 19세기에 대해 설명하기

(C) 과제 제시하기

(D) 어려운 숙제에 대해 경고하기

instead of ~ 대신에 period 기간, 시기; (발달 과정의) 단계 scene (영화나 책 등에 나오는) 장면

정답 및 해설 **[화자의 의도를 묻는 문제]** 역사 수업 시간에 선생님이 이번 과는 좀 다른 방식으로 진행할 것이라면서, "우리가 방금 토론한 시대에 대한 보고서 대신 그것과 관련한 연극을 할 것(**Instead of writing a paper about the time period we just discussed, we're going to put on a play about it.**)"이라고 말한다. 그리고 "그룹을 만들어서 한 장면을 쓰라(**I'd like you to get into groups and each write one scene.**)"고 지시한다. 즉, 화자의 목적은 연극 준비라는 '과제를 소개하는 것'이므로, 정답은 (C)이다.

Conversation Question Types

Unit 1 Main Idea Questions

□ Example Dialogue Excerpt

두 친구의 대화를 들으세요.

남 안녕, Sally. 어떻게 지내?

여 잘 지내, Paul, 넌 어때?

남 아주 좋아. 다음 주에 시내에서 가을 축제가 열리는데, 너 갈 거니?

여 모르겠어. 친구들 중에 가고 싶어 하는 애가 하나도 없거든. 혼자 가긴 싫고.

남 나랑 내 친구들이랑 갈래? 우리는 다음 주 토요일에 갈 거야.

여 그거 좋겠다. 몇 시에 만날까?

남 저녁 7시에 축제장 정문에서 만나자. 일찍 도착해서 줄 서서 기다리는 일이 없도록 하고 싶어.

Q. 두 사람은 주로 무슨 얘기를 하고 있나요?

(A) 시내에서 열리는 축세가 언제인지

(B) 여학생이 축제에 가고 싶은지

(C) 축제에 일찍 가려는 이유가 뭔지

(D) 다음 주 수요일 언제쯤 만날 것인지

fair 축제; 박람회 main gate 정문, 앞문 wait in line 줄을 서서 기다리다 get in 들어가다

□ Example Dialogue Excerpt

도서관 사서와 학생의 대화를 들으세요.

학생 안녕하세요.

사서 안녕하세요, 어떻게 도와줄까요, 학생?

학생 이 학교가 처음이라 그러는데 도서관에서 책을 어떻게 빌리는지 알려 주세요.

사서 그거라면 도와줄 수 있어요. 학생증이 있나요?

학생 네, 있습니다. 보여드릴까요?

사서 네, 봅시다. 책을 빌리려면, 내가 학생의 학생증과 학생이 빌리려는 책을 스캔만 하면 됩니다. 책을 반납할 때는, 내가 다시 스캔하고 (빌린 내역을) 학생 계정에서 삭제하면 되죠.

학생 아, 간단하네요. 고맙습니다.

사서 천만에요. 다른 도움이 필요하면 또 찾아오도록 해요.

Q. 대화의 주제는 무엇인가요?

(A) 학생증을 사용하는 방법

(B) 책을 반납하는 방법

(C) 책을 빌리는 방법

(D) 학생 계정을 사용하는 방법

student card 학생증 scan (컴퓨터로 데이터를) 훑다; 정밀 검사하다; (스캐너로) 스캔하다 remove 없애다, 제거하다 account (정보 서비스) 이용 계정

□ Conversation Example

두 친구의 대화를 들으세요.

남 안녕, Joanie. 잘 지내니?

여 안녕, Rex. 잘 지내, 넌?

남 좋아. 물어보고 싶은 게 있는데, 나 이번 겨울에 선택 과목을 어떤 걸로 하는 게 좋을까?

여 글쎄, 난 스키를 선택 과목으로 할 생각인데, 너도 가자.

남 좋겠다. 재미있을 거야. 나도 가고 싶었지만, 그건 너무 비싸서. 그거 말고 제일 괜찮은 선택 과목은 뭐라고 생각해?

여 아마도 하키이지 않을까. 네가 장비를 갖고 있으면, 일주일에 10달러밖에 안 해.

남 괜찮다. 한 달 동안 매주 금요일마다 하키를 하면 좋을 거야. 게다가 가격도 괜찮고.

여 네가 스키 과목에 들어올 수 없는 건 무척 아쉽지만, 넌 하키를 하는 것도 무척 재미있어 할 것 같아.

남 나도 그렇게 생각해. 조언 고마워, Joanie. 나중에 보자.

Q. 두 학생은 주로 무슨 얘기를 하나요?

(A) 어떤 선택 과목을 고를지
(B) 선택 과목 비용이 얼마나 드는지
(C) 남학생이 왜 스키 타러 갈 수 없는지
(D) 남학생이 언제 하키 경기를 할지

elective 선택 과목, 선택 강좌   second best 둘째로 가장 좋은   equipment 장비, 용품   affordable (가격이) 알맞은

□ Dictation

Listen to a conversation between a teacher and a student. (S: student, T: teacher)

S Hello, Mr. Wilson. Can I talk to you for a minute?

T Sure, Genie. What can I do for you?

S Well, sir, I wanted to know ①how to run for school president.

T Really! Excellent. First, you need to have good grades. Do you have an 80% average?

S I have a 92% average. ②What else do I need?

T You need to officially apply to run for presidency. ③Fill out this application form. Return it to me when you are finished.

S OK. Is that all?

T No. You need ④to get students to vote for you, so you'll need to run a campaign. If you win the vote, you'll be school president.

S Great! Thanks for your help, Mr. Wilson. Bye!

T See you soon, Genie.

번역 선생님과 학생의 대화를 들으세요.

학생 안녕하세요, Wilson 선생님. 잠깐 말씀 드릴 게 있는데요.

교사 좋아, Genie. 무엇을 도와줄까?

학생 저, 선생님, 학생 회장에 출마하려면 어떻게 해야 하는지 알고 싶습니다.

교사 그래? 멋지구나. 우선, 성적이 좋아야 하지. 평균 80점 이상이 되니?

학생 평균 92점이에요. 그리고 또 뭐가 필요한가요?

교사 공식적으로 회장 출마를 신청해야 해. 이 신청서를 작성하거라. 그리고 다 작성하면 선생님한테 주면 돼.

학생 알겠습니다. 이게 다인가요?

교사 아니다. 다른 학생들이 너에게 투표하도록 해야 하니까 캠페인 활동을 시작해야 할 거다. 표를 많이 얻으면 학생 회장이 되는 거란다.

학생 네, 도와주셔서 고맙습니다, Wilson 선생님. 안녕히 계세요.

교사 또 보자꾸나, Genie.

Q. 두 사람은 주로 무슨 얘기를 하나요?

(A) 대통령 선거 캠페인
(B) 학생 회장 출마
(C) 학생 회장의 성적
(D) 학교 교장직 신청

run for 출마하다   average 평균의; 평균(수준)   officially 공식적으로   apply to 신청하다   application form 신청서, 신청 용지
vote 투표하다; 표, 총 투표수   campaign 캠페인

정답 및 해설 [주제를 묻는 문제] 학생이 선생님께 "학생 회장에 출마할 수 있는 방법을 알고 싶다(I wanted to know how to run for school president.)"라고 말하자 선생님이 자세하게 출마 조건 및 방법을 설명하고 있다. 따라서 정답은 (B)이다.

□ Practice Test

1. (C)	2. (D)	3. (B)	4. (C)	5. (C)	6. (B)	7. (B)	8. (B)

[1-4] Listen to a conversation between a student and a school nurse. (S: student, N: nurse)

N Hi, Jackie. How can I help you today?

S Hi, Mrs. Collette. I'm here because my brother's at home with lice. My mother wanted me to come in to get my head checked, just to make sure I don't have them, either.

N Oh, no! I'm sorry to hear that Dylan has lice.

S Yes, he's been scratching his head for the past three days.

N Well, it's no problem to give you a head check. Let me ask you— have you shared any brushes or hats with Dylan?

S Not recently, but my mother's worried anyway. She says that lice can live on furniture or on stuffed animals.

N She's right. It's important to be careful. Now, come sit down over here so I can look for lice.

S Okay.

N *(pause)* I can't find any lice or eggs, so it looks like you're fine. Please be careful at home. You could still catch lice from Dylan.

S Thanks, Mrs. Collette. I'll be extra careful.

번역 **학생과 양호 선생님의 대화를 들으세요.**

교사 안녕, Jackie. 오늘은 어떤 일을 도와줄까?

학생 안녕하세요, Collette 선생님. 남동생이 이(*사람 몸에 기생하며 피를 빨아 먹는 곤충)가 생겨서 집에 있거든요. 엄마가 선생님한테 가서 머리 검사를 받아보라고 하셨어요. 저한테 이가 없는지 확인하라고요.

교사 어머나, 저런! Dylan한테 이가 생겼다니 안됐구나.

학생 네, 지난 3일간 계속 머리를 긁고 있어요.

교사 음, 네 머리를 검사해보는 건 별로 어려운 일이 아니지. 근데 물어보자꾸나, 너 Dylan이랑 빗이나 모자를 같이 사용하니?

학생 요즘은 아니에요, 그래도 엄마가 걱정하셔서요. 엄마 말씀이 이는 가구나 봉제 동물 인형 같은 데서도 살 수가 있대요.

교사 맞는 말씀이시다. 조심하는 게 중요하지. 자, 여기 와서 앉아보렴. 선생님이 이가 있는지 보게.

학생 네.

교사 (잠시 후) 이나 그 알은 보이지 않는 걸 보니, 넌 괜찮은 것 같다. 그래도 집에서 신경 쓰려무나. 여전히 Dylan한테 옮을 가능성은 있으니까.

학생 고맙습니다, Collette 선생님. 정말 조심할게요.

lice (*louse의 복수) [곤충]이	scratch (가려운 데를)긁다	share 공유하다, 같이 쓰다	brush 빗	stuffed animal 봉제 동물 인형

1. Jackie의 문제는 무엇인가요?

(A) Dylan한테서 이를 옮았다.

(B) 엄마가 Jackie를 걱정하신다.

(C) Dylan 때문에 이가 옮을지도 모른다.

(D) 양호 선생님을 자주 방문하지 않는다.

정답 및 해설 [주제를 묻는 문제] 여학생이 "남동생의 머리에 이가 생겨서 엄마가 자신한테도 이가 있는지 확인해보라고 했다(~ my brother's at home with lice. My mother wanted me to come in to get my head checked, just to make sure I don't have them, too)"고 말한다. 즉 여학생이 Dylan한테서 이가 옮을지도 몰라 걱정하고 있는 상황이다. 따라서 정답은 (C)이다. 여학생의 머리에서 이나 그 알이 발견되지 않았으므로 (A)는 오답이다.

2. Jackie는 Dylan에 대해 뭐라고 하나요?

(A) 지금 학교에 있다.

(B) 지난주에 양호 선생님을 방문했었다.

(C) 가장 친한 친구한테서 이가 옮았다.

(D) 머리를 많이 긁고 있다.

정답 및 해설 **[세부사항을 묻는 문제]** Dylan한테 이가 생겨서 안됐다는 선생님의 말에 여학생은 "Dylan이 지난 3일 동안 머리를 긁었다(he's been scratching his head for the past three days.)"고 말한다. 따라서 정답은 (D)이다. (B)와 (C)에 대한 언급은 없다.

3. 양호 선생님의 다음 말이 의미하는 것은 무엇인가요? *(have you shared any brushes or hats with Dylan?)*

(A) 여학생과 그녀의 남동생이 같은 모자를 쓰던 걸 봤다.

(B) 이런 물건에서 이가 옮을 수도 있다는 걸 안다.

(C) 여학생이 이에 관해 알고 있다는 사실을 믿지 않는다.

(D) 여학생이 학교로 빗이나 모자를 가져오는 게 걱정이다.

정답 및 해설 **[화자의 어조를 묻는 문제]** 여학생은 남동생한테 이가 생겼고, 그래서 엄마가 자신에게도 이가 생겼는지 걱정하고 계신다면서 "엄마가 선생님한테 가서 머리에 이가 있는지 검사 받으라고 했다(My mother wanted me to come in to get my head checked, ~)"고 한다. 이 말에 선생님이 "Dylan과 빗이나 모자를 같이 썼냐(have you shared any brushes or hats with Dylan?)"고 물어 본 것이다. 즉, 빗이나 모자를 함께 사용하면, 이런 물건들을 통해 이가 옮을 수 있다는 의미가 암시되어 있다. 따라서 정답은 (B)이다.

4. 양호 선생님이 집에서 조심하라고 말한 이유는 무엇인가요?

(A) Jackie는 더 이상 수업에 빠져서는 안 된다.

(B) Dylan의 베개에 이의 알이 있다.

(C) Dylan이 여전히 Jackie에게 이를 옮길 가능성이 있다.

(D) Jackie의 엄마는 두 아이를 모두 돌볼 수 없다.

정답 및 해설 **[수사학적 구조를 묻는 문제]** 선생님은 여학생에게 집에서 주의하라고 말한 이후에 바로 "Dylan으로부터 이를 옮을 수 있다(You could still catch lice from Dylan)"고 한다. 즉, Dylan 때문에 이가 생길 수 있으니까 조심하라는 의미로 해석된다. 따라서 정답은 (C)이다.

[5-8] Listen to a conversation between two students as they leave a classroom. (G: girl, B: boy)

G So Billy, what did you think of Mr. Jackson's idea to enter the school science fair?

B I think it's a great idea, but it sounds like it's going to be really competitive.

G I know. A lot of the best students are going to enter and they'll be hard to beat. I have a great idea for a project, though.

B Oh, really? What is it?

G I'm going to grow a bunch of plants. I'll start by treating them all the same way—giving them the same sunlight, shadow, water, fertilizer, and soil. After they start to grow, I'll change these things to see what happens.

B That sounds like a really interesting project. What kinds of plants are you going to grow?

G I'm not sure. Do you have any ideas?

B You should grow vegetables. That way, you can see what factors make the healthiest and most delicious food.

G Wow! That would be great. Then I can taste the vegetables once they're ripe.

B Exactly.

번역 **두 학생이 교실을 나오면서 나누는 대화를 들으세요.**

여 그래서 말인데, Billy, Jackson 선생님께서 교내 과학 박람회에 참가하라고 말씀하신 거에 대해 어떻게 생각해?

남 좋은 생각인 것 같아, 하지만 무척 경쟁이 심할 것 같던걸.

여 알아. 공부 잘하는 애들이 많이 참가할 테고 그러면 걔들 이기기가 힘들겠지. 그렇지만 나한테 좋은 생각이 있어.

남 아, 정말? 뭔데?

여 식물 한 묶음을 재배할 거야. 처음엔 그 식물들을 동일한 방식으로 기르는 거지. 햇빛도 그림자도, 물이나 비료, 흙까지 똑같이 주는 거야. 그리고 자라기 시작한 후에는 이 조건들에 변화를 준 다음 어떻게 바뀌는지를 관찰하는 거지.

남 정말 재미있는 프로젝트가 될 것 같다. 어떤 식물들을 재배할 거야?

여 잘 모르겠어. 좋은 아이디어 있니?

남 채소를 길러 봐. 그러면 (네가 말한)그런 요소들 중 어떤 게 더 건강하고 맛있는 먹거리를 만들어 내는지 알 수 있겠지.

여 와! 정말 괜찮다. 그럼 다 자란 다음엔 채소를 먹을 수도 있을 거고.

남 그렇지.

G Hey, Mr. Jackson said that two people could work on one project. Do you want to work on this with me?

B I'd love to. Are you sure that's okay? Do you think I can help you?

G Of course! Your vegetable idea was awesome! Plus, it will be much more fun to work as a team!

여 있잖아, Jackson 선생님이 한 프로젝트에 두 사람씩 작업해도 좋다고 하셨잖아. 너 나랑 같이 이 프로젝트 하지 않을래?

남 좋지. 그런데 정말 괜찮겠어? 내가 도움이 될까?

여 물론이지! 네가 말한 채소 아이디어는 정말 좋았어! 게다가, 팀으로 일하면 훨씬 더 재미있을 거야.

enter (대회 등에) 출전하다, 참가하다; 들어가다 **science fair** 과학 박람회 **competitive** 경쟁을 하는; (사람이) 경쟁력 있는
a bunch of 한 묶음의 ~, 한 꾸러미의 ~ **treat** 다루다, 대하다, 취급하다 **fertilizer** 비료 **factor** 요인, 요소, 인자
ripe (과일이나 곡물이) 익은 **awesome** 경탄할 만한, 어마어마한, 엄청난

5. 두 사람은 주로 무엇에 관해 논의하고 있나요?

(A) Jackson 선생님의 과학 수업
(B) 채소밭을 가꾸는 것
(C) 교내 과학 박람회를 위한 아이디어
(D) 과학 박람회가 얼마나 경쟁력이 셀 것인지

정답 및 해설 **[주제를 묻는 문제]** 여학생이 남학생에게 "과학 박람회에 들어가라는 Jackson 선생님의 생각이 어떠냐(What did you think of Mr. Jackson's idea to enter the school science fair?)"라고 물어보자 남학생은 "좋은 생각 같지만 정말 경쟁이 심할 것 같다(I think it's a great idea, but it sounds like it's going to be really competitive.)"고 대답한다. 이어서 여학생이 "나한테 프로젝트를 위한 좋은 아이디어가 있다(I have a great idea for a project, though.)"고 말한 후, 박람회 프로젝트에 대한 세부적인 내용들을 설명한다. 따라서 정답은 (C)이다. 여학생이 말한 프로젝트는 실험용 채소를 기르는 것이지 채소밭을 가꾸는 게 아니므로 (B)는 오답이고, (D)는 대화 중에 언급되었으나 세부 사항에 해당하므로 정답이 될 수 없다.

6. 남학생은 여학생에게 어떤 아이디어를 주나요?

(A) (함께 작업할) 파트너를 찾아야 한다.
(B) 채소를 길러야 한다.
(C) 채소 맛을 보아야 한다.
(D) 식물 재배에 쓰는 흙을 바꾸어야 한다.

정답 및 해설 **[세부사항을 묻는 문제]** 여학생이 어떤 식물을 심을지에 대해 "좋은 생각 있나(Do you have any ideas?)"라고 물어보자 남학생이 "채소를 길러야 한다(You should grow vegetables.)"라고 말한다. 따라서 정답은 (B)이다.

7. 여학생이 남학생의 채소 아이디어가 훌륭하다고 말한 의미는 무엇인가요?

(A) 그가 자신보다 더 똑똑하다.
(B) 그는 파트너로서 무척 도움이 될 것이다.
(C) 그는 지금껏 훌륭한 아이디어를 내놓은 적이 없었다.
(D) 그는 채소에 관해 많이 알고 있다.

정답 및 해설 **[추론 문제]** 프로젝트를 같이 하자고 제안하는 여학생에게 남학생은 "내가 도움이 될 수 있을까(Do you think I can help you?)"라고 물어본다. 이 말에 여학생은 "네가 말한 채소 아이디어는 굉장했다(Your vegetable idea was awesome.)"며, "함께 작업하면 훨씬 더 재미있을 것 같다(~ it will be much more fun to work as a team!)"라고 긍정적인 답변을 한다. 이를 볼 때 여학생은 '남학생이 파트너로서 무척 도움이 될 것'이라고 생각함을 알 수 있다. 따라서 정답은 (B)이다.

8. 남학생에 관해 추론할 수 있는 것은 무엇인가요?

(A) 자기 프로젝트를 위한 아이디어를 낼 것이다.
(B) 여학생과 프로젝트 일을 같이 하기로 동의할 것이다.
(C) 채소와 관련된 다른 프로젝트를 생각해 볼 것이다.
(D) Jackson 선생님한테 과학 박람회 규칙을 물어볼 것이다.

정답 및 해설 **[추론 문제]** 여학생이 "이 프로젝트를 나와 같이 하지 않을래(Do you want to work on this with me?)"라고 물어보자 남학생은 "하고 싶다(I'd love to.)"라고 말하면서 "내가 도움이 될 수 있을까(Do you think I can help you?)"라고 물어본다. 이에 여학생은 "물론(Of course!)"이라고 대답했다. 이를 볼 때 남학생은 '프로젝트를 같이 하기로 동의할 것'임을 유추할 수 있다. 따라서 정답은 (B)이다.

Unit 2	Details Questions

□ Example Dialogue Excerpt

두 친구의 대화를 들으세요.

남 안녕, Jessie.
여 안녕, Joe. 잘 지내니?
남 좋아. 넌 어때?
여 잘 지내. 수족관으로 현장 학습 가는 게 정말 기대돼. 넌 표 끊었니?
남 응. 10달러밖에 안 해서 정말 좋아. 보통 가격은 19.99달러잖아.
여 학생들이 많이 가니까 학교에서 흥정을 잘 한 거지.
남 얼마나 많은 애들이 간대?
여 참가 가능한 연령대가 전부 75명인데, 그 중 약 50명이 가. 정말 재미있을 거야.
남 맞아. 진짜 기다려진다.

Q. 학생들은 무엇에 대한 값을 지불해야 했나요?

(A) 점심값
(B) 티켓값
(C) 버스표
(D) 기념품

aquarium 수족관 pay (값, 비용 등을) 지불하다, 내다 cost (값, 비용이) ~이다 regular 보통의, 평상시의; 규칙적인, 정기적인 deal 거래, (사업상의) 합의

□ Example Dialogue Excerpt

두 친구의 대화를 들으세요.

남 저기, Brianna!
여 안녕, Brandon. 너 좀 정신 없어 보인다. 괜찮니?
남 괜찮아, 그런데 좀 도와 줘. 학교 연극 하는 데 9학년은 강당 몇 번째 줄에 앉니?
여 너희 반은 뒷줄이야, G열부터 I열까지. 너희 반 애들 중 몇 명은 지금 거기 있을 거야.
남 그래? 알겠어, 다행이야. 가서 찾아봐야겠다. 고마워, Bri.
여 도움이 돼서 기뻐. 안녕.

Q. 남학생은 학교 연극을 하는 동안 어디에 앉게 될까요?

(A) A에서 C열
(B) D에서 F열
(C) G에서 I열
(D) J에서 L열

confused (사람이) 혼란스러워 하는 row 열

□ Example Dialogue Excerpt

학생과 선생님의 대화를 들으세요.

학생 안녕하세요, Jameson 선생님. 어떻게 지내세요?
교사 잘 지내고 있지, Allen. 오늘은 뭘 도와줄까?
학생 저희 미술 프로젝트가 언제까지인지 여쭤보려고 왔습니다.
교사 유화 작품을 4월 7일까지 먼저 내고, 점토 조각상은 14일까지 내면 된다.
학생 네, 감사합니다.
교사 도움이 돼서 기쁘구나. 나중에 미술 수업 시간에 보자.
학생 네! 안녕히 계세요, Jameson 선생님.

Q. 유화 프로젝트의 제출 기한은 언제인가요?

(A) 4월 7일 (B) 4월 14일

(C) 4월 21일 (D) 4월 28일

oil paint 유화 clay 찰흙, 점토 statue 조각상

□ Conversation Example

학생과 선생님의 대화를 들으세요.

학생 안녕하세요, Smith 선생님. 잠깐 시간 좀 내주시겠어요?

교사 좋아, Laura. 무슨 문제가 있니?

학생 제가 이번 여름 학교에서 수학 과목 수업을 들어야 될지도 모르는데, 그래서 걱정입니다.

교사 아, 그렇지. 네 성적이 지금 55점밖에 안되더구나. 문제가 심각해.

학생 알고 있습니다만, 여름 학교에 가고 싶지 않아요. 밴드에서 캠프를 가기로 되어 있거든요. 거기 가서 제 실력을 발휘할 수 있게 하려고 일년 동안 플루트 연습을 정말 열심히 했거든요.

교사 음, 선생님도 네가 밴드 캠프를 못 가게 되는 건 바라지 않는다. 그럼 너한테 도움이 될 추가 연습 과제를 내주마. 그리고 원한다면 선생님이 점식 시간에 도와 줄 수도 있고.

학생 정말이세요? 그럼 정말 큰 도움이 될 거예요. 그렇지만 저 때문에 선생님 점심 시간을 뺏고 싶시는 않습니다.

교사 음, 선생님은 네가 훌륭한 플루트 연주자가 되었으면 한단다. 점심 시간 한두 번쯤 놓친다고 크게 문제 될 건 없으니까.

학생 네, 그럼 점심 시간에 와서 선생님께 도움이 필요한 부분을 말씀 드릴게요. 고맙습니다, Smith 선생님.

교사 도움이 돼서 다행이다. 나중에 보자, Laura!

Q. 선생님은 학생의 수학 과목을 어떻게 도와줄까요?

(A) 여름 학교에서 가르친다. (B) 추가로 연습할 시험 문제를 준다.

(C) 수업 시간에 학생에게 주목한다. (D) 점심 시간에 (공부하는 걸)도와준다.

scared 무서워하는, 겁먹은 flute 플루트 show off ~을 자랑하다, 보여주다, 으스대다 flutist 플루트 연주자

□ Dictation

Listen to a conversation between two friends.

(B: boy, G: girl)

B Hollo, Jenny.

G Hey, Paul. What's up?

B Not much. I am ① just reading the novel for our English class. What do you think of it?

G I really don't like it. The story is ② not very interesting for a girl. What about you?

B I guess that is why I enjoy it. I understand ③ what the main character is going through.

G I heard the book is very popular with male readers.

B It is about a teenage boy growing up, so I guess it is hard for a girl ④ to appreciate it as much as a boy does.

G True. That's OK. I've already read next month's book. It's great. Oh, I'm late for my next class. Bye, Paul.

B Cool, see you later.

번역 **두 친구의 대화를 들으세요.**

남 안녕, Jenny.

여 안녕, Paul. 뭐하고 있니?

남 별로. 그냥 영어 수업 시간에 필요한 소설을 읽고 있어. 넌 이 소설 어떻게 생각해?

여 난 사실 별로 안 좋았어. 여자 애들이 흥미로워할 만한 이야기는 아니야. 넌 어때?

남 난 아무래도 그래서 재미있는 것 같아. (남자) 주인공이 겪는 일들이 이해가 되거든.

여 남성 독자들한테 굉장히 인기가 많다는 얘긴 들었어.

남 십대 소년의 성장에 관한 이야기지. 그래서 여자들은 남자들이 느끼는 것만큼의 진면목을 알기는 힘들 것 같아.

여 맞아. 어쨌든 좋아. 나 벌써 다음 달에 볼 소설을 읽었는데, 정말 좋더라. 어머, 다음 수업 시간에 늦었다. 안녕, Paul.

남 그래, 나중에 보자

Q. 남학생은 소설에 대해 어떻게 느끼고 있나요?
(A) 재미있어한다.
(B) 좋아하지 않는다.
(C) 재미없다고 생각한다.
(D) 남자 아이에게 좋은 소설은 아니라고 생각한다.

main character 주인공 go through 겪다, 경험하다 appreciate 진가를 알아보다; 고마워하다

정답 및 해설 **[세부사항을 묻는 문제]** 두 학생이 영어 수업을 위해 읽은 소설에 대해 대화하고 있다. 여학생이 소설이 재미없었다면서 "여자 애들이 흥미로워할 만한 이야기가 아니었다(**The story is not very interesting for a girl.**)"고 말하자 남학생은 "그래서 나는 재미있었던 것 같다(**I guess that is why I enjoy it.**)"고 말하는데, 이 말은 여학생들이 좋아하지 않는 스토리라 오히려 남학생들이 더 좋아할 만하다라는 의미이다. 이어서 "난 주인공이 겪은 상황이 이해된다(**I understand what the main character is going through.**)"라고 덧붙인다. 이런 대화를 볼 때 남학생은 이 소설을 재미있게 읽고 있다고 짐작할 수 있다. 따라서 정답은 (A)이다.

□ Practice Test

1. **(D)**	2. **(C)**	3. **(D)**	4. **(B)**	5. **(B)**	6. **(B)**	7. **(D)**	8. **(B)**

[1-4] Listen to a conversation between a student and a science teacher. (S: student, T: teacher)

S Hi, Mr. Clemmons. How did the experiment go yesterday?

T It went well. All your classmates really enjoyed it. Where were you? Why didn't you come?

S I was sick with a stomach bug yesterday so I didn't come to school. I'm disappointed that I missed the experiment. I know that I need to complete the lab report about it.

T I'm sorry to hear you were sick, but it's true that you need to do the work.

S Are you going to have another lab session for students that weren't there yesterday?

T Yes. It's going to be during tomorrow's lunch break. Tina, Tara, Ben, and James also missed the lab, so they'll be coming, too.

S Okay, great. Is there anything I need to bring?

T Just make sure you wear sneakers instead of sandals in case anything spills or breaks. Of course, don't forget your science textbook and your notebook.

S Okay. I'm excited to do the experiment. Labs are my favorite part of class. Thanks so much for holding another session.

T It's no problem at all. I'll see you tomorrow.

번역 **학생과 과학 선생님의 대화를 들으세요.**

학생 안녕하세요, Clemmons 선생님. 어제 실험은 어땠나요?

교사 잘 됐단다. 너희 반 친구들 모두 재미있게 실험했지. 넌 어디 있었니? 왜 참석을 안 했지?

학생 어제 배탈이 나서 아팠어요. 그래서 학교에 못 왔습니다. 실험을 놓쳐서 저도 속상합니다. 실험 보고서도 써야 하잖아요.

교사 아팠다니 유감이구나. 하지만 너도 보고서를 써야 하는 건 맞아.

학생 어제 참석 안 한 학생들을 위해 또 다른 실험을 하실 계획이신가요?

교사 그래. 내일 점심 시간에 할 거란다. Tina, Tara, Ben, 그리고 James도 실험에 참석을 못 했어. 그래서 걔들도 올 거야.

학생 네, 잘됐네요. 뭐 가져가야 할 게 있을까요?

교사 뭔가 흘리거나 깨질 수도 있으니까 샌들 대신 스니커즈를 신고 오너라. 그리고 물론 과학 교과서랑 노트를 잊지 말고.

학생 알겠습니다. 실험하게 돼서 신나요. 실험은 제가 수업 중 가장 좋아하는 부분이거든요. 다른 실험을 만들어 주셔서 고맙습니다.

교사 천만에. 내일 보자.

stomach bug 배탈　disappointed 실망한, 낙담한　session (특별 활동을 위한) 시간, 기간
make it (모임 등에) 참석하다; (어떤 곳에 간신히) 시간 맞춰 가다　spill (액체 등을) 엎지르다, 쏟다, 흘리다
hold (회의 등을) 열다, 하다, 개최하다

1. 학생이 선생님을 찾아간 이유는 무엇인가요?
(A) 실험 보고서 제출 기한이 언제인지 알아보려고
(B) 실험에 빠진 다른 학생들이 있는지 알아보려고
(C) 배탈이 나서 더 이상 수업에 참석할 수 없다고 말하려고
(D) 실험에 참가하지 못한 이유를 설명하고 또 다른 실험이 있을지 여쭤보려고

정답 및 해설 **[주제를 묻는 문제]** 선생님이 학생에게 실험에 불참한 이유를 묻자 학생은 "배탈이 나서 학교에 올 수가 없었고, 실험에 못 와서 속상하다(I was sick with a stomach bug yesterday so I didn't come to school. I'm disappointed that I missed the experiment.)"라고 대답한다. 그러면서 "어제 참석 안 한 학생들을 위해 추가 실험을 하실 거냐(Are you going to have another lab session for students that weren't there yesterday?)"고 물어본다. 이에 선생님은 추가 실험이 있다면서 몇 가지 주의 사항을 전달한다. 이런 상황을 정리하면, 학생이 선생님에게 간 이유는 '실험에 빠진 이유를 설명하고 추가 실험이 있을 것인지 물어 보기 위함'이라는 것을 알 수 있다. 따라서 정답은 (D)이다.

2. 여학생이 과학 실험에 빠진 이유는 무엇인가요?
(A) 병원에 있었다.
(B) 점심 시간 휴식을 취하고 있었다.
(C) 배탈이 나서 아팠다.
(D) Tina, Tara, Ben, 그리고 James와 함께 있었다.

정답 및 해설 **[세부사항을 묻는 문제]** 선생님이 왜 어제 실험에 불참했냐고 묻자 학생은 "어제 배탈이 나서 아팠기 때문에 학교에 못 왔다(I was sick with a stomach bug yesterday so I didn't come to school.)"라고 대답한다. 따라서 정답은 (C)이다.

3. Clemmons 선생님이 Tina, Tara, Ben, 그리고 James를 언급한 이유는 무엇인가요?
(A) 보고서를 잘 쓴 학생들을 예로 들기 위해
(B) 여학생이 이들 학생을 편하게 대할 수 있도록 만들기 위해
(C) 여학생에게 배탈이 난 다른 학생들이 많다는 걸 설명하기 위해
(D) 여학생에게 추가 실험에 참가할 다른 학생들에 대해 얘기하기 위해

정답 및 해설 **[수사학적 구조를 묻는 문제]** 학생이 "어제 참석 안 한 학생들을 위해 추가 실험을 하실 거냐(Are you going to have another lab session for students that weren't there yesterday?)"라고 묻자, 선생님은 내일 점심 시간에 할 예정이라며, "Tina, Tara, Ben, James도 어제 실험에 빠졌기 때문에 내일 참석할 것(Tina, Tara, Ben, and James also missed the lab, so they'll be coming, too.)"이라고 말한다. 즉 선생님이 이 아이들을 언급한 것은 '여학생에게 (내일) 실험에 참석할 예정인 다른 아이들에 대해 말해주기 위함'이다. 따라서 정답은 (D)이다.

4. 여학생에 관해 사실인 것은 무엇일까요?
(A) 실험을 지겨워한다.
(B) 과학 실험을 좋아한다.
(C) Clemmons 선생님을 좋아하지 않는다.
(D) 매주 실험 보고서를 쓴다.

정답 및 해설 **[추론 문제]** 선생님이 빠진 실험을 해야 한다고 말하면서 준비물을 알려주자 학생은 "실험을 하게 되어 신난다, 실험은 내가 수업에서 가장 좋아하는 부분이다(I'm excited to do the experiment. Labs are my favorite part of class.)"라고 대답한다. 이를 볼 때 학생은 '과학 실험 하는 것을 좋아한다'고 유추할 수 있다. 따라서 정답은 (B)이다. (A)는 정답과 반대되는 내용이고, (C)나 (D)와 관련된 내용은 언급되지 않았다.

[5-8] Listen to a conversation between a student and a math teacher. (S: student, T: teacher)

S Hi, Mrs. LeClaire. Do you have a minute?

T Sure, Billy. What's going on?

S Well, I got my midterm back and I'm not happy with my grade. I was wondering if I could take the exam again.

T I'm sorry to say that you can't retake the midterm exam. It's against my class rules. If I let you take it, then I have to let everybody else take it.

S So what can I do?

T I teach a two-hour study session every Wednesday after school. Many of your classmates have started coming to get extra help. I highly recommend that you join us.

S Okay, I can come on Wednesdays. But, Mrs. LeClaire, what about my grade on the midterm? How can I fix that?

T You can't change your grade on the midterm, but you can work to do well on the final. If you work hard during Wednesday sessions and always complete your homework, then you'll have an excellent chance of doing well on the final exam.

번역 학생과 수학 선생님의 대화를 들으세요.

학생 안녕하세요, LeClaire 선생님. 시간 있으세요?

교사 그래, Billy. 무슨 일이니?

학생 저, 중간 고사 시험지를 받았는데, 점수가 만족스럽지 못해서요. 시험을 다시 치를 수 있을지 여쭤 보러 왔습니다.

교사 유감이지만, 중간 고사는 다시 볼 수 없단다. 선생님 수업 규정에 어긋나. 너한테 다시 기회를 준다면 다른 아이들에게도 모두 다시 기회를 줘야 하잖니.

학생 그럼 어떻게 해야 할까요?

교사 매주 수요일 방과 후에 선생님이 2시간짜리 (보충) 수업을 진행하고 있어. 너희 반 아이들도 추가 수업을 하려고 많이 온단다. 너도 그 반 수업에 꼭 오라고 하고 싶구나.

학생 좋습니다. 수요일에 갈게요. 그런데, LeClaire 선생님, 중간 고사 성적은 어쩌죠? 어떻게 해야 만회할 수 있을까요?

교사 중간 고사 성적은 바꿀 수 없지만 기말 시험을 잘 보면 되지. 수요일 수업 시간에 열심히 듣고 숙제도 항상 다 하면 기말 시험을 잘 볼 확률이 꽤 높을 거다.

wonder if ~인지 아닌지 궁금하다 **rule** 규칙, 원칙 **highly** 매우, 대단히 **recommend** 추천하다 **join** 함께 하다, 합류하다; 가입하다 **fix** 고치다, 바로잡다

5. 학생이 선생님께 찾아간 이유는 무엇인가요?

(A) 기말 시험에 대해 걱정이 된다.
(B) 중간 고사를 다시 보고 싶다.
(C) 숙제가 이해되지 않는다.
(D) 수요일 복습 수업에 참가하고 싶다.

정답 및 해설 **[주제를 묻는 문제]** 수학 선생님과 학생이 재시험에 대해 나누는 대화이다. 학생이 "중간 고사 시험지를 받았는데 점수가 만족스럽지 않다(**I got my midterm back and I'm not happy with my grade.**)"라고 말하면서 "재시험을 볼 수 있는지 알고 싶다(**I was wondering if I could take the exam again.**)"고 한다. 이를 볼 때 학생이 선생님을 찾아 간 목적은 '중간 고사를 다시 보고 싶기 때문'이라고 짐작할 수 있다. 따라서 정답은 (B)이다. '수요일 복습 수업 참가(D)'는 선생님이 재시험 대신 제안한 내용이므로, 학생이 선생님을 찾아간 원래의 목적으로 볼 수 없다.

6. 선생님이 남학생에게 중간 고사 재시험의 기회를 줄 수 없는 이유는 무엇인가요?

(A) 시험이 쉬웠었다고 생각한다.
(B) 수업 규정에 어긋난다고 생각한다.
(C) 남학생에게 이미 재시험의 기회를 주었다.
(D) 다른 선생님이 기회를 주었다는 것을 안다.

정답 및 해설 **[세부사항을 묻는 문제]** 학생이 "재시험을 볼 수 있는지 알고 싶다(**I was wondering if I could take the exam again.**)"라고 말하자 선생님은 "유감이지만 재시험은 볼 수 없다. 수업 규정에 어긋난다(**I'm sorry to say that you can't retake the midterm exam. It's against my class rules.**)"라고 답한다. 이어서 "네게 재시험을 볼 수 있게 해주면 다른 아이들에게도 모두 기회를 줘야 된다(**If I let you take it, then I have to let everybody else take it.**)"라며 구체적인 불가 이유를 덧붙인다. 따라서 정답은 (B)이다. (A), (D)는 언급되지 않았고, (C)는 논리적으로 옳지 않다.

7. 선생님은 기말 시험에 대해 무엇이라고 하나요?
(A) 중간 고사보다 쉽고 짧을 것이다.
(B) 중간 고사만큼 많은 학생들이 보지는 않을 것이다.
(C) 수요일 복습 시간에 학생들이 만들 것이다.
(D) 학생이 복습 시간에 참여하고 숙제를 다 하면 (기말 시험을) 잘 볼 수 있을 것이다.

정답 및 해설 **[세부사항을 묻는 문제]** 학생이 중간 고사 성적에 대해 걱정하자 선생님은 이미 치른 중간 고사 점수는 바꿀 수 없지만 기말 고사를 잘 보면 된다고 말한다. 그러면서 "수요일 보충 시간에 열심히 공부하고 숙제를 항상 하면 기말 고사를 잘 볼 수 있는 확률이 높다(If you work hard during Wednesday sessions and always complete your homework, then you'll have an excellent chance of doing well on the final exam.)"며 격려한다. 따라서 정답은 (D)이다.

8. 수요일 복습 시간에 대해 무엇을 추론할 수 있나요?
(A) 남학생은 항상 참여한다.
(B) 남학생에게 유용할 것이다.
(C) 2주에 한번씩이다.
(D) LeClaire 선생님이 이 수업을 광고하고 싶어 한다.

정답 및 해설 **[추론 문제]** 선생님이 학생에게 수요일 복습 보충에 대해 소개하면서 "너희 반 아이들도 추가 수업을 하려고 많이 온다. 너도 그 반 수업에 꼭 오라고 하고 싶다(Many of your classmates have started coming to get extra help. I highly recommend that you join us.)"고 한다. 이어서 수요일 보충 수업을 열심히 듣고 항상 숙제를 하면 기말고사를 잘 볼 수 있다고도 말한다. 이를 볼 때 수요일 복습 보충 수업이 '남학생에게 도움이 될 것'이라고 유추할 수 있다. 따라서 정답은 (B)이다.

Unit 3 Inference Questions

□ Example Dialogue Excerpt

두 친구의 대화를 들으세요.

여 안녕, Devin. 잘 지내니?
남 잘 지내. 넌?
여 난 좀 걱정스런 일이 있어. Azzano 선생님께서 나더러 학교 뮤지컬에 나가서 플루트를 연주하라고 하셔.
남 그게 왜 걱정이야? 너 플루트 잘 불잖아. 해야지!
여 나도 그러고 싶긴 한데, 연습일이 교회 청년팀 모이는 날이랑 같아.
남 그렇구나. 그러면 청년팀 가는 걸 몇 주 정도만 중단하면 되잖아.
여 그럴 수는 있지만, 그러고 싶지가 않아. 정말 재미있거든.
남 글쎄, 잘 모르겠다. 나 수학 수업 들어가야 해. 나중에 얘기하자. 안녕!

Q. 여학생에 관해 추론할 수 있는 것은 무엇인가요?
(A) 훌륭한 플루트 연주자이다.
(B) Azzano 선생님과 얘기해 볼 것이다.
(C) 교회 청년팀 모임을 정말 좋아한다.
(D) 교회 청년팀에 가는 걸 중단할 것이다.

upset 근심되는; 속상한, 마음이 상한 youth 젊은이, 청년

□ Example Dialogue Excerpt

두 친구의 대화를 들으세요.

여 James, 잘 지내니?

남 안녕, Lacey. 난 잘 지내. 넌?

여 이보다 더 좋을 순 없지. 이제 곧 여름 방학이잖아. 넌 방학 때 뭐 할 거니?

남 여름 캠프에 가고 싶었는데, 우리 아빠는 우리가 국내 여행 하길 원하셔.

여 우리 나라(미국) 여행을 하면 멋진 경험이 될 거야. 넌 왜 캠프에 더 가고 싶은데?

남 내 친구들 대부분이 가거든. 나도 걔네와 같이 하고 싶어.

Q. 남학생에 관해 사실인 것은 무엇일까요?

(A) 여행을 좋아하지 않는다.

(B) 친구들과 가깝게 지낸다.

(C) 여름 캠프에 갈 것이다.

(D) Lacey와 함께 시간을 보내고 싶어 한다.

break (짧은)휴가, 휴식(시간)

□ Example Dialogue Excerpt

학생과 선생님의 대화를 들으세요.

교사 안녕, Madison. 어떻게 지내니?

학생 그다지 좋지는 않아요. 선생님은 어떻게 지내세요?

교사 잘 지낸단다. 그런데 무슨 문제가 있니? 선생님이 도와 줄까?

학생 시험 때문에 스트레스가 쌓여서요. 시험 볼 준비가 안됐어요.

교사 그거 문제구나. 중요한 부분들에 대해서 다른 사람한테 문제를 내봐 달라고 하지 그랬니?

학생 해봤어요. 수업 끝나면 엄마가 밤마다 시험 문제를 내 주세요.

교사 그래, 그럼 어머니와 계속 그렇게 해보렴. 넌 (평소)시험 점수가 높고 공부도 열심히 하잖니. 괜찮을 거다.

학생 네, 고맙습니다, Welsh 선생님. 수업 때 뵐게요.

Q. 여학생에 관해 무엇을 추론할 수 있나요?

(A) 외향적인 성격이다.

(B) 동기 부여가 되어 있지 않다.

(C) 자신감이 없다.

(D) 불량 학생이다.

stressed out 스트레스가 쌓인, 스트레스로 지친 quiz (간단히)시험을 보다, 테스트하다

□ Conversation Example

학생과 선생님의 대화를 들으세요.

교사 안녕, Suzie, 잘 지내니?

학생 잘 지내요. 그런데 도움이 필요한 일이 있습니다, Wayne 선생님.

교사 어떻게 도와줄까?

학생 학교 댄스 파티 주제로 어떤 걸 선택하는 게 좋을지, 선생님 생각을 알고 싶어요.

교사 학생 자치 위원회에서는 어떤 주제를 생각하고 있니?

학생 가장 인기 있는 주제 두 가지는 〈Under the Sea (바다 아래서)〉와 〈첩보원〉이에요.

교사 <Under the Sea>는 해변가 파티 같구나. 지금은 1월이고 좀 춥잖니. 게다가, 수영복을 입는 건 학교 복장 규정에 위배될 것 같구나.

학생 일리 있는 말씀이세요, 하지만 비치볼 놀이를 하면 재미있을 거예요.

교사 그 말도 맞지만, 다들 스파이 복장을 하는 것도 재미있어 할 것 같은걸.

학생 선생님 말씀이 맞는 것 같아요. 어떤 주제를 해야 할지 이제 알 것 같네요.

교사 그래. 아무튼 선생님은 올해도 또 〈고대 로마〉라는 주제는 아니라서 다행이구나.

Q. 학교 댄스 파티 주제에 관해 추론할 수 있는 것은 무엇인가요?

(A) 주제가 〈첩보원〉이 될 것이다.
(B) 주제가 〈학교 댄스 파티〉가 될 것이다.
(C) 주제가 〈고대 로마〉가 될 것이다.
(D) 주제가 〈바다 아래서〉가 될 것이다.

theme 주제, 테마 student council 학생 자치 위원회 secret agent 첩보원, 간첩 swim suit 수영복 spy 스파이, 간첩 ancient 고대의, 먼 옛날의

□ Dictation

Listen to a conversation between a student and a school secretary. (St: student, Se: secretary)

St Hi, Mrs. Scott.
Se Hello, Alf. What can I help you with today?
St Mr. Pierce sent me here ①for detention.
Se Again? This is the third time this week. What did you do this time?
St I ②put gum on Kathy West's chair. The class thought it was funny, but Mr. Pierce didn't.
Se No, that is ③not funny or nice. Did you say sorry to Kathy?
St No. I was sent straight here.
Se Well, you ④go back to class and say sorry. Then come right back here to do your detention.
St Oh man! Okay, Mrs. Scott. I'll be back in five minutes.

번역 **학생과 학교 총무의 대화를 들으세요.**

학생 안녕하세요, Scott 선생님.
총무 안녕, Alf. 오늘은 뭘 도와줄까?
학생 Pierce 선생님께서 벌로 방과 후에 남아있으라며 이리로 보내셨어요.
총무 또? 이번 주에 벌써 세 번째야. 이번엔 무슨 일을 저질렀니?
학생 Kathy West의 의자에 껌을 붙였어요. 반 애들은 다 재미있다고 하는데, Pierce 선생님만 아니에요.
총무 아니지, 그건 재미있는 일도 올바른 일도 아니야. Kathy에게 미안하다고 말했니?
학생 아뇨, 곧장 여기로 가라고 하셔서요.
총무 그럼, 교실에 돌아가서 미안하다고 얘기하거라. 그런 다음 다시 이리로 와서 방과 후에 남아 있는 벌을 받아야지.
학생 어휴… 알겠습니다, Scott 선생님. 5분 안에 올게요.

Q. 남학생에 관해 사실인 것은 무엇일까요?

(A) Scott 선생님을 좋아한다.
(B) 문제를 많이 일으킨다.
(C) 의자에 껌을 붙이는 걸 좋아한다.
(D) 부모님이 놀랄만한 일을 했다.

detention (학생에 대한 벌로서)방과 후에 남게 하는 일 straight 곧장, 곧바로

정답 및 해설 [추론 문제] 남학생이 "Pierce 선생님이 방과 후에 남아있으라고 이곳에 보냈다(Mr. Pierce sent me here for detention.)"고 하자, Scott 선생님은 "또? 오늘이 이번 주 들어 세 번째다. 이번엔 무슨 일을 했냐(Again? This is the third time this week. What did you do this time?)"라고 묻는다. 이를 볼 때 남학생은 평소에도 '문제를 많이 일으키는 학생'이라는 것을 추론할 수 있다. 따라서 정답은 (B)이다.

□ Practice Test

1. (C)	2. (C)	3. (B)	4. (B)	5. (C)	6. (D)	7. (A)	8. (C)

[1-4] Listen to a conversation between a student and a guidance counselor. (S: student, C: counselor)

C Hello, Toby. What brings you into my office today?

S I'm having some problems sorting out my schedule. I signed up for honors English but got placed in the lower level. Also, I wanted to take the art elective, but I got put in music class instead.

C Hmm... what time is your English class?

S It's at 1:30.

C Is it with Mr. Viggers or Mr. Cohan?

S It's with Mr. Viggers.

C Okay, well, there isn't an honors English class available at 1:30. There's only a class with Mr. Cohan. If you want to take honors English, you'll have to change your elective.

S Well, that's perfect. I don't want to be in the music elective anyway.

C Okay, I know you said you wanted an art elective, but there's only one art elective that isn't full... and that's printmaking. I know printmaking isn't a traditional art class.

S Printmaking is fine with me. Can I take another art elective next semester that is more closely related to my interests?

C Of course! Just make sure you sign up as soon as classes are posted so that your first choice doesn't get filled up.

S Okay, I will. Thanks. Let's make those changes to the schedule.

번역 **학생과 생활지도 선생님의 대화를 들으세요.**

교사 안녕, Toby. 오늘은 선생님 방에 무슨 일로 왔나요?

학생 수업 시간표 짜는 데 문제가 좀 생겼습니다. 영어 우등반을 신청했는데, 하급반을 배정받았어요. 또 선택 과목으로 미술 수업을 신청했는데, 대신 음악반을 배정받았습니다.

교사 흠… 영어 수업 시간이 언제죠?

학생 1시 30분이에요.

교사 Viggers 선생님 수업인가요, 아니면 Cohan 선생님 수업인가요?

학생 Viggers 선생님 수업이에요.

교사 그래요, 음, 1시 30분에는 영어 우등반이 없어요. Cohan 선생님 수업이 하나 있네요. 학생이 영어 우등반 수업을 듣고 싶으면 선택 과목을 변경해야 해요.

학생 네, 잘됐네요. 어쨌든 음악 수업을 듣고 싶었던 건 아니니까요.

교사 좋아요, 학생이 미술 수업을 듣고 싶다고 했는데, 정원이 다 차지 않은 미술 수업은 딱 하나 남았는데… 그건 판화 제작 수업이네요. 판화 제작은 전통적인 미술 수업은 아니지만요.

학생 판화 제작 수업도 괜찮습니다. 그런데 다음 학기에는 제가 원하는 분야랑 좀더 밀접한 미술 수업을 들을 수 있을까요?

교사 물론이죠! 다만 학생이 1순위로 듣고 싶어하는 과목이 다 차기 전에 수업이 게시되자마자 등록하는 게 좋을 겁니다.

학생 네, 그럴게요. 고맙습니다. 그럼 이대로 시간표 변경을 하겠습니다.

sort out 골라내다, 분류하다, 가려내다 sign up for ~을 신청하다 honors English 영어 우등반
available 이용할 수 있는, 사용할 수 있는 printmaking 판화 제작 related to ~와 관계가 있는

1. 생활지도 선생님은 남학생에게 무엇을 설명하고 있나요?

(A) 판화 제작 수업이 흥미로운 이유

(B) 선택 과목이 교육적으로 중요한 이유

(C) 남학생 시간표에서 변경할 수 있는 것들

(D) Viggers 선생님과 Cohan 선생님 반 중 하나를 선택하는 방법

정답 및 해설 **[주제를 묻는 문제]** 학생과 생활지도 선생님이 수업 시간표 변경에 관해 나누는 대화이다. 학생이 "수업 시간표 정리에 문제가 생겼다(I'm having some problems sorting out my schedule.)"고 하자, 선생님은 수업 시간과 담당 선생님을 확인한 후 1시 30분에는 Cohan 선생님 수업만 있다며, "우등반 수업을 듣고 싶으면 선택 과목을 바꿔야 한다(If you want to take honors English, you'll have to change your elective.)"고 말한다. 이런 대화 내용을 볼 때, 선생님이 '수업 스케줄에 무엇을 변경해야 하는지'를 설명하는 대화임을 알 수 있다. 따라서 정답은 (C)이다.

2. 생활지도 선생님은 판화 제작에 관해 어떤 점을 암시하나요?

(A) 음악 수업보다 덜 재미있다.

(B) 무척 열정적인 선생님이 지도하신다.

(C) 일반적인 미술 수업보다 선호도가 덜하다.

(D) 이 수업에는 Toby의 친구들이 하나도 없다.

정답 및 해설 **[추론 문제]** 학생이 음악 과목 말고 미술 과목을 원한다고 하자, 선생님은 "아직 학생 수가 차지 않은 미술 과목은 하나밖에 없는데, 그 과목은 판화 제작 수업이다(~ but there's only one art elective that isn't full... and that's printmaking.)"라고 말한다. 이처럼 정원이 차지 않을 걸로 봐서 '판화 과목이 일반적인 미술 수업만큼 선호되지 않는다'는 것을 알 수 있다. 따라서 정답은 (C)이다.

3. 두 사람은 다음에 무엇을 할까요?

(A) 판화 제작 수업에 들어간다.

(B) Toby의 수업 시간표를 변경한다.

(C) 서로에게 작별 인사를 한다.

(D) 다음 학기 수업에 등록한다.

정답 및 해설 **[예측 문제]** 선생님과 학생이 수업 시간표 변경에 관한 대화를 한 후 마지막에 남학생이 "그렇게 스케줄을 변경하자(Let's make those changes to the schedule.)"라고 말한다. 그러니까 두 사람은 앞에서 논의한 대로 'Toby의 시간표를 변경할 것'이다. 따라서 정답은 (B)이다.

4. 남학생이 다음 학기 미술 수업을 가능한 빨리 등록해야 하는 이유는 무엇인가요?

(A) Viggers 선생님이 가르칠 것이다.

(B) 미술 수업은 아마도 정원이 일찍 마감될 것이다.

(C) 남학생은 미술 수업을 들을 자격이 없다.

(D) 남학생은 판화 제작 수업을 다시 들어야 할 것이다.

정답 및 해설 **[세부사항을 묻는 문제]** 남학생이 "다음 학기에는 자신이 원하는 분야와 좀더 관련이 있는 미술 수업을 들을 수 있냐(Can I take another art elective next semester that is more closely related to my interests?)"고 물어보자, 선생님은 가능하다고 답하면서, "단 1순위로 듣고 싶은 수업을 수강하려면 수업 시간이 게시되자마자 등록해라(Just make sure you sign up as soon as classes are posted so that your first choice doesn't get filled up.)"라고 말한다. 즉 일반적인 미술 수업의 경우 '비교적 빨리 정원이 마감된다'고 볼 수 있다. 따라서 정답은 (B)이다.

[5-8] Listen to a conversation between two friends.

(B: boy, G: girl)

B Did you see the storm last night, Elizabeth?

G I didn't see it, but I could feel it. It was so loud! I was too nervous to watch it. Oh, I really hate storms! I hid under my bed for the whole thing.

B It was a scary storm, but I loved it. I climbed up into my attic to watch it.

G Could you see the lightning? I can't remember ever hearing louder thunder.

B Yes, I saw the lightning, but the scary part of the storm was the wind. It was unbelievable.

G I know. When I woke up this morning there were trees on the ground everywhere. An oak tree fell on my dad's truck.

B Oh my goodness! It's good that the tree didn't hit the house.

G I know. That would have been terrible.

B Well, I am glad that nothing else bad happened. How did you get to school?

번역 **두 친구의 대화를 들으세요.**

남 Elizabeth, 너 어젯밤 폭풍 봤니?

여 아니, 보진 못했는데, 그래도 다 느껴졌어. 소리가 엄청 컸잖아. 겁나서 보지는 못하겠더라. 난 정말 폭풍이 싫어. 내내 침대 밑에 숨어 있었어.

남 폭풍이 무섭긴 했지만, 그래도 난 좋았어. 다락방에 올라가서 폭풍을 지켜봤어.

여 번개도 봤어? 어젯밤 천둥소리보다 더 큰 소리는 들어본 적이 없는 것 같아.

남 응, 번개도 보긴 했는데, 가장 무서운 건 바람이었어. 믿기 어려울 정도로 굉장했어.

여 맞아. 오늘 아침에 일어났더니 사방에 나무가 쓰러져 있더라. 참나무 한 그루는 우리 아빠 트럭 위로 넘어져 있었어.

남 저런, 세상에! 그 나무가 집으로 쓰러지지 않은 게 다행이다.

여 그래. 만약 그랬으면 끔찍했겠지.

남 아무튼, 그것 말고 다른 나쁜 일은 일어나지 않아서 다행이야. 학교에는 어떻게 왔니?

G My mom drove me and then she went home to help my dad. Dad said that it will take a few days to clean up our yard and fix the truck.

B Wow! You'll have a great story to write about in your English class today.

G I know! I hope Mrs. Williams likes it. I never have any interesting things to write about, but today I have a really good story.

여 엄마가 차로 태워다 주시고 아빠 도우러 다시 집으로 가셨어. 아빠 말씀이 마당을 치우고 트럭을 수리하려면 며칠이 더 걸릴 거래.

남 와~ 너 오늘 영어 수업 시간에 정말 굉장한 얘기를 쓸 수 있겠다.

여 그래. Williams 선생님이 맘에 들어 하셨으면 좋겠어. 지금까지는 쓸만한 재미있는 얘깃거리가 없었는데, 오늘은 정말 좋은 소재가 생겼어.

attic 다락, 다락방 **lightning** 번개, 번갯불 **thunder** 천둥, 우레 **unbelievable** 믿기 어려울 정도인, 믿기 힘든 **oak tree** 참나무 **clean up** ~을 치우다, 청소하다

5. 두 사람이 어젯밤에 깨어 있었던 이유는 무엇인가요?

(A) TV를 보고 있었다.
(B) 폭풍 게임을 하고 있었다.
(C) 악천후에 놀라서 깼다.
(D) 폭풍에 관한 조사를 하고 있었다.

정답 및 해설 **[세부사항을 묻는 문제]** 남학생이 "무서운 폭풍이었다(It was a scary storm ~)"고 하면서 "폭풍을 보기 위해 다락방에 올라갔다(I climbed up into my attic to watch it)"고 하자, 여학생은 "그처럼 큰 천둥 소리는 들어본 기억이 없다(I can't remember ever hearing louder thunder.)"고 한다. 이런 대화 내용으로 볼 때 두 사람은 폭풍이라는 악천후에 놀라 잠이 깨어 있었음을 알 수 있다. 따라서 정답은 (C)이다.

6. 여학생은 폭풍에 관해 어떤 점을 암시하나요?

(A) 폭풍이 무척 마음에 들었다.
(B) 무척 오랫동안 지속되었다.
(C) 비가 엄청 많이 왔다.
(D) 폭풍이 무서웠다.

정답 및 해설 **[추론 문제]** 여학생은 어젯밤에 폭풍을 봤냐는 남학생의 질문에 "겁나서 볼 수가 없었다. 침대 밑에 숨어 있었다(I was too nervous to watch it. ~ I hid under my bed for the whole thing.)"라고 답한다. 이 말에서 여학생은 폭풍을 무서워했다는 것을 알 수 있다. 따라서 정답은 (D)이다.

7. 여학생 아버지의 트럭에 무슨 일이 있었나요?

(A) 나무에 부딪혀 찌그러졌다.
(B) 많은 문제를 일으켰다.
(C) 폭풍이 일어났을 때 (다른) 차와 충돌했다.
(D) 엔진 고장이 났다.

정답 및 해설 **[세부사항을 묻는 문제]** 여학생이 아침에 일어나 보니 "참나무가 아버지 트럭 위에 쓰러져 있었다(An oak tree fell on my dad's truck.)"라고 했으므로, (A)가 정답이다.

8. 여학생은 영어 수업 시간에 무엇을 할까요?

(A) 남학생에게서 펜이나 연필을 빌린다.
(B) 아빠를 도울 수 있게 집에 일찍 보내달라고 한다.
(C) 글쓰기에 나무가 트럭 위로 넘어진 일을 쓴다.
(D) Williams 선생님에게 (폭풍 때문에) 숙제를 못 했다고 말한다.

정답 및 해설 **[예측 문제]** 남학생이 "오늘 영어 수업 시간에 정말 굉장한 이야기를 쓸 수 있겠다(You'll have a great story to write about in your English class today.)"고 말하자, 여학생도 이에 수긍하며 "지금까지는 재미있는 쓸 거리가 없었는데, 오늘은 정말 좋은 얘깃거리가 생겼다(I never have any interesting things to write about, but today I have a really good story.)"고 했으므로, 여학생이 '나무가 트럭 위로 쓰러진 일을 쓸 것'임을 짐작할 수 있다. 따라서 정답은 (C)이다.

Unit 4 Prediction Questions

□ Example Dialogue Excerpt

두 친구의 대화를 들으세요.

여 안녕, John. 또 만나서 반가워!
남 안녕, Mary. 오랜만이다, 그지?
여 너한테 전화해서 다음 학기 가정 수업 듣지 않을지 물어보려고 했어. 그 반에 (수업 같이 들을)친구가 있으면 좋겠어.
남 글쎄, 그 수업은 대부분 여학생들뿐이잖아. 나한테 맞지 않을 거야.
여 넌 여자 친구 많잖아. 그렇게 나쁘지 않을 거야.
남 그럴지도 모르지, 하지만 아무튼 난 요리나 바느질에는 별 관심이 없어. 게다가 그 시간에 컴퓨터 과학 수업에 등록했거든.
여 알겠어. 어쩌면 Natalie가 가겠다고 할지도 모르겠다.
남 Natalie한테 물어 봐. 좀 전에 도서관에 있는 걸 봤어.
여 좋아. 가서 찾아볼게. 나중에 보자.

Q. 다음 학기에 무슨 일이 생길까요?

(A) 남학생은 두 가지 수업을 모두 들을 것이다.
(B) 남학생은 두 가지 수업을 다 듣지 않을 것이다.
(C) 남학생은 가정 수업을 들을 것이다.
(D) 남학생은 컴퓨터 과학 수업을 들을 것이다.

fit 적합한, 알맞은, 어울리는 sewing 바느질, 재봉

□ Example Dialogue Excerpt

두 친구의 대화를 들으세요.

남 안녕, Emily.
여 안녕, Jordon, 어떻게 지내니?
남 잘 지내. 너 나랑 같이 〈철자 맞춤법 대회〉에 나가지 않을지 물어보려고 왔어.
여 내가? 철자법 대회에? 난 철자 엉망이야.
남 너 그렇게까지 나쁘지 않아. 누구 나랑 같이 참여할 사람이 필요하단 말이야. 같이 가자.
여 흠… 나 그날 피아노 수업이 있어.
남 수업 한번쯤이야 취소할 수 있잖아.
여 그렇긴 해. 그럼 취소할게. 그런데 대회 참가하는 데 특별히 필요한 게 있니?
남 응, 오늘 등록해야 해. 영어반에 신청서가 있어.
여 좋아, 알겠어. 나 다음 시간이 영어 수업이야. 아무튼 지금 수업에 들어가야 해. 안녕!
남 그래. 나중에 보자.

Q. 여학생은 다음에 무엇을 할까요?

(A) 피아노 수업에 간다.
(B) 친구와 수업에 들어간다.
(C) 철자법 대회 참가 신청을 한다.
(D) 철자법 대회 연습을 한다.

(good, bad, terrible) speller 철자법에 (능한/부족한/엉망인) 사람 sheet (종이)한 장; 시트

□ Conversation Example

두 친구의 대화를 들으세요.

여 안녕, Mark. 네가 이 수업 듣는지 몰랐어.
남 수업 시간을 변경했어. 오늘 어떻게 지냈니?
여 좋아. 너 과학 실습 실험 파트너 있니?

남 아니, 넌?
여 없어. 아직 그룹 프로젝트를 안 했는데, 다음 주에 첫 실험이 있어.
남 오늘 수업 시간에 파트너를 정하기로 되어 있지 않아?
여 맞아. 그렇게 되면 좋지. 그러면 실험을 시작할 수 있을 거야.
남 그래, 맞아. 정말 기다려져.

Q. 두 사람은 수업 시간에 무엇을 하게 될까요?
(A) 혼자 작업하기로 결정한다.
(B) 수업 시간을 변경한다.
(C) 숙제 계획을 세운다.
(D) 실험 파트너를 찾는다.

partner 파트너; 동업자 agree 동의하다, 의견이 일치하다

□ Dictation

Listen to a conversation between a student and school cafeteria cook. (S: student, C: cook)

S Hi, Mr. Webb. I've got a question for you.
C Sure, Kelly. What is it? Are you wondering about the menu?
S No, it's not that. I've noticed that many students are throwing away their cans and bottles ① instead of recycling them. That upsets me. Anyway, I'm wondering if you can get the students to start recycling.
C Well, Kelly, the staff at this school has been trying to get the kids to recycle for many years. At this point, we believe ② it's the students' responsibility.
S Well, I'm a student. Don't you think I can do something?
C Sure! I'm sure if you talk to your friends and classmates ③ about your concerns, they'll listen to you.
S Hmm... okay... maybe there are other students who feel the same way.
C Exactly. You can work together ④ to convince your classmates to recycle.
S Okay, great idea! Thanks, Mr. Webb.

번역 학생과 카페테리아 요리사와의 대화를 들으세요.

학 생 안녕하세요, Webb 씨. 질문이 있는데요.
요리사 그래, Kelly, 뭐지? 메뉴가 궁금하니?
학 생 아뇨, 그런 건 아니에요. 학생들이 캔이나 병을 재활용하지 않고 쓰레기 통에 많이들 버리더라고요. 그게 맘에 걸려서요. 아무튼, 제가 궁금한 건 아저씨가 학생들이 재활용을 하게 하실 수 없나 해서요.
요리사 글쎄다, Kelly, 지난 수년 간 학교 직원들이 아이들이 재활용하게 하려고 애써왔다. 그런 점에서 보면 이건 학생들 문제인 것 같다.
학 생 음, 저도 학생이잖아요. 제가 뭔가 할 수 있을 거라고 생각지 않으세요?
요리사 물론이지! 네가 걱정하고 있는 것에 관해 친구들이나 반 아이들에게 말하면 아이들도 네 말에 귀 기울일 게다.
학 생 흠… 알겠어요. 아마 저처럼 느끼는 학생들이 또 있을 거예요.
요리사 바로 그거지. 반 아이들이 재활용을 할 수 있도록 너희들이 함께 얘기해 보렴.
학 생 알겠어요, 좋은 생각이에요. 고맙습니다, Webb 씨.

Q. 다음에 무슨 일이 일어날까요?
(A) 요리사가 스스로 재활용을 하려고 애쓸 것이다.
(B) 여학생이 친구들과 재활용에 관해 얘기할 것이다.
(C) 전교생이 재활용을 시작할 것이다.
(D) 요리사가 새로운 재활용 계획안을 내놓을 것이다.

throw away (필요 없는 것을) 버리다, 없애다 bottle 병 recycle 재활용하다, 재생하다 responsibility 책임, 책임감
concern 걱정, 우려; 관심사 feel the same way 똑같이 느끼다

정답 및 해설 **[예측 문제]** 여학생이 요리사에게 학생들의 재활용 활성화를 위해 자신이 할 일이 없겠냐고 묻는다. 그러자 요리사는 "만약 네가 친구들이나 반 아이들에게 네가 걱정하는 부분에 대해 말한다면 네 말을 들을 것이라고 확신한다(I'm sure if you talk to your friends and classmates about your concerns, they'll listen to you.)"라고 말한다. 그러자 여학생이 이에 동의하며 "아마 자신과 똑같이 생각하고 있는 다른 학생들이 있을 것이다(~ maybe there are other students who feel the same way.)"라고 대답한다. 따라서 '여학생은 자신의 친구들에게 재활용에 대해 말할 것'임을 예측할 수 있다. 그러므로 정답은 (B)이다.

□ Practice Test

1. (A)	2. (C)	3. (D)	4. (C)	5. (B)	6. (C)	7. (B)	8. (D)

[1-4] Listen to a conversation between a student and a bus driver. (S: student, D: driver)

S Good morning, Mr. Marshall. I have a problem.

D What is it, Amy? How can I help you?

S Well, it seems I've lost my bus pass.

D Don't worry. This happens all the time. Today and tomorrow I'll let you ride the school bus without a pass. I need you to get a new pass by Friday though, okay?

S Sure! Thanks, Mr. Marshall. But wait... where do I get a new pass?

D You can go to the front office and ask the receptionist. Since your information is in the computer, she'll be able to print out a new one for you.

S Is it going to cost any money?

D I'm not sure. I think there's a small fee of about $5.00. You should bring some money just in case.

S Okay, thanks.

D One more thing, Amy. You should tell the receptionist that your pass is lost. If someone else is using your pass, the two of you could get into some trouble. That's happened before!

S Thanks for the advice, Mr. Marshall. I'll get a new pass as soon as I can.

번역 **학생과 버스 기사의 대화를 들으세요.**

학생 안녕하세요, Marshall 씨. 저 문제가 하나 있는데요.

기사 뭐지, Amy? 어떻게 도와줄까?

학생 음, 제가 버스 승차권을 잃어버린 것 같아요.

기사 걱정 마라. 늘 일어나는 일이니까. 오늘과 내일은 승차권 없이 버스를 태워 주마. 그렇지만 금요일까지는 새 승차권을 가져와야 한다, 알겠니?

학생 그럼요! 고맙습니다, Marshall 씨. 그런데, 잠깐만요… 새 승차권은 어디서 구하죠?

기사 학교 사무실에 가서 접수 담당자한테 물어보면 돼. 네 정보가 컴퓨터에 기록되어 있을 테니 그 분이 곧 새 승차권을 출력해 줄 거란다.

학생 돈이 들까요?

기사 글쎄다. 5달러 정도는 들지도 모르지. 만일을 대비해서 돈을 좀 가져가는 게 좋겠지.

학생 네, 고맙습니다.

기사 한 가지만 더, Amy. 접수 담당자한테 네가 승차권을 잃어버렸다는 걸 말해야 한다. 만약 다른 사람이 네 승차권을 쓰고 있다면 너랑 그 사람 둘 다 문제가 생길 테니까 말이야. 전에도 그런 적이 있었거든.

학생 충고 고맙습니다, Marshall 씨. 될 수 있는 대로 빨리 승차권을 구입할게요.

pass 패스, 통행증, 정기권 **receptionist** 접수원, 접수 담당자 **fee** 수수료, 요금 **just in case** 만약을 위해서
get into trouble 귀찮게 되다, 곤란하게 되다

1. Amy의 문제는 무엇인가요?

(A) 버스 승차권을 찾을 수가 없다.
(B) 친구가 그녀의 버스 승차권을 가지고 있다.
(C) 버스 승차권이 너무 비싸다.
(D) 그녀는 접수 담당자를 알지 못한다.

정답 및 해설 **[주제를 묻는 문제]** 학교 버스 기사와 학생과의 대화이다. 학생이 문제가 생겼다고 하면서 "버스 승차권을 잃어버린 것 같다(**Well, it seems I've lost my bus pass.**)"라고 말한다. 그러자 버스 기사는 오늘과 내일은 승차권 없이 태워주겠다면서 새로 버스 승차권을 구입할 수 있는 방법을 알려 준다. 따라서 정답은 (A)이다.

2. 버스 기사는 Amy에게 무엇을 하라고 하나요?

(A) 친구에게 무엇을 해야 할지 물어 봐라.
(B) 항상 승차권 없이 버스를 타라.
(C) 금요일까지 사무실에 가서 버스 승차권을 구입하라.
(D) 학교 컴퓨터에 그녀의 정보를 입력하라.

정답 및 해설 **[세부사항을 묻는 문제]** 버스 기사는 승차권을 잃어버린 학생에게 "금요일까지 새 승차권을 사야 한다(**I need you to get a new pass by Friday though, okay?**)"라고 당부한다. 따라서 정답은 (C)이다.

3. 버스 기사에 관해 사실인 것은 무엇일까요?

(A) 아침에만 버스를 몬다.

(B) Amy에게 돈을 빌려주고 싶어 한다.

(C) 학교 접수 담당자를 만나본 적이 없다.

(D) 전에 다른 학생들이 승차권을 분실한 경우를 본 적이 있다.

정답 및 해설 **[추론 문제]** 학생이 버스 승차권을 잃어버린 것 같다고 하자 버스 기사는 "걱정 마라. 이런 일은 항상 일어난다(Don't worry. This happens all the time.)"라고 말한다. 이를 볼 때 '버스 기사는 예전에도 학생들이 승차권을 잃어버린 것을 보았다'고 논리적으로 추론할 수 있다. 그러므로 정답은 (D)이다. (A), (B), (C)와 관련된 내용은 언급되지 않았다.

4. 여학생은 학교에 가서 무엇을 할까요?

(A) 자기 주머니에서 5달러를 찾는다.

(B) 엄마한테 전화해서 집까지 태워다 달라고 한다.

(C) 새 버스 승차권을 구입하러 사무실에 간다.

(D) 다른 사람이 자신의 버스 승차권을 쓰고 있는 걸 발견한다.

정답 및 해설 **[예측 문제]** 버스 기사는 "새로운 승차권을 어디서 얻냐(~ where do I get a new pass?)"라고 묻는 학생에게 "사무실에 가서 접수 담당자에게 물어보면 된다(You can go to the front office and ask the receptionist.)"고 가르쳐 준 후 승차권을 사는 데 필요한 정보를 말해 준다. 대화의 마지막에 학생이 "가능한 빨리 새 승차권을 사겠다(I'll get a new pass as soon as I can.)"고 말한 것을 볼 때, 학생은 학교에 도착한 후 '사무실에 가서 새 승차권을 살 것'이라고 예측할 수 있다. 따라서 정답은 (C)이다.

[5-8] Listen to a conversation between two students.

(G: girl, B: boy)

G Hey, Steve. How are you?

B I'm great. How are you doing?

G I'm really good. I have a tennis match today and I'm so excited.

B I didn't know you played tennis. There's a tennis court at my local park and sometimes I play with my brother. It's a great game. How long have you been playing?

G I've been playing for about three years. I've met a lot of nice kids on the team. Hey, are you doing anything this afternoon?

B No, I don't have any plans.

G You should definitely come watch the matches. You can meet some of the kids on the team.

B Sure, I'd love to come watch you play. Is there any chance that your team is looking for more members?

G Yes, of course. We're always looking for new members. We're having a tryout in two weeks actually. You should come!

B I'm not sure I'm good enough for the team, but I'll definitely try out.

G Great! It would be awesome to have you on the tennis team.

번역 **두 친구의 대화를 들으세요.**

여 안녕, Steve. 어떻게 지내니?

남 아주 좋아. 넌 어때?

여 나도 정말 좋아. 오늘 테니스 시합이 있어서 무척 흥분돼.

남 네가 테니스 치는 줄 몰랐어. 우리 집 근처 공원에도 테니스 코트가 있어서 나도 가끔 동생이랑 테니스를 쳐. 정말 좋은 게임이야. 넌 테니스 친 지 얼마나 됐니?

여 약 3년 정도 됐어. 테니스 팀에서 좋은 친구들도 많이 만났고. 저기, 너 오늘 오후에 일이 있니?

남 아니, 아무 계획 없어.

여 그럼 나 경기하는 데 꼭 와라. 테니스 팀 애들도 만나 볼 수 있어.

남 좋아, 나도 가서 네가 경기하는 거 보고 싶다. 너희 팀에서 새 멤버를 모집할 가능성도 있니?

여 그럼, 물론이지. 우리는 항상 새 멤버를 모집하고 있어. 사실 2주 안에 (멤버 선발을 위한) 테스트가 있을 거야. 너도 와!

남 내가 팀에 들어갈 만큼 잘할지는 모르겠지만, 한번 시도는 해볼게.

여 좋아. 네가 우리 테니스 팀에 들어오면 정말 좋을 거야.

local 지역의, 현지의 definitely 분명히, 틀림없이 tryout (스포츠 등의) 실력 시험, 적격 시험

5. 두 학생은 주로 무슨 얘기를 하고 있나요?
(A) 남학생이 치르는 중요한 테니스 시합
(B) 여학생과 남학생의 테니스에 대한 관심
(C) 마을에서 운동 경기를 하기에 가장 적합한 장소
(D) 여학생이 테니스 경기에 할애하는 시간의 양

정답 및 해설 **[주제를 묻는 문제]** 두 학생이 테니스에 대해 나누는 대화이다. 여학생이 오늘 테니스 시합이 있으니 보러 오라고 제안하자 남학생이 가고 싶다고 말하며, "너의 팀이 새 멤버를 뽑을 가능성이 있나(**Is there any chance that your team is looking for more members?**)"라고 물어본다. 그러자 여학생은 2주 안에 열리는 선발 테스트에 대해 소개하며 꼭 참석하라고 한다. 이처럼 두 사람은 전반적으로 테니스에 높은 관심을 보이며 대화를 나누고 있다. 따라서 정답은 (B)이다. 시합을 치르는 건 여학생이므로 (A)는 오답이고, (C), (D)는 언급되지 않았다.

6. 남학생은 테니스에 대해 뭐라고 하나요?
(A) 자신은 한번도 테니스를 쳐 본 적이 없다.
(B) 자신은 테니스 팀원이었었다.
(C) 가끔 동생과 테니스를 친다.
(D) 그의 동생은 학교 대표로 테니스를 친다.

정답 및 해설 **[세부사항을 묻는 문제]** 남학생은 여학생에게 "우리 동네 공원에 테니스 코트가 있는데 가끔 동생과 함께 테니스를 친다(**There's a tennis court at my local park and sometimes I play with my brother.**)"라고 말한다. 그러므로 정답은 (C)이다. 이 사실에 비추어 (A)는 틀린 내용이고, (B), (D)는 언급되지 않았다.

7. 여학생의 다음 말이 의미하는 것은 무엇인가요? *(Hey, are you doing anything this afternoon?)*
(A) 그녀는 남학생이 바쁘기를 바란다.
(B) 그녀는 남학생이 자신의 시합을 보러 오길 원한다.
(C) 그녀는 남학생이 오늘 팀 선발 시험을 치르기를 기대한다.
(D) 그녀는 남학생이 화요일에 테니스 수업이 있다는 걸 안다.

정답 및 해설 **[화자의 어조를 묻는 문제]** 여학생이 "오늘 테니스 시합이 있어서 무척 흥분된다(**I have a tennis match today and I'm so excited.**)"면서 남학생에게 "오늘 오후에 할 일이 있나(**~ are you doing anything this afternoon?**)"라고 묻자 남학생은 계획이 없다고 대답한다. 이어서 여학생이 "꼭 시합 보러 오라(**You should definitely come watch the matches.**)"라고 말한 것을 볼 때 여학생은 '남학생이 그녀의 시합을 보러 오기를 원한다'고 짐작할 수 있다. 따라서 정답은 (B)이다.

8. 남학생은 오늘 오후에 무엇을 하게 될까요?
(A) 테니스 팀에 가입한다.
(B) 테니스 선발 시험에 참여한다.
(C) 남동생과 테니스를 친다.
(D) 여학생의 테니스 시합을 보러 간다.

정답 및 해설 **[예측 문제]** 여학생이 남학생에게 "오늘 꼭 시합 보러 와야 한다(**~ you should definitely come watch the matches.**)"라고 말하자 남학생은 "가서 네가 치는 것 꼭 보고 싶다(**I'd love to come watch you play.**)"라고 대답한다. 이를 볼 때 남학생은 오후에 '여학생의 테니스 시합에 갈 것'이라고 예측할 수 있다. 따라서 정답은 (D)이다. 테니스 선발 시험은 2주 안에 있다고 했기 때문에 (B)는 오답이다.

Unit 5 Rhetorical Device Questions

□ Example Dialogue Excerpt

두 친구의 대화를 들으세요.

남 안녕, Miki.
여 안녕, Adam. 너 어디 갔다 왔어? 많이 늦었네.
남 알아. 오늘은 정말 이상한 날이었어.
여 왜? 무슨 일이 있었어?

남 음, 처음엔 자명종 맞춰놓는 걸 깜빡했지 뭐야. 그래서 버스를 놓쳤어.
여 그래서 이렇게 늦은 거야?
남 아니. 엄마가 학교까지 태워 주겠다고 하셨는데, 차까지 가다가 미끄러지는 바람에 물 웅덩이에 넘어졌어. 옷이 다 젖어서 갈아입어야 했거든.
여 어머나. 오늘은 운이 없네.
남 (신랄하게) 아니, 더 좋아지고 있나 본데. 숙제를 집에다 놔두고 안 가져 온 것 같아!
여 에고, 저런. June 선생님께서 숙제 확인하러 오셔.

Q. 남학생이 자신의 하루가 더 좋아지고 있다고 말한 이유는 무엇인가요?
(A) 보통의 평범한 하루임을 보여주려고
(B) 자신의 하루가 굉장히 좋을 것임을 암시하려고
(C) 자신의 하루가 나아지고 있음을 지적하려고
(D) 자신의 하루가 점점 더 나빠지고 있음을 지적하려고

alarm clock 자명종 on the way to ~로 가는 길에 slip 미끄러지다 puddle 물웅덩이 soak 흠뻑 적시다

□ Example Dialogue Excerpt

두 친구의 대화를 들으세요.
여 안녕, Peter. 너 무척 기분 좋아 보이네?
남 금요일은 피자 먹는 날이잖아. 일주일 중에 제일 좋아.
여 그럼 점심 때 피자를 먹을 모양이지?
남 당연하지. 엄마가 점심 값으로 5달러 주셨어. 피자 3조각 살 수 있어.
여 좀 비싸다. 피자 가게에 가면 6달러 99센트에 피자 한 판을 살 수 있잖아.
남 그래, 하지만 학교 밖으로 나가지 못하잖아.
여 방과 후에 가면 되지. 학교에서 나오는 피자 조각은 작고 기름지잖아. 나라면 방과 후까지 기다렸다가 먹겠다.
남 충고는 고맙지만, 난 그냥 다른 애들이랑 (학교에서) 피자를 먹을래.

Q. 여학생이 학교 피자의 크기와 기름기를 언급한 이유는 무엇인가요?
(A) 그 피자가 싸다고 말하려고
(B) 자신이 그 피자를 좋아하는 이유를 설명하려고
(C) 그 피자가 좋지 않다는 점을 지적하려고
(D) 건강한 점심 식사임을 증명하려고

pizza parlor 피자 가게 property 건물, 건물 구내 greasy 기름이 많은, 기름 투성이의

□ Example Dialogue Excerpt

학생과 선생님의 대화를 들으세요.
교사 안녕, Joe. 어서 오렴.
학생 안녕하세요, Wells 선생님. 잘 지내시죠?
교사 그래, 고맙구나. 네가 수학 기말 고사에 대해 어떻게 생각하는지 물어보고 싶어서 불렀단다.
학생 문제가 너무 많았던 것 같아요. 시간이 부족해서 모두 다 풀지 못했어요.
교사 그래? 다른 학생들은 대부분 일찍 끝낸 것 같던데.
학생 아마 걔네는 저보다 수학을 잘하나 봐요. 전 심지어 모르는 공식들도 몇 개 있었어요.
교사 안타깝구나. 공식은 시험 전에 모두 다 알려준 것들이야.

Q. 선생님이 시험을 일찍 끝낸 학생들에 관해 말하는 이유는 무엇인가요?
(A) 남학생이 시험을 빨리 치른 것이라고 말하려고
(B) 남학생이 공부를 열심히 했음을 지적하려고
(C) 대부분의 학생들에게는 시험이 더 쉬웠음을 알려주려고
(D) 시험이 무척 어려웠음을 표시하려고

recognize (무엇인지) 알아보다, 알아채다 formula 공식, 식

□ Conversation Example

학생과 선생님의 대화를 들으세요.

학생 또 뵙습니다, Robins 선생님.

교사 반갑구나, Jane. 학교 첫날 잘 보냈니?

학생 네, 그런데 오늘 아침에 수업료를 내다가 깜짝 놀랐어요.

교사 그래, 지난해보다 수업료가 올랐지.

학생 학교에서 왜 올린 거죠?

교사 학교가 선택한 일이 아니다. 학교에서 노트와 플래너, 폴더 인쇄를 의뢰하는 회사에서 가격을 올렸기 때문이야.

학생 음, 정말 비싸요.

교사 글쎄다, 다음 번에는 그런 학교 물품들을 가게에서 직접 살 수도 있겠지.

학생 그렇게 할 수도 있지만, 전 Fillmore 학교 로고가 찍힌 물품을 갖는 게 좋거든요.

교사 그래, 이해한단다. 가격이 인상된 건 정말 유감이야.

학생 네, 정말 그래요.

Q. 여학생이 학교의 수업료 인상 결정에 관해 물어보는 이유는 무엇인가요?

(A) 수업료가 인상된 이유를 이해하려고

(B) 새로운 플래너 때문에 얼마나 기분 좋은지 보여주려고

(C) 수업료는 인상되면 안 된다고 주장하려고

(D) 선생님으로부터 올해 수업에 관한 정보를 얻으려고

student fees 수업료 **go up** (가격 등이)오르다 **planner** 일정 계획표(수첩) **folder** 서류철, 폴더 **raise** (양, 수준 등을)올리다, 인상하다 **supplies** 공급물, 지급품

□ Dictation

Listen to a conversation between two friends.

(B: boy, G: girl)

G Morning, Jason.

B Hey, Brittany, how was your morning?

G Good, ① except for the letter I got from the school.

B What does it say?

G It is about the changes to the school dress code. The girls ② can't wear anything anymore, while the boys can wear whatever they want.

B Really? What are ③ some specific rules?

G Girls can no longer wear short skirts or shirts that show our shoulders.

B That isn't too bad. What's the big deal?

G I feel like I should wear what I want to.

B ④ It could be worse. At least we do not need to wear uniforms to school.

G I guess that is true, but I got to get to gym. See you.

B Bye, Brit.

번역 **두 친구의 대화를 들으세요.**

여 안녕, Jason.

남 안녕, Brittany, 오늘 아침 기분 어때?

여 좋아, 학교에서 온 편지만 빼곤.

남 뭐라고 써 있는데?

여 학교 복장 규칙 변경에 관한 거야. 여학생들은 이제부터 아무거나 못 입어. 남학생들은 뭐든 입어도 되는데 말이야.

남 그래? 특정한 규칙이 뭔데?

여 여학생들은 이제 짧은 치마나 어깨를 드러내는 셔츠를 입을 수 없어.

남 그렇게 나쁠 것도 없는데 뭐. 뭐가 큰 문제야?

여 난 내가 입고 싶은 걸 입길 원해.

남 그것보다 더 안 좋을 수도 있었어. 적어도 교복은 안 입어도 되잖아.

여 그건 맞는 말인 것 같다, 그런데 나 이제 체육관 가 봐야 해. 나중에 봐.

남 안녕, Brit.

Q. 여학생이 남학생들은 뭐든 입을 수 있다고 말한 이유는 무엇인가요?

(A) 남학생들이 화가 난 이유를 설명하려고

(B) 복장 규칙이 긍정적으로 변화했음을 주장하려고

(C) 새로운 복장 규칙이 여학생에게 불공평함을 암시하려고

(D) 여학생들이 왜 교복을 입을 필요가 없는지 설명하려고

except for ~을 제외하고는 whatever 어떤 ~이든, 어떤 ~일지라도 no longer 더 이상 ~이 아닌, 더 이상 ~하지 않는
big deal 큰 일, 대단한 것 gym 체육관

정답 및 해설 **[수사학적 구조를 묻는 문제]** 여학생이 바뀐 복장 규칙에 대해 불평하고 있다. "여학생은 더 이상 아무거나 입을 수 없다. 반면에 남학생은 원하는 것은 아무거나 입을 수 있다(**The girls can't wear anything anymore, while the boys can wear whatever they want.**)" 라고 말한 것을 볼 때, 여학생은 '새 복장 규정이 여학생에게 불공평하다'고 생각하고 있음을 알 수 있다. 따라서 정답은 (C)이다.

□ Practice Test

1. **(C)**	2. **(D)**	3. **(B)**	4. **(C)**	5. **(C)**	6. **(B)**	7. **(D)**	8. **(B)**

[1~4] Listen to a conversation between a student and a health teacher. (S: student, T: teacher)

S Miss McHenry, I get a cold every fall. What's the best way to avoid getting one?

T Molly, it might be difficult to avoid getting a cold. A lot of people catch colds in the fall. But there are a few things you can do to protect yourself.

S Like what?

T Well, don't share drinks or food with anyone, even your family. Make sure you wash your hands throughout the day so that you wash away the germs. Germs can easily get on your hands, so make sure you keep them away from your mouth.

S If I get a cold, should I go to the doctor? My parents always say I shouldn't go.

T If you're sick for longer than five days, you should go to the doctor. Otherwise, staying home and taking a rest is fine. Drink a lot of tea, try to get some sleep, and make sure you eat healthy foods.

S Do you think some people are more likely to get colds than other people?

T Yes, I think some people are more likely to get colds. Keep your immune system strong by exercising and eating right. That should help protect you.

S Okay, Miss McHenry. Thanks for the advice.

번역 **학생과 보건 선생님의 대화를 들으세요.**

학생 McHenry 선생님, 제가 매년 가을이면 감기에 걸리는데요. 감기에 안 걸리는 제일 좋은 방법이 뭘까요?

교사 Molly, 감기에 안 걸리기란 어려울 거다. 가을이면 감기에 걸리는 사람들이 많단다. 하지만 감기에 안 걸리게 할 수 있는 방법이 몇 가지 있긴 하지.

학생 예를 들면요?

교사 음, 다른 사람과 음료나 음식을 함께 먹지 말아야 해. 가족들과도 말이다. 그리고 병균을 씻어낼 수 있도록 하루에도 여러 차례 꼭 손을 씻도록 하고. 병균은 손에 쉽게 붙으니까 손을 입에 대지 않도록 주의하고.

학생 만약 감기에 걸리면 병원에 가야 하나요? 저희 부모님은 병원에 갈 필요가 없다고 항상 말씀하시거든요.

교사 5일이 넘도록 아프면 병원에 가 보는 게 좋지. 그렇지 않으면 그냥 집에 있으면서 휴식을 취하는 것만으로도 괜찮다. 차를 많이 마시고 잠을 잘 자고 몸에 좋은 음식을 먹도록 해.

학생 선생님 생각에 어떤 사람들은 다른 사람들보다 더 쉽게 감기에 걸리기도 하나요?

교사 그렇지, 감기에 좀더 쉽게 걸리는 사람들이 있는 것 같단다. 그러니까 운동과 올바른 식습관으로 네 면역 체계를 잘 지켜야 한다. 그러면 네 자신을 (병균으로부터)보호하는 데 도움이 될 거야.

학생 알겠습니다, McHenry 선생님. 도움 말씀 고맙습니다.

avoid 피하다; (~이 일어나는 것을)막다, 예방하다 protect 보호하다, 막다, 지키다 throughout 죽, 처음부터 끝까지
germ 세균, 병균, 병원균 keep ~ away from ... ~을 …로부터 멀리하다 otherwise 그렇지 않으면, 그 외에는
take a rest 쉬다, 휴식하다 immune system 면역 체계

1. 선생님은 여학생에게 무엇을 설명하고 있나요?

(A) 의사 선생님을 찾아갈 시기

(B) 감기가 위험한 이유

(C) 감기 예방 방법

(D) 일부 사람들이 다른 사람들보다 감기에 더 많이 걸리는 이유

정답 및 해설 **[주제를 묻는 문제]** 보건 선생님과 학생과의 대화이다. 여학생이 자신은 매년 가을이면 감기에 걸린다며 "감기를 피하는 가장 좋은 방법이 뭐냐(What's the best way to avoid getting one?)"고 물어본다. 이에 선생님은 감기를 예방할 수 있는 몇 가지 구체적인 방법을 알려준다. 따라서 정답은 (C)이다. (A)는 여러 방법 중의 하나이고, (B), (D)는 언급되지 않은 내용이므로 오답이다.

2. 여학생이 자신은 매년 가을이면 감기에 걸린다고 말한 이유는 무엇인가요?

(A) 선생님의 동정심을 얻으려고
(B) 그런 문제를 갖고 있는 사람이 자신 뿐인지 알아보려고
(C) 감기가 특정 계절에만 발생하는지 물어보려고
(D) 자신이 감기 예방을 원하는 이유를 설명하려고

정답 및 해설 **[수사학적 구조를 묻는 문제]** 여학생은 자신이 매년 가을마다 감기에 걸린다고 말한 후 "감기를 피하는 가장 좋은 방법이 뭐냐(What's the best way to avoid getting one?)"라고 물어본다. 이어서 선생님이 감기 예방법을 세부적으로 설명한다. 즉 여학생은 '자신을 감기로부터 보호하고 싶은 이유를 설명하기 위해서' 이같이 말한 것을 알 수 있다. 따라서 정답은 (D)이다.

3. 선생님은 사람들 손에 대해 무엇을 암시하나요?

(A) 주머니에 넣으면 안 된다.
(B) 수많은 세균들과 접촉한다.
(C) 하루에 한 번만 씻어야 한다.
(D) 신체 가운데 병이 발생하는 최초 지점이다.

정답 및 해설 **[추론 문제]** 선생님이 감기 예방법에 대해 설명하면서 손을 자주 씻어서 세균을 없애라고 지시한다. 이에 덧붙여 "세균은 손에 쉽게 달라붙기 때문에 입에서 멀리 하라(Germs can easily get on your hands, so make sure you keep them away from your mouth.)"고 당부한다. 이를 볼 때 '손이 수많은 세균과 접촉한다'고 논리적으로 추론할 수 있다. 따라서 정답은 (B)이다.

4. 여학생은 부모님에 관해 뭐라고 하나요?

(A) 감기로 종종 병이 난다.
(B) 학교 간호사와 친분이 있다.
(C) 자신이 감기에 걸려도 병원에 데려가지 않는다.
(D) 감기 치료를 위해 차를 많이 마시고 몸에 좋은 음식을 먹는다.

정답 및 해설 **[세부사항을 묻는 문제]** 학생은 선생님에게 감기에 걸리면 병원에 가야 하는지 물으면서 "우리 부모님은 병원에 갈 필요가 없다고 항상 말씀하신다(My parents always say I shouldn't go.)"라고 말한다. 따라서 정답은 (C)이다. (D)는 부모님이 아니라 선생님이 감기 예방법에 대해 말한 내용이므로 오답이다.

[5-8] Listen to a conversation between two students.

(B: boy, G: girl)

B Hi, Meredith. Do you have plans for Friday night?
G No, not yet. Why do you ask?
B Well, the eighth grade class is hosting a roller-skate night at the Skate Palace. Ten percent of the money is going towards our class trip. Do you want to come?
G Sure, but I don't have any skates.
B That's okay. You can rent skates. The Skate Palace recently got new ones and has them in every size.
G Won't the rental be expensive?
B No, the skates come with your ticket and the tickets are only $5.00
G Oh, wow. That's a pretty good deal. Are there any seventh graders going?
B I talked to Molly, Sidd, and Becky. They're all going to come.
G Oh great. They are all friends of mine. I'd rather not be the only seventh grader.

번역 **두 친구의 대화를 들으세요.**

남 안녕, Meredith. 금요일 밤에 계획 있니?
여 아니, 아직. 왜?
남 음, 8학년생들이 Skate Palace에서 〈롤러스케이트 나잇〉을 주최하거든. 수익금의 10 퍼센트는 수학 여행에 쓰일 거야. 너도 올래?
여 가고 싶지만, 나 스케이트가 없어.
남 괜찮아. 빌리면 돼. Skate Palace에서 최근에 새 스케이트를 구매했는데 모든 사이즈가 다 있어.
여 대여료가 비싸지 않을까?
남 아냐, 티켓 값에 포함되어 있는데, 티켓 값은 겨우 5달러밖에 안 해.
여 와~. 꽤 좋은 가격이네. 거기 7학년생들도 와?
남 Molly, Sidd, 그리고 Becky한테도 얘기했어. 모두 다 온대.
여 잘됐다. 다들 내 친구들이야. 7학년생이 나 혼자만은 아니겠다.

B Don't worry. I think lots of kids from the middle school are going. Plus, I'll be there! I know I'm in eighth grade, but still, you won't be alone.

G Oh—one last thing. What time does the roller-skate night start?

B It starts at 6:30. Don't be late!

남 걱정 마. 중학생 아이들이 많이 올 것 같아. 또 나도 가는걸! 나는 8학년이지만, 아무튼 너 혼자는 아닐 거야.

여 참, 마지막으로 한 가지만 더. 〈롤러스케이트 나잇〉은 몇 시에 시작해?

남 6시 30분 시작이야. 늦지 마!

class trip 학급 수학 여행 **rent** (사용료를 내고 단기간) 빌리다 **rental** 사용료, 임대료

5. 남학생이 여학생에게 찾아가 얘기하는 이유는 무엇인가요?

(A) 여학생이 롤러스케이트를 가지고 있는지 보려고

(B) 여학생에게 자신으로부터 티켓을 구입하라고 부탁하려고

(C) 〈롤러스케이트 나잇〉에 오라고 요청하려고

(D) 8학년 학급에 돈을 기부하라고 부탁하려고

정답 및 해설 **[주제를 묻는 문제]** 두 학생은 금요일에 열리는 〈롤러스케이트 나잇〉에 대해서 대화를 나누고 있다. 남학생은 여학생에게 "8학년생들이 Skate Palace에서 롤러스케이트 나잇을 개최한다(Well, the eighth grade class is hosting a roller-skate night at the Skate Palace.)"면서 "오지 않겠냐(Do you want to come?)"고 물어본다. 이를 볼 때 남학생이 여학생에게 '〈롤러 스케이트 나잇〉에 오라고 요청하기 위해서' 말을 건넨 것을 알 수 있다. 따라서 정답은 (C)이다.

6. 8학년 학생들이 〈롤러스케이트 나잇〉을 주최하는 이유는 무엇인가요?

(A) 새 롤러스케이트를 신어보려고

(B) 수학 여행 경비를 모으려고

(C) 학생들에게 티켓을 싸게 팔려고

(D) 다른 중학교 학생들과 즐거운 시간을 보내려고

정답 및 해설 **[세부사항을 묻는 문제]** 남학생은 〈롤러스케이트 나잇〉을 소개한 후 "수익금의 10 퍼센트는 수학 여행에 쓰일 것이다(Ten percent of the money is going towards our class trip.)"라고 말한다. 따라서 정답은 (B)이다. (A), (C), (D)는 언급되지 않았다.

7. 여학생이 남학생에게 롤러스케이트 대여 비용이 비싸지 않냐고 물어본 바가 암시하는 것은 무엇인가요?

(A) 그녀의 부모님이 비용을 내 줄 것이다.

(B) 그녀는 자신의 스케이트를 가지고 있지 않다.

(C) 그녀는 차라리 친구에게서 빌릴 것이다.

(D) 그녀는 대여비가 비싸서 (롤러스케이트 나잇 모임에) 가지 못할까 봐 걱정이다.

정답 및 해설 **[추론 문제]** 여학생이 "대여비가 비싸지 않을까(Won't the rental be expensive?)"라고 묻자 남학생은 그렇지 않다며 "티켓 값에 스케이트 대여 비용이 포함되며, 티켓 값은 겨우 5달러다(~ the skates come with your ticket and the tickets are only $5.00.)"라고 대답한다. 그러자 여학생은 "꽤 좋은 가격이다(That's a pretty good deal.)"라며 반색한다. 이 대화를 근거로 여학생이 스케이트 대여비가 비싼지를 물은 것은 '가격 때문에 가지 못할까 봐 걱정'하기 때문임을 유추할 수 있다. 따라서 정답은 (D)이다.

8. 여학생이 7학년 학생들이 가는지를 물어본 이유는 무엇인가요?

(A) 7학년생들 중 몇 명과 함께 가기 싫다.

(B) 자신만이 유일한 7학년 학생인 것이 싫다.

(C) 8학년 중에는 친구가 하나도 없다.

(D) 같은 반 학생들과는 잘 어울리지 못한다.

정답 및 해설 **[수사학적 구조를 묻는 문제]** 여학생이 "다른 7학년 학생들도 가냐(Are there any seventh graders going?)"라고 묻자 남학생이 가기로 한 친구들의 이름을 말해준다. 이에 대해서 여학생은 잘됐다며 "모두 내 친구들이고, 나만 7학년인 것은 싫다(They are all friends of mine. I'd rather not be the only seventh grader.)"라고 말한다. 따라서 정답은 (B)이다. (A), (C), (D)는 언급되지 않았다.

Unit 6 Prosody Questions

□ Example Dialogue Excerpt

학생과 선생님의 대화를 들으세요.

학생 안녕하세요, Biggs 선생님. 잠깐 시간 되세요?

교사 물론이지. 뭘 도와 줄까?

학생 영어 숙제를 다 못 끝냈습니다. 기한 연장을 할 수 있을지 알고 싶은데요.

교사 기한은 내일이다, Zach. 미안하구나.

학생 하지만, Biggs 선생님. 저 지난주에 하키 시합이 있었거든요.

교사 (엄격하게) 마감까지 한 달이나 있었잖니. 내일까지 내 책상에 숙제를 갖다 놓아라. 잘 가거라, Zach.

Q. 선생님의 다음 말이 의미하는 것은 무엇인가요? *(You had a month to finish.)*

(A) 남학생이 하키를 너무 많이 한다고 생각한다.

(B) 남학생의 변명이 타당치 않다고 생각한다.

(C) 남학생에게 기간 연장해 주는 걸 고려해 보겠다.

(D) 앞으로는 1개월 기한의 숙제는 더 이상 주지 않겠다.

extension (기간의) 연장

□ Example Dialogue Excerpt

두 친구의 대화를 들으세요.

남 안녕, Selena. 뭐 새로운 일이라도 있니?

여 아무것도. 넌?

남 오늘 체육 수업에 파트너가 필요해. 나랑 같이 할래?

여 글쎄, Dave. Jennifer가 나랑 한 팀이 되고 싶어 하는 것 같아. 넌 Nathan이랑 파트너가 되는 게 좋겠어.

남 괜찮은 생각이네. Nathan은 체육을 잘 하는데다, 걔는 키가 커서 같이 농구하면 좋아.

여 나도 너랑 함께 하고 싶지만, Jen이 먼저 하자고 해서 말이야.

남 괜찮아. Nate가 아직 팀을 안 정했는지 볼게.

여 잘 되길 바라. 다음 시간에 보자.

Q. 남학생의 다음 말이 의미하는 것은 무엇인가요? *(No big deal.)*

(A) 여학생과 파트너가 되지 못했지만 괜찮다.

(B) 여학생이 자신의 파트너가 될 수 없어서 슬프다.

(C) 여학생이 자신의 파트너가 되지 않아서 다행이다.

(D) 여학생이 자신의 파트너가 되고 싶어 하지 않는다고 생각한다.

no big deal 별 일 아니다, 대수롭지 않다 teammate 팀 동료, 팀 메이트

□ Example Dialogue Excerpt

학생과 선생님의 대화를 들으세요.

교사 Nicole!

학생 네, Ranger 선생님?

교사 (소리 높여) 지금 뭘 하고 있다고 생각하죠?

학생 아무것도 아니에요, Ranger 선생님. 죄송합니다.

교사 좋아요. 자, 주목하세요.

Q. 선생님의 다음 말이 의미하는 것은 무엇인가요? *(What do you think you are doing?)*

(A) 학생이 주의 깊게 듣고 있다.

(B) 학생이 수업 과제를 하고 있다.

(C) 학생이 뭔가 좋지 않은 일을 하고 있다.

(D) 학생이 무엇을 해야 할지 알지 못한다.

pay attention 주목하다, 주의를 기울이다

□ Conversation Example

학생과 생활지도 상담사의 대화를 들으세요.

상담사 어서 와요, Ray. 자리에 앉아요.
학 생 안녕하세요, Clancy 선생님. 저한테 문제가 있나요?
상담사 아니에요, Ray, 그렇지 않아요. 학생이 다른 학생들에게 수학 과목 과외를 할 생각이 있는지 물어보려고 불렀어요.
학 생 사람들을 돕는 걸 좋아합니다. 좋은 경험도 될 테고요. 일주일에 몇 시간씩 해야 하나요?
상담사 그건 학생한테 달렸죠. 여기 목록에 있는 학생들 중 아무나 골라 이메일을 보내요. 도움을 받겠다고 하면 두 사람이 만나는 겁니다.
학 생 좋습니다. 제가 너무 바빠지면 시간을 줄일 수도 있나요?
상담사 물론, 그럴 수 있어요. 그리고 학생이 과외 하는 데 들인 시간은 모두 사회 봉사 시간으로 처리될 거예요. 졸업하려면 필요할 겁니다.
학 생 이렇게 알려 주셔서 고맙습니다, Clancy 선생님.
상담사 천만에요, Ray. 좋은 하루 보내요.
학 생 안녕히 계세요!

Q. 상담사의 다음 말이 의미하는 것은 무엇인가요? *(It's up to you.)*
(A) 남학생이 누구를 가르칠지 결정한다.
(B) 남학생은 과외를 하겠다고 신청해야 한다.
(C) 남학생은 10시간까지 가르쳐야 한다.
(D) 남학생은 과외 시간을 결정할 수 있다.

be in trouble 곤경에 처하다, 어려움에 처하다 tutor (과외로서) 가르치다, 개인 지도하다 list 목록
community service 사회 봉사 활동 graduate (고등학교나 대학교) 학업을 마치다, 졸업하다

□ Dictation

Listen to a conversation between a teacher and a student. (T: teacher, S: student)

S Hi, Mr. Irving. How is your day going?
T Good, Stacey. What can I do for you?
S I wanted to ask you about the score you gave me ① on my mid-term.
T Okay, what is your question?
S Well, I think I got this question right, but ② it was marked incorrect.
T Let me take a look. ③ Look at that! The answer is right. Sorry about that, Stacey.
S It's OK, Mr. Irving, but ④ can you fix my grade please?
T Of course. I'm giving you ⑤ an extra one percent for proving me wrong, too!

번역 **학생과 선생님의 대화를 들으세요.**

학생 안녕하세요, Irving 선생님. 오늘 하루 어떠셨어요?
교사 좋았다, Stacey. 뭘 도와줄까?
학생 선생님이 채점하신 제 중간 고사 점수에 대해 여쭤보고 싶습니다.
교사 좋아, 물어볼 게 뭐지?
학생 저, 제 생각엔 이 문제 답이 맞는 것 같은데, 틀렸다고 채점이 되어 있어서요.
교사 어디 보자. 이것 봐라! 답이 맞네. 미안하구나, Stacey.
학생 괜찮습니다, Irving 선생님. 헌데 점수는 수정해 주시는 거죠?
교사 물론이지. 선생님이 틀린 걸 찾아냈으니 추가로 1점 더 주겠다.

Q. 선생님의 다음 말이 의미하는 것은 무엇인가요? *(Look at that!)*
(A) 자신이 옳았다고 생각한다.
(B) 학생이 틀렸다는 것을 안다.
(C) 학생의 말이 맞아서 놀랐다.
(D) 학생이 자신의 실수를 봐서 화가 난다.

mark (표나 기호 등으로) 표시하다 incorrect 맞지 않는, 부정확한 fix 바로 잡다; 수리하다

정답 및 해설 [화자의 어조를 묻는 문제] 여학생이 선생님에게 중간 고사 점수에 대해 물어보러 왔다면서 "이 문제를 맞힌 것 같은데 틀리게 표시되어 있다(Well, I think I got this question right, but it was marked incorrect.)"라고 말한다. 이에 선생님은 "어디 보자. 정답이 맞네. 미안하다(Let me take a look. ~ The answer is right.)"라고 한다. 여기서 이 말은 여학생의 답이 옳은 것에 대한 놀람을 표현하는 것으로 볼 수 있다. 따라서 정답은 (C)이다.

□ Practice Test

1. (D)	2. (A)	3. (A)	4. (C)	5. (D)	6. (C)	7. (A)	8. (B)

[1-4] Listen to a conversation between a student and the school soccer coach. (S: student, C: coach)

S Hi, Coach Evans. I'm excited for practice today.
C I'm glad you're excited. We're going to be practicing a lot for the game against Portland.
S I hope we can beat them in the game. We were so close to winning last time.
C Our team is definitely strong enough to beat Portland. We'll work this week to enhance our defense skills so that we'll be ready on Friday.
S What!? The game is on Friday!? Is it the game against Portland? I thought it was on Monday.
C No, Alanna, it's on Friday. Is that a problem?
S Well, my mom told me this morning that I have a dentist appointment on Friday.
C You're a very valuable player and this is a big game for our team, so I think it's important that you try to make it.
S Of course! I know I can't miss the game. It seems like I'll have to cancel the appointment.
C I'm sure you can get an appointment for sometime next week when we don't have any games.
S Thanks, Coach. I'm just glad I found out today!

번역 학생과 축구 코치의 대화를 들으세요.

학생 안녕하세요, Evans 코치님. 오늘 연습이 정말 기대돼요.
코치 네가 기대하고 있다니 기쁘구나. 포트랜드 전에 대비해서 연습을 많이 할 거다.
학생 우리 팀이 경기에서 이겼으면 좋겠어요. 지난번에는 거의 이길 뻔했잖아요.
코치 우리 팀이 포트랜드 팀에 이길 만큼 충분히 강하긴 하지. 금요일 경기에 대비할 수 있도록 이번 주에는 방어력 향상에 집중할 거다.
학생 네!? 경기가 금요일이에요!? 포트랜드 전이요? 전 월요일이라고 생각했었어요.
코치 아냐, Alanna, 금요일이다. 문제가 있니?
학생 저, 오늘 아침에 엄마가 말씀하시길 제가 금요일에 치과 예약이 되어 있대요.
코치 너는 우리 팀 중요 선수야. 그리고 이번 경기는 우리 팀한테 중요한 경기이고. 그러니까 네가 어떻게든 경기에 참여하는 게 중요하다고 생각한다.
학생 물론입니다. 저 역시도 경기에 빠지면 안 된다는 건 알아요. 아무래도 치과 예약을 취소해야겠어요.
코치 다음 주에 우리가 경기가 없을 때 아무 때라도 예약 일정을 다시 잡을 수 있을 게다.
학생 고맙습니다, 코치님. 오늘이라도 알게 돼서 다행이에요.

> against ~에 맞서 close (경쟁 등이) 접전인, (세력이) 백중한 enhance (실력 등을) 높이다, 강화하다
> defense 수비, 방어 dentist appointment 치과 진료 예약 valuable 매우 유용한; 값진, 귀중한 cancel 취소하다

1. 여학생의 문제는 무엇인가요?

(A) 포트랜드 전에 맞설 준비가 되어 있지 않다.
(B) 약속이 있기 때문에 금요일 경기에 빠져야 한다.
(C) 자신의 스케줄 때문에 오늘 연습에 참가할 수 없다.
(D) 대결전의 날과 같은 날에 치과 진료 예약이 있다.

정답 및 해설 [주제를 묻는 문제] 축구 코치가 학생에게 금요일에 포트랜드 팀과의 경기가 있다고 하자 학생은 "월요일이라고 생각했다(I thought it was on Monday.)"면서, "엄마가 오늘 아침에 금요일에 치과 예약이 있다고 했다(Well, my mom told me this morning that I have a dentist appointment on Friday.)"고 답한다. 따라서 정답은 (D)이다. (A), (B), (C)는 모두 틀린 내용이다.

2. 여학생의 다음 말이 의미하는 것은 무엇인가요? *(I thought it was on Monday.)*

(A) 경기 일자가 헷갈렸다.
(B) 오직 월요일에 경기가 하고 싶다.
(C) 금요일에 경기를 할 준비가 되어 있지 않다.
(D) 이번 주에는 경기를 하고 싶지 않다.

정답 및 해설 **[화자의 어조를 묻는 문제]** 코치가 금요일 경기에 대해 말하자 학생은 무척 놀라며 "경기가 월요일이라고 생각했다(I thought it was on Monday.)"라고 말한다. 즉, 학생이 경기 요일을 헷갈린 것을 나타낸다. 따라서 정답은 (A)이다.

3. 코치의 다음 말이 의미하는 것은 무엇인가요? *(I think it's important that you try to make it.)*

(A) 여학생이 경기에 참여할 필요가 있다.
(B) 팀은 여학생의 수비 기술이 필요하다.
(C) 다른 선수들은 이미 약속을 취소했다.
(D) 여학생이 치과에 간다고 하더라도 이해하겠다.

정답 및 해설 **[화자의 어조를 묻는 문제]** 학생이 "엄마가 오늘 아침에 금요일에 치과 예약이 있다고 했다(my mom told me this morning that I have a dentist appointment on Friday.)"며 난감해 하자, 코치는 여학생에게 "너는 우리 팀 중요 선수이고 이번 시합은 우리 팀에게 중요한 시합이므로, 참가할 수 있도록 노력하는 것이 중요하다고 생각한다(You're a very valuable player and this is a big game for our team, so I think it's important that you try to make it.)"라고 말한다. 이를 근거로 추론해 볼 때 코치는 '학생이 시합에 꼭 와야 한다'고 생각하고 있음을 알 수 있다. 따라서 정답은 (A)이다.

4. 여학생은 치과 진료 예약에 대해 뭐라고 말하나요?

(A) 치과 진료를 받으러 꼭 가야 한다.
(B) 치과 진료에 가고 싶다.
(C) 치과 진료 예약을 취소할 것이다.
(D) 목요일로 예약 일정을 옮길 것이다.

정답 및 해설 **[세부사항을 묻는 문제]** 코치는 경기하는 날 치과 예약을 했다는 여학생에게 "너는 매우 중요한 선수이고 우리 팀에게 중요한 경기이기 때문에 꼭 참가해야 한다(You're a very valuable player and this is a big game for our team, so I think it's important that you try to make it.)"라고 말한다. 이에 대해 학생은 "물론이다. 예약은 취소해야겠다(Of Course! ~ I'll have to cancel the appointment.)"라고 한다. 그러므로 정답은 (C)이다.

[5-8] Listen to a conversation between two students.
(B: boy, G: girl)

G So, what do you want to do our history project on?
B I was thinking it would be fun to do it on the knights in the Middle Ages. What a cool topic!
G Hmm... well... to be honest, I'm not all that interested in researching knights and their armor. The Middle Ages is an interesting time period, though. Is there anything else we could do it on?
B How about the Black Plague? It killed nearly a third of Europe and changed a lot of things in European society.
G That might be interesting. I'd love to do some research on the reasons why the plague was so deadly. Do you know much about the Black Plague?
B Not really, but I'd love to find out more. It would make a good presentation because other people in our class will probably be interested in learning about it, don't you think?
G Yes, I think it's a great idea. Now all we have to do is ask Mrs. Edwards to approve the project.

번역 **두 친구의 대화를 들으세요.**

여 그래서 넌 역사 과제를 어떤 걸로 하고 싶어?
남 중세 시대 기사들에 관해서 하면 재미있을 것 같아. 정말 멋진 주제잖아!
여 흠… 글쎄… 솔직히 말하면, 난 기사들이나 갑옷에 대해 조사하는 데 전혀 흥미가 안 생겨. 중세 시대가 흥미로운 시대이긴 하지만 말이야. 그 시대에 관해 다른 건 할 게 없을까?
남 흑사병에 관해선 어때? 유럽 인구의 거의 1/3이 사망했고 유럽 사회의 여러 부분에 변화를 가져왔지.
여 그거 재미있겠다. 흑사병이 왜 그렇게 치명적이었는지에 관해 조사해 보고 싶어. 너 흑사병에 관해 많이 아니?
남 그렇진 않아, 하지만 좀더 조사해 보고 싶어. 우리 반 애들도 아마 그 사건에 흥미를 느낄 거고, 그러면 꽤 괜찮은 발표가 될 거 같아. 어떻게 생각해?
여 맞아, 나도 좋은 생각 같아. 이제 Edwards 선생님께 이 주제가 괜찮은지 여쭤보기만 하면 되겠다.

B Do you think she'll say yes?
G I don't see why not. As long as we include a lot of historical details and facts, the project will make Mrs. Edwards happy.
B Okay, sounds good. Let's start researching for our proposal.

남 선생님이 좋다고 하실까?
여 왜 안 된다고 하시겠어? 역사와 관련된 세부 사항과 역사적 사실들만 많이 포함한다면 선생님도 이 프로젝트가 맘에 드실 거야.
남 좋아, 괜찮은 것 같아. 그럼 우리가 생각한 대로 조사를 시작해 보자.

knight 기사 armor 갑옷, 철갑 the Middle Ages 중세(*유럽 역사에서 서기 500~1450년경) black plague 페스트, 흑사병, 폐결핵
deadly 치명적인, 생명을 앗아가는 approve 찬성하다, 괜찮다고 생각하다 historical 역사상의, 역사와 관련된
proposal 제안, 제의

5. 두 사람은 주로 무엇에 관해 논의하고 있나요?
(A) 중세 시대
(B) 발표를 잘 하기
(C) Edwards 선생님의 승인
(D) 역사 과제 주제

정답 및 해설 **[주제를 묻는 문제]** 두 학생이 역사 프로젝트에 대해 대화를 나누고 있다. 처음에 여학생이 "우리 역사 프로젝트에 뭘 하고 싶은가(~ what do you want to do our history project on?)"라고 물은 후, 두 학생이 발표 주제를 정하는 대화가 이어진다. 따라서 정답은 (D)이다. (A), (B), (C)는 대화 중에 언급되긴 했으나, 각각의 세부적인 내용이므로 전체 주제는 될 수 없다.

6. 여학생의 다음 말이 의미하는 것은 무엇인가요? *(Is there anything else we could do it on?)*
(A) 그녀는 언제나 남학생의 의견에 동의하지 않는다.
(B) 중세 시대와 관련해서는 전혀 관심이 없다.
(C) (중세 시대에 관해) 기사와 갑옷 외에 다른 주제를 하고 싶다.
(D) 자신이 관심을 갖지 않는 분야에 관해 프로젝트를 하고 싶다.

정답 및 해설 **[화자의 어조를 묻는 문제]** 남학생이 중세 시대 기사에 대한 프로젝트를 제안하자 여학생은 "기사와 갑옷에 대해 조사하는 것이 전혀 흥미롭지 않다. 그래도 중세 시대는 흥미로운 시기인 것 같다(I'm not all that interested in researching knights and their armor. The Middle Ages is an interesting time period, though.)"라며, "그것 말고 다른 것은 없나(Is there anything else we could do it on?)"라고 물어 본 것이다. 즉, 중세 시대라는 시기는 마음에 드니까, '기사와 갑옷 외에 다른 주제를 원한다'고 볼 수 있다. 따라서 정답은 (C)이다.

7. 여학생은 무엇을 조사하고 싶어 하나요?
(A) 흑사병이 왜 그렇게 치명적이었는지
(B) 기사들이 왜 그처럼 무거운 갑옷을 입었는지
(C) 흑사병이 어떻게 그처럼 많은 아이들을 죽게 했는지
(D) 흑사병이 왜 유럽에서만 발병했는지

정답 및 해설 **[세부사항을 묻는 문제]** 남학생이 "흑사병은 어떠나(How about the Black Plague?)"며 다른 제안을 하자 여학생은 "흥미로울 것 같다. 왜 그렇게 흑사병이 치명적이었는지 그 이유에 대해 조사하고 싶다(That might be interesting. I'd love to do some research on the reasons why the plague was so deadly.)"라고 말한다. 따라서 정답은 (A)이다.

8. 여학생의 다음 말이 의미하는 것은 무엇인가요? *(I don't see why not.)*
(A) 그녀 생각에 Edwards 선생님을 기쁘게 하기는 쉽다.
(B) Edwards 선생님이 자신들의 프로젝트를 승인할 거라고 생각한다..
(C) Edwards 선생님이 자신들을 돕는 데 동의할 거라고 생각하지 않는다.
(D) 그녀는 중세 시대가 프로젝트 주제로 좋은 이유를 모르겠다.

정답 및 해설 **[화자의 어조를 묻는 문제]** 남학생이 "선생님이 허락해주실까(Do you think she'll say yes?)"하고 묻자 여학생은 "안 될 이유 없다(I don't see why not.)"라며, "역사와 관련된 세부 사항과 역사적 사실들을 많이 포함하는 한 선생님이 그 프로젝트를 맘에 들어 할 것이다(As long as we include a lot of historical details and facts, the project will make Mrs. Edwards happy.)"라고 대답한다. 즉 여학생은 '선생님이 그들의 프로젝트를 승인할 것으로 생각한다'고 볼 수 있다. 따라서 정답은 (B)이다.

Actual Test

1. (B)	2. (B)	3. (C)	4. (C)	5. (B)	6. (B)	7. (B)	8. (B)	9. (D)	10. (C)	11. (B)	12. (B)
13. (A)	14. (C)	15. (D)	16. (C)	17. (C)	18. (D)	19. (B)	20. (D)	21. (D)	22. (B)	23. (D)	24. (D)
25. (A)	26. (D)	27. (B)	28. (C)	29. (C)	30. (D)	31. (B)	32. (B)	33. (A)	34. (D)	35. (D)	36. (C)
37. (D)	38. (D)	39. (C)	40. (C)	41. (D)	42. (C)						

1 Listen to a teacher talking to students.

W Writing on the desks is not appropriate. I've had to clean off the desks every day for the past three weeks. It doesn't matter if you write in pencil. It is still destructive behavior. If I catch you writing on a desk, then you will be staying after school to clean off your desk and any others that have been written on.

번역 **선생님이 학생들에게 하는 말을 들으세요.**

여 책상 위에 낙서하는 것은 옳지 못한 일입니다. 지난 3주 간 선생님이 매일 책상의 낙서를 닦아야 했었어요. 연필로 쓴다고 해도 다르지 않습니다. 그것 역시 나쁜 행동이에요. 책상 위에 낙서하다 걸리면 방과 후에 남게 해서 여러분들 책상은 물론 낙서가 되어 있는 다른 책상들까지 닦게 하겠어요.

1. 선생님에 관해 사실은 무엇일까요?

(A) 방과 후에 남아 책상을 닦고 싶어 한다.

(B) 학생들이 책상 위에 낙서하는 걸 그만두길 원한다.

(C) 전에 학교 책상을 망가뜨리려 했었다.

(D) 학생들이 책상에 낙서할 때는 연필로 하길 바란다.

appropriate 적절한, 알맞은 clean off ~을 닦아내다, 쓸어 내다 destructive 파괴적인, 해를 끼치는; 부정적인

정답 및 해설 **[추론 문제]** 선생님이 학생들에게 "책상에 낙서하는 것은 옳지 못하다(Writing on the desks is not appropriate.)"라고 말한다. 지난 3주 동안 매일 선생님이 책상을 닦았다면서 "책상에 낙서하는 것을 보면 방과 후에 낙서가 된 책상을 모두 닦게 하겠다(If I catch you writing on a desk, ~ to clean off your desk and any others that have been written on.)"라고 말한다. 이를 볼 때 선생님은 '학생들이 책상에 낙서하는 것을 그만두기를 원한다'고 추론할 수 있다. 따라서 정답은 (B)이다.

2 Listen to a school principal talking to a group of students.

M The cafeteria workers have recently complained that students are not cleaning up after themselves in the cafeteria. If you bring your own lunch from home, make sure to throw away your wrappers. If you buy lunch at school, please return your dishes and tray. It is not difficult to clean up, so please do it.

번역 **교장 선생님이 몇몇 학생들에게 하는 말을 들으세요.**

남 학교 식당 직원들이 최근 여러분들이 식당에서 식사를 마친 후 제대로 정리를 안 하고 있다며 불만을 제기했습니다. 집에서 점심 식사를 가져와서 먹을 경우, (다 먹고 난)포장지는 반드시 제대로 버려 주세요. 학교에서 점심을 사먹는 경우라면, (식사를 마친 후)식기와 쟁반을 반납해 주시기 바랍니다. 이렇게 정리하는 게 어려운 일은 아니니까, 반드시 지켜주시기 바랍니다.

2. 교장 선생님은 학생들에게 무엇을 지시하나요?

(A) 식당에서 점심을 사 먹어라.

(B) 점심 식사 후에는 (먹은 것에 대해)정리하라.

(C) 식당 직원과 대화를 나눠라.

(D) 점심 식사는 운동장 밖에서 하라.

complain 불평하다, 불만을 털어놓다 wrapper 포장지; 싸는 것 tray 쟁반; 쟁반 모양의 접시

정답 및 해설 **[세부사항을 묻는 문제]** 교장 선생님이 학생들에게 "최근에 학교 식당 직원들이 학생들이 식사 후 치우지 않아 불평하고 있다(The cafeteria workers have recently complained that students are not cleaning up after themselves in the cafeteria.)"라고 말한 후, 집에서 점심 식사를 가져왔을 때나 학교에서 점심을 사 먹을 경우에 대한 두 가지 정리 방법을 지시한다. 따라서 정답은 (B)이다. (A), (C), (D)는 언급되지 않았다.

3 Listen to a teacher talking to students.

W Over the past month, I've collected a variety of items that students have left behind. I'm going to give you a few minutes to check the Lost and Found box in the back of my classroom to see if you've misplaced anything. In the future, try not to leave your clothing behind. It's important to keep track of your belongings. Okay, everyone, go ahead and check.

번역 선생님이 학생들에게 하는 말을 들으세요.

여 지난달에 선생님은 여러분들이 남기고 간 다양한 종류의 물건들을 모아두었습니다. 선생님이 잠깐 시간을 줄 테니, 여러분들이 잃어버린 물건이 없는지 교실 뒤쪽에 있는 분실물 박스를 확인해보기 바랍니다. 앞으로는 옷을 교실에 두고 가지 마세요. 여러분들 소지품을 잘 챙기는 일은 아주 중요합니다. 좋아요, 여러분, 가서 확인해 보세요.

3. 화자의 목적은 무엇인가요?

(A) 분실물 보관 박스 만들기

(B) 학생들에게 가방을 점검해 보라고 말하기

(C) 학생들에게 분실물 보관 박스를 확인해보라고 하기

(D) 학부모들한테 자녀들에게 새 옷을 사주라고 하기

collect 모으다, 수집하다 **a variety of** 다양한 ~, 여러 가지의 ~ **leave behind** 두다, 두고 가다 **Lost and Found** 분실물 취급소 **misplace** 제자리에 두지 않다, 잘못 두다, 둔 곳을 잊다 **keep track of** ~의 흔적을 더듬다, ~을 놓치지 않고 따라가다 **belongings** 소유물, 재산

정답 및 해설 **[화자의 의도를 묻는 문제]** 선생님이 학생들에게 분실물 보관 상자를 확인할 것과 소지품을 잃어버리지 않을 것을 당부하고 있다. "여러분들이 잃어버린 물건이 없는지 교실 뒤쪽에 있는 분실물 박스를 확인해보기 바란다(**~ to check the Lost and Found box in the back of my classroom to see if you've misplaced anything.**)"라고 말하며, 마지막에 "가서 확인해 보라(**~ go ahead and check.**)"라고 지시한다. 이를 볼 때, 선생님의 목적은 '학생들이 분실물 상자를 확인하도록 하는 것'임을 알 수 있다. 따라서 정답은 (C)이다.

4 Listen to a school nurse talking to students.

M Students, as we approach flu season, the school will be giving flu shots. If you're interested in getting one, the shots will be given on this Wednesday. They will be given all day. You can sign up at my office. Don't forget to bring your insurance card and a permission slip from your parents.

번역 보건 선생님이 학생들에게 하는 말을 들으세요.

남 학생 여러분, 독감의 계절이 다가오고 있습니다. 그래서 학교에서 독감 예방 주사 접종을 할 겁니다. 예방 주사 접종을 원한다면, 이번 수요일에 실시하니 알아두세요. 주사 접종은 하루 종일 실시됩니다. (주사를 맞고 싶은 학생은) 선생님 사무실에서 신청하면 됩니다. 보험 카드와 부모님 허가서를 꼭 갖고 오도록 하세요.

4. 공지사항의 주제는 무엇인가요?

(A) 독감의 계절의 위험성

(B) 보험 카드 가져오기

(C) 학교에서 치르는 독감 주사 예방 접종

(D) 독감 주사 예방 접종 신청 장소

approach 다가오다, 다가가다 **flu shot** 독감 예방 주사 **sign up** 등록하다, 가입하다, 참가하다 **insurance** 보험 **permission** 허락, 허가 **slip** 메모 용지, 종이 조각

정답 및 해설 **[주제를 묻는 문제]** 보건 선생님이 학생들에게 독감 예방 주사 접종에 대해 안내하고 있다. 처음에 "독감의 계절이 다가오고 있으므로 학교에서 독감 예방 주사 접종을 실시하겠다(**~ as we approach flu season, the school will be giving flu shots.**)"라고 말한다. 이어서 주사를 맞는 요일과 가져와야 할 것에 대해 언급한다. 따라서 정답은 (C)이다. (A)에 대해서는 구체적으로 언급하지 않았고, (B)와 (D)는 세부적인 내용이므로 전체를 아우르는 주제가 될 수 없다.

5 Listen to an art teacher talking to his class.

M This month we're going to work on drawing the human body. We're going to start by working on drawing the human face. If you look closely at a human face, you'll see that the eyes are not actually near the top of the head, but closer to the middle. There are lots of things to remember when drawing a face. Here, I'll tell you how you can make a perfect face shape.

번역 **미술 선생님이 학생들에게 하는 말을 들으세요.**

남 이번 달에는 인간의 신체를 그릴 겁니다. 먼저 우리 얼굴을 그리는 것부터 시작합니다. 여러분들이 얼굴을 자세히 살펴보면 알겠지만, 사실 눈은 이마 위쪽과 가까이 위치해 있지 않고 오히려 중간 쪽에 더 가까이 위치해 있습니다. 이처럼 얼굴을 그릴 때 기억해 둬야 할 것들이 많습니다. 이제 여러분들에게 어떻게 완벽한 얼굴 모양을 그릴 수 있는지 알려 주겠습니다.

5. 선생님은 다음에 무엇을 할까요?
(A) 학생들에게 얼굴 그림을 보여준다.
(B) 얼굴을 정확하게 그리는 방법을 설명한다.
(C) 학생들에게 다양한 사진들을 보여준다.
(D) 학생 한 명을 예로 들어 얼굴 수치 측정법을 보여준다.

human body 인체　face shape 얼굴 모양

정답 및 해설 **[예측 문제]** 미술 선생님이 학생들에게 "이번 달에는 인간의 몸을 그리겠다(This month we're going to work on drawing the human body.)"라고 말한다. 먼저 얼굴 그리기부터 시작하겠다며, "얼굴을 그리는 데 기억해야 할 것들이 많다. 완벽한 얼굴을 그리는 방법을 말하겠다(There are lots of things to remember when drawing a face. Here, I'll tell you how you can make a perfect face shape.)"라고 한다. 이를 볼 때, 선생님이 곧이어 '얼굴을 정확히 그리는 방법을 설명할 것'이라고 예측할 수 있다. 따라서 정답은 (B)이다.

6 Listen to a teacher talking to her class.

W Next week we're going to go to the library. We're going to find some books to help you write your reports. The library has a lot of books on every subject. If you are worried about finding the books that you need, I will be there to help each student. The librarians will also be very helpful.

번역 **선생님이 반 학생들에게 하는 말을 들으세요.**

여 다음주에 우리는 도서관에 갈 겁니다. 여러분들이 리포트 쓰는 데 도움이 될만한 책을 찾을 거예요. 도서관에는 모든 주제를 망라하는 다양한 도서들이 있습니다. 여러분들이 필요한 책을 제대로 찾을 수 있을지 걱정이 된다면 제가 옆에서 도와줄 테니 걱정 말도록 하세요. 도서관 사서들도 역시 도움을 줄 것입니다.

6. 선생님이 학생들에게 도움을 주는 것에 대해 말한 이유는 무엇인가요?
(A) 학생들에게 어떤 주제를 제시하려고
(B) 학생들에게 걱정하지 말라고 말하려고
(C) 도서관 규모가 크다는 것을 증명하려고
(D) 학생들이 길을 잃지 않도록 경고하려고

helpful 유용한, 도움이 되는

정답 및 해설 **[화자의 의도를 묻는 문제]** 선생님이 학생들에게 다음 주에 도서관에 간다고 공지하면서 "여러분들이 필요한 책을 제대로 찾을 수 있을지 걱정이 된다면 선생님이 옆에서 도와줄 테니 걱정 마라(If you are worried about finding the books that you need, I will be there to help each student.)"라고 말한다. 또한 도서관 사서의 도움도 받을 수 있다고 했다. 따라서 정답은 (B)이다.

7 Listen to a music teacher talking to a group of students.

M The school band is having tryouts next week. The band needs trumpet and trombone players, which is why I'm talking to you. Tryouts will be after school on Monday, Tuesday, and Wednesday of next week. You are all good musicians so I think you should try out. It's really fun to be in the school band.

번역 **음악 선생님이 몇몇 학생들에게 하는 말을 들으세요.**

남 학교 밴드부에서 다음 주에 선발 시험을 치를 예정입니다. 밴드부에서는 트럼펫 연주자와 트롬본 연주자를 구하고 있는데요, 제가 여러분에게 얘기하는 이유도 그 때문입니다. 선발 시험은 다음 주 월요일, 화요일, 수요일 방과 후에 치러집니다. 여러분들 모두 실력 있는 연주자들이니까 꼭 시험에 응시해 보도록 하세요. 학교 밴드에 들어가면 정말 재미있습니다

7. 선생님은 주로 무엇에 대해 얘기하나요?
(A) 실력 있는 음악가들
(B) 밴드 선발 시험에 응시하기
(C) 트럼펫과 트럼본 연주자들
(D) 밴드에서 연주하는 것이 얼마나 재미있는지

trumpet 트럼펫(*금관악기) trombone 트럼본(*금관악기) musician 음악가, 뮤지션

정답 및 해설 [주제를 묻는 문제] 음악 선생님이 학생들에게 "학교 밴드부에서 다음 주에 선발 시험을 치를 예정이다(The school band is having tryouts next week.)"라고 공지하고 있다. 트럼펫 연주자와 트롬본 연주자를 구하고 있는 것과 시험 날짜를 안내하면서 "여러분들은 실력 있는 연주자들이니까 꼭 시험에 응시해 보도록 하라(You are all good musicians so I think you should try out.)"라고 말하고 있다. 따라서 정답은 (B)이다.

8 Listen to a teacher talking to students.

M I finished correcting your tests last night. You all did very well. I am so pleased that you all studied hard and listened carefully. There was no one in the class who got a failing grade. In fact, everyone got over 80% correct. You should all be proud of your hard work. Nice job!

번역 **선생님이 학생들에게 하는 얘기를 들으세요.**

남 어젯밤에 선생님이 여러분들 시험 채점을 마쳤습니다. 모두들 아주 잘했어요. 여러분들 모두 공부를 열심히 하고 (수업을) 잘 들었다고 생각하니 무척 기쁩니다. 우리 반에서 낙제점을 받은 학생은 아무도 없었습니다. 사실, 모두들 80점 이상을 맞았어요. 이렇게 열심히 했으니 스스로 자부심을 느껴도 되겠어요. 아주 잘했습니다.

8. 선생님에 관해 사실은 무엇일까요?
(A) (학생들에게) 점수를 나쁘게 준 적이 한번도 없었다.
(B) 학생들을 자랑스러워한다.
(C) 시험 채점을 아직 마치지 못했다.
(D) 학생들이 좀더 잘 할 수 있을 거라고 기대했다.

correct 고치다, 바로잡다; 첨삭하다 failing grade 낙제점

정답 및 해설 [추론 문제] 선생님이 학생들에게 "어젯밤에 여러분들 시험 채점을 마쳤는데 모두들 아주 잘했다(I finished correcting your tests last night. You all did very well.)"라고 칭찬하고 있다. 덧붙여 낙제점을 받은 학생은 아무도 없었고 모두 80점 이상을 맞았다고 말하면서 "이렇게 열심히 했으니 스스로 자부심을 느껴도 되겠다. 아주 잘했다(You should all be proud of your hard work. Nice job!)"라고 다시 한번 칭찬한다. 이를 볼 때 선생님이 '학생들을 자랑스러워한다'라고 추론할 수 있다. 따라서 정답은 (B)이다. (A)와 관련된 내용은 언급되지 않았고, (C), (D)는 내용과 상반되므로 오답이다.

9 Listen to a school principal talking to a group of students.

W On Friday we're going to have a small pizza party. The pizza party is to thank you for helping to clean the school. The school looks clean and beautiful because your group planted flowers and trees outside. I'll buy the pizza, but please bring some snacks to the pizza party. Let's make sure we have a lot of food!

번역 **교장 선생님이 몇몇 학생들에게 하는 말을 들으세요.**

여 금요일에 조촐한 피자 파티를 열려고 합니다. 여러분들이 학교 청소에 도움을 주어서 그 감사 표시로 파티를 여는 거예요. 여러분들이 교정에 꽃과 나무를 심은 덕분에 학교가 깨끗하고 예뻐 보여요. 선생님이 피자를 살 테니, 간단한 스낵류는 여러분들이 가져오면 좋겠군요. 음식이 많으면 좋겠습니다.

9. 교장 선생님은 학생들에게 무엇을 지시하나요?
(A) 피자를 사라.
(B) 밖에서 점심을 먹어라.
(C) 꽃과 나무를 심어라.
(D) 파티에 스낵을 가져와라.

plant (나무나 씨앗을) 심다; 식물, 초목, 나무

정답 및 해설 **[세부사항을 묻는 문제]** 교장 선생님이 금요일에 있을 피자 파티에 대해 안내하고 있다. "선생님이 피자를 살 테니, 간단한 스낵류는 여러분들이 가져오면 좋겠다(**I'll buy the pizza, but please bring some snacks to the pizza party.**)"라고 말한 것을 통해 (D)가 정답임을 알 수 있다.

10 Listen to an art teacher talking to her class.

W Today we're going to show the pictures that we drew last week. Do you remember? We drew pictures of fruit. We're going to talk about what's good about the pictures and what's bad about them. When we're talking, please be kind to the other students. To start, you'll all need to hang your pictures on this wall.

번역 **미술 선생님이 학생들에게 하는 말을 들으세요.**

여 오늘은 여러분들이 지난 주에 그린 그림을 전시하려고 합니다. 기억나죠? 과일 그림을 그렸었잖아요. 그림을 보고 (서로)어떤 점이 좋고 어떤 점이 나쁜지 얘기를 해보도록 할 거예요. (다른 사람 그림에 대해) 얘기할 때는 다른 학생들에게 상냥하게 말하도록 하세요. 시작하기에 앞서 여러분 모두 여기 벽에 그림을 걸어 놓으세요.

10. 학생들은 다음에 무엇을 할까요?
(A) 과일에 대해 얘기한다.
(B) 과일 그림을 그린다.
(C) 자신들이 그린 그림을 (벽에) 건다.
(D) 선생님에게 질문을 한다.

show 전시하다, 전시되다; 보여주다, 제시하다 hang 걸다, 매달다 wall 벽

정답 및 해설 **[예측 문제]** 미술 선생님이 학생들에게 지난주에 그린 과일 그림을 전시할 것에 대해 안내하고 있다. 서로의 그림에 대해 상냥하게 평가할 것을 당부한 후 "시작하기에 앞서 모두 여기 벽에 그림을 걸어라(**To start, you'll all need to hang your pictures on this wall.**)"라고 지시한다. 따라서 정답은 (C)이다. 과일이 아니라 과일 그림에 대한 얘기를 할 것이고, 그 그림도 이미 지난주에 그렸으므로 (A)와 (B) 모두 오답이다. (D)는 언급되지 않았다.

[11-14] Listen to a conversation between a student and a librarian. (L: librarian, S: student)

S Hi, Mrs. Waldorf. Can you help me with something?
L Of course, Jesse. What do you need?
S Well, when I was here yesterday, I forgot to take my books with me. I left them here in the library. You weren't here, though. Mr. Anderson helped me to check out the books.
L Hmm... what books were they?
S They were three books on the Civil War. I forgot the names, but one had a black cover. Another had a red cover.
L Okay, why don't you follow me to the desk? I'll check and see if any books were set aside.
S Thanks, Mrs. Waldorf.
L *(pause)* Oh! Are these your books? They all seem to be about the Civil War.
S Yes, that's them. Thank you so much for your help.

번역 **학생과 도서관 사서의 대화를 들으세요.**

학생 안녕하세요, Waldorf 선생님. 저 좀 도와주실 수 있으세요?
사서 물론이지, Jesse. 어떤 도움이 필요하니?
학생 저기, 제가 어제 여기 왔을 때, 깜박 잊고 책을 안 가져갔어요. 여기 도서관에 두고 갔습니다. 그땐 선생님이 여기 안 계셨고, Anderson 선생님께서 책을 대출해 주셨어요.
사서 흠… 어떤 책들이었니?
학생 남북전쟁과 관련된 책들 3권이에요. 책 제목은 까먹었는데, 하나는 검은색 표지였습니다. 다른 하나는 빨간색 표지였고요.
사서 좋아, 선생님 책상까지 따라오겠니? 옆으로 치워둔 책이 있는지 살펴보자꾸나.
학생 고맙습니다, Waldorf 선생님.
사서 (잠시 후)아, 이 책들이니? 전부 다 남북전쟁과 관련된 책들인 것 같구나.
학생 네, 그것들이에요. 도와주셔서 정말 고맙습니다.

L It's no problem, Jesse. Try to remember to take them with you next time. You're lucky that these books weren't put back on the shelf.

S I understand that. Thanks, again.

사서 천만에, Jesse. 그렇지만 다음 번에는 책을 잊지 말고 꼭 챙겨가도록 해라. 책을 다시 서가에 꽂아두지 않았던 건 순전히 운이니까 말이야.

학생 알겠습니다. 다시 한번 감사합니다.

leave (어떤 장소 등에 계속)있게 만들다, 그대로 두다 **the Civil War** (미국)남북전쟁(*1861~1865) **cover** (책의)표지; 덮개, 커버 **set aside** 한쪽으로 치워 놓다, 따로 떼어 놓다

11. 학생이 도서관 사서를 찾아간 이유는 무엇인가요?

(A) 보고서 작성에 도움이 필요하다.

(B) 도서관에 책을 두고 갔다.

(C) 컴퓨터 사용하는 데 도움이 필요하다.

(D) 도서관 사서가 남북전쟁에 대해 알고 있다.

정답 및 해설 **[주제를 묻는 문제]** 학생과 도서관 사서와의 대화이다. 사서가 "어떤 도움이 필요하냐(What do you need?)"라고 묻자 학생이 "깜박 잊고 빌린 책을 도서관에 두고 갔다(I forgot to take my books with me. I left them here in the library.)"라며 도움이 필요한 이유를 말한다. 따라서 정답은 (B)이다.

12. 도서관 사서의 다음 말이 의미하는 것은 무엇인가요? *(You're lucky that these books weren't put back on the shelf.)*

(A) Jesse는 일반적으로 운이 좋은 학생이다.

(B) 도서관에 남겨진 책들은 보통 서가에 다시 꽂아둔다

(C) Jesse가 정리정돈을 잘 하는 학생이라고 생각하지 않는다.

(D) 남북전쟁에 관한 책들은 보통 도서관 대출이 되지 않는다.

정답 및 해설 **[화자의 어조를 묻는 문제]** 사서는 학생이 놓고 간 책을 찾아 주면서 "이 책들이 서가에 다시 꽂히지 않은 것은 운이 좋은 것이다(You're lucky that these books weren't put back on the shelf.)"라고 말한다. 이말은 곧 '도서관에 놓고 간 책들은 대개 치워진다'는 의미이다. 따라서 정답은 (B)이다.

13. 학생이 자신의 책의 생김새를 설명하는 이유는 무엇인가요?

(A) 도서관 사서가 책을 찾는 데 도움을 주려고

(B) Anderson 선생님의 도서관 업무 능력에 대해 불만을 표시하려고

(C) 도서관 사서에게 자신의 책들이 재미있었다고 말하려고

(D) 평상시 자신이 공부하지 않는 이유에 대해 논의하려고

정답 및 해설 **[수사학적 구조를 묻는 문제]** 사서가 어떤 책이었는지를 묻자 학생은 "남북전쟁에 대한 세 권의 책으로, 이름은 잊어버렸지만 한 권은 검은색 표지였고 또 다른 책은 빨간색 표지였다(They were three books on the Civil War. I forgot the names, but one had a black cover. Another had a red cover.)"라고 대답한다. 이에 사서가 "따로 둔 책이 있는지 확인해보겠다(I'll check and see if any books were set aside.)"라고 말한 것을 볼 때, 학생은 '사서가 책을 찾는 데 도움을 주려고' 책의 생김새를 말했다고 짐작할 수 있다. 따라서 정답은 (A)이다.

14. 도서관 사서는 학생에게 무엇을 지시하나요?

(A) 책상 위에 책을 두어라.

(B) 3주 안에 책을 반납하라.

(C) 잊지 말고 책을 챙겨가도록 하라.

(D) Anderson 선생님과 대화하려면 며칠 기다려라.

정답 및 해설 **[세부사항을 묻는 문제]** 대화의 마지막 부분에서 사서는 "다음 번에는 책을 잊지 말고 꼭 챙겨가도록 해라(Try to remember to take them with you next time.)"라고 당부한다. 따라서 정답은 (C)이다. (A), (B), (D)는 언급되지 않았다.

[15-18] Listen to a conversation between a student and a teacher. (T: teacher, S: student)

S Hi, Mr. Jordan. How are you?

T I'm doing well, Bobby. I just heard about a contest you might be interested in.

S Oh, really? What's the contest?

T It's a junior biology contest and the prize includes a one-week trip to Hawaii.

번역 **학생과 선생님의 대화를 들으세요.**

학생 안녕하세요, Jordan 선생님. 어떻게 지내세요?

교사 잘 지내고 있단다, Bobby. 선생님이 방금 네가 관심을 보일 것 같은 대회에 대해 들었다.

학생 네, 그래요? 어떤 대회인가요?

교사 주니어 생물학 대회인데 상으로 1주일간의 하와이 여행이 주어진단다.

S Hawaii! Really? How do I enter?

T Well, you'll have to make a short video about one of your biology projects. You need to include your name, age, and school. Besides that, you can be creative.

S Oh no, but Mr. Jordan, I don't have a video camera to use.

T The school has video cameras that you can borrow. You can go to the technology room and rent one for a few days. Be careful though, the cameras are expensive and fragile.

S Okay, I think I can handle it.

T Sounds good. Let me tell you a bit more about the contest.

학생 하와이라고요? 정말이요? 어떻게 참가하면 되나요?

교사 음, 너의 생물 프로젝트 중 하나와 관련된 짧은 동영상을 하나 만들어야 한다. 네 이름과 나이 그리고 학교명을 포함해서 말이야. 그 외에는 네 맘껏 창의성을 발휘하면 돼.

학생 음, 그런데 Jordan 선생님, 저한테는 비디오 카메라가 없어요.

교사 학교 비디오 카메라를 빌리면 되지. 기술실에 가서 며칠 간 빌려 쓰거라. 그렇지만 조심해야 한다. 카메라는 비싸고 손상되기 쉬운 물건이니까.

학생 네, 잘 다룰 수 있을 겁니다.

교사 좋다. 그럼 대회에 대해 몇 가지 더 말하마.

contest 대회, 시합, 콘테스트 **enter** (대회 등에)출전하다, 참가하다 **prize** 상, 포상, 상품 **besides** ~외에; 게다가
creative 창조적인, 창의적인 **fragile** 부서지기 쉬운, 손상되기 쉬운

15. 두 사람은 주로 무슨 얘기를 하고 있나요?
(A) 대회 참가용 비디오 제작
(B) 하와이 동물과 관련한 생물학
(C) 학교 소유의 비디오 카메라
(D) 주니어 생물학 대회에 참가하는 남학생

정답 및 해설 **[주제를 묻는 문제]** 선생님이 학생에게 "방금 네가 흥미를 가질 만한 대회에 대해 들었다(**I just heard about a contest you might be interested in.**)"라고 말한 후 "주니어 생물학 대회이고 상으로 일주일간 하와이 여행이 주어진다(**It's a junior biology contest and the prize includes a one-week trip to Hawaii.**)"라고 덧붙인다. 학생이 관심을 가지고 참가 방법을 묻자 이에 대해 구체적으로 설명해 준다. 따라서 정답은 (D)이다. (B)는 언급되지 않았고, (A), (C)는 언급되었으나 일부 내용에 해당하므로 전체 주제로 볼 수 없다.

16. 선생님은 대회에서 주어지는 상에 대해 뭐라고 하나요?
(A) 새 비디오 카메라가 주어진다.
(B) 여러 학생들에게 주어진다.
(C) 일주일간의 하와이 여행이 주어진다.
(D) 비디오에 따라 (시상 내역이) 바뀐다.

정답 및 해설 **[세부사항을 묻는 문제]** 선생님은 어떤 대회인지를 묻는 학생에게 주니어 생물학 대회라며 "상으로 일주일간의 하와이 여행이 주어진다(**~ the prize is a one-week trip to Hawaii.**)"라고 말한다. 따라서 정답은 (C)이다. (A), (B), (D)는 언급되지 않았다.

17. 남학생의 다음 말이 의미하는 것은 무엇인가요? *(Okay, I think I can handle it.)*
(A) 지금껏 카메라를 사용해 본 적이 없다.
(B) 친구한테 카메라를 빌릴 것이다.
(C) 자신이 카메라를 잘 다룰 수 있다고 믿는다.
(D) 자신은 언제나 학교에서 카메라를 빌린다.

정답 및 해설 **[화자의 어조를 묻는 문제]** 학생이 비디오 카메라가 없다고 하자 선생님은 "학교에서 카메라를 빌릴 수 있다(**The school has video cameras that you can borrow.**)"라고 하면서 구체적인 방법을 설명한다. 그러면서 "그렇지만 카메라는 비싸고 손상되기 쉬운 물건이니까 조심해야 한다(**Be careful though, the cameras are expensive and fragile.**)"라고 덧붙인다. 이에 학생이 "알겠다. 잘 다룰 수 있을 것이다(**Okay, I think I can handle it**)."라고 한 것이다. 이를 근거로 추론해 볼 때, 학생은 자신이 '카메라를 조심해서 잘 사용할 수 있다고 생각한다'고 볼 수 있다. 따라서 정답은 (C)이다.

18. 두 사람은 다음에 무엇을 할까요?
(A) 하와이 여행 계획을 짠다.
(B) 남학생이 찍을 영화 대본을 쓴다.
(C) 비디오 카메라 사용 방법에 대해 논의한다.
(D) 대회와 대회 규칙에 대해 좀더 얘기한다.

정답 및 해설 **[예측 문제]** 선생님이 학생에게 대회 참가 방법과 비디오 대여 문제에 대해 알려준 후 마지막에 "대회에 대해서 좀 더 말해주겠다(Let me tell you a bit more about the contest.)"라고 말한다. 그러므로 뒤이어 '대회와 대회 규칙에 관해 좀더 자세한 대화를 나눈다'고 유추할 수 있다. 따라서 정답은 (D)이다.

[19-22] Listen to a conversation between two students as they leave a classroom.

(G: girl, B: boy)

B Hi, Rachel. How are you?

G I'm fine, Steve. How are you doing?

B I'm fine. What did you think of the exam?

G I thought it was really hard. I studied a lot and thought that I would do well, but now I'm not sure.

B I feel the same way. The test was full of things that we didn't study in class.

G Do you think other students feel like we do?

B I'm sure they do. We should ask them during lunch.

G Yeah, and maybe we should talk to Mr. Brooklyn about the test. I'm really worried I got a bad grade.

B I'm worried, too. Maybe Mr. Brooklyn doesn't realize how hard the test actually was.

G Yeah, the last test he gave us was really easy. That might be the reason that he made it hard this time.

B Yes, that's true. OK, let's go to the cafeteria and talk to our friends from class.

G Good idea. If they agree with us, then we can go talk to Mr. Brooklyn.

번역 두 학생이 교실을 나서면서 나누는 대화를 들으세요.

남 안녕, Rachel. 기분 어떠니?

여 좋아, Steve. 넌 어때?

남 좋아. 넌 이번 시험 어떻게 생각해?

여 정말 어려웠던 것 같아. 공부를 많이 했기 때문에 시험을 잘 볼 줄 알았는데, 지금은 잘 모르겠어.

남 나도 같아. 수업 시간에 안 배웠던 내용들이 시험에 많이 나왔더라.

여 다른 애들도 같은 생각일까?

남 분명 그럴 거야. 점심 시간에 물어 보자.

여 그래, 그런 다음 Brooklyn 선생님한테 시험에 관해 말씀 드려 볼 수도 있겠지. 난 시험 점수가 나쁠까 봐 정말 걱정스러워.

남 나도 걱정돼. 아마 Brooklyn 선생님은 시험이 얼마나 어려웠는지 짐작 못하실 것 같아.

여 그래, 지난번 선생님이 내준 시험은 정말 쉬웠잖아. 아마 그래서 이번에 이렇게 어렵게 만드신 것 같아.

남 응, 그래. 좋아, 식당에 가서 반 애들하고 얘기해 보자.

여 좋은 생각이야. 걔들도 우리 생각에 동의하면 Brooklyn 선생님한테 가서 말씀 드려 볼 수 있을 거야.

realize 깨닫다, 알아차리다, 인식하다 agree 동의하다, 의견이 일치하다

19. 두 학생은 주로 무슨 얘기를 하고 있나요?

(A) Brooklyn 선생님의 부당한 채점 체계
(B) 시험이 너무 어려워서 시험 점수가 나쁠지도 모른다는 것
(C) Brooklyn 선생님 수업을 위해 얼마나 많이 공부하는지
(D) 시험의 어려움에 대해 반 아이들에게 의견을 물어보기

정답 및 해설 **[주제를 묻는 문제]** 두 학생이 Brooklyn 선생님 수업의 시험에 대해 나누는 대화이다. 여학생은 "시험이 정말 어려웠던 것 같다. 공부를 많이 했기 때문에 시험을 잘 볼 줄 알았지만 지금은 모르겠다(I thought it was really hard. I studied a lot and thought that I would do well, ~)"라며, "시험 점수가 나쁠까 봐 정말 걱정이다(I'm really worried I got a bad grade.)"라고 말한다. 남학생 역시 이 생각에 동의하며 반 아이들의 의견을 물어보자고 제안한다. 이어서 두 사람은 시험 출제자인 Brooklyn 선생님과의 상담을 언급하면서 대화를 마무리하고 있다. 이런 점을 볼 때, 대화의 전반적인 주제는 '나쁜 점수로 이어질 수도 있는 어려웠던 시험'과 관련되었다고 볼 수 있다. 따라서 정답은 (B)이다. (A)는 언급되지 않았고, (C), (D)는 일부 내용이므로 주제로 볼 수 없다.

20. 남학생은 시험에 관해 뭐라고 하나요?

(A) 식당에서 시험을 치렀다.
(B) 생각보다 쉬웠다.
(C) Brooklyn 선생님이 출제하지 않았을 것이다.
(D) 수업 시간에 배우지 않은 내용들로 가득했다.

정답 및 해설 **[세부사항을 묻는 문제]** 두 학생 모두 시험이 어려웠다고 말한 후에 남학생은 "수업 시간에 안 배웠던 내용들이 시험에 많이 나왔다(The test was full of things that we didn't study in class.)"라고 말한다. 따라서 정답은 (D)이다. (A)는 상식적으로 옳지 않고, 대화 내내 시험이 어려웠다고 했으므로 (B)는 오답이다. 또한 "지난번 선생님이 내신 시험은 아주 쉬웠는데, (덕분에 학생들 성적이 좋았을 것이고 그래서) 이번에는 어렵게 출제한 것 같다(~ the last test he gave us was really easy. That might be the reason that he made it hard this time.)"라고 했으므로 (C) 역시 오답이다.

21. 학생들은 다음에 무엇을 할까요?

(A) Brooklyn 선생님과 얘기를 나눈다.
(B) 서로 작별 인사를 한다.
(C) 식당에서 시험을 치른다.
(D) 시험에 관해 친구들과 얘기를 나눈다.

정답 및 해설 **[예측 문제]** 두 학생들이 어려웠던 이번 시험에 대해 얘기를 나누다가 남학생이 "식당에 가서 반 애들하고 얘기해 보자(let's go to the cafeteria and talk to our friends from class.)"라고 제안한다. 이에 대해 여학생이 좋은 생각이라며 "걔들도 우리 생각에 동의하면 Brooklyn 선생님한테 가서 말씀 드려 볼 수 있을 것이다(If they agree with us, then we can go talk to Mr. Brooklyn.)"라고 동의한다. 그러므로 두 학생이 곧이어 '시험에 관해 친구들과 얘기를 나눌 것'이라고 유추할 수 있다. 따라서 정답은 (D)이다. Brooklyn 선생님과의 상담은 반 아이들과 얘기를 나눠본 이후의 일이기 때문에 (A)는 틀린 답이다.

22. 여학생이 지난번 시험이 쉬웠다고 말한 이유는 무엇인가요?

(A) 자신은 그 수업을 좋아하지 않는다는 것을 보여주려고
(B) Brooklyn 선생님의 시험이 어려웠던 이유를 설명하려고
(C) 자신은 남학생보다 더 많이 공부했다는 것을 증명하려고
(D) 자신이 A 학점을 받았던 때를 예로 들려고

정답 및 해설 **[수사학적 구조를 묻는 문제]** 여학생이 시험 점수가 나쁠까 봐 걱정된다고 하자 남학생도 동의한다. 이에 여학생은 "지난번 선생님이 내준 시험은 정말 쉬웠는데, 아마 그래서 이번에 이렇게 어렵게 낸 것 같다(~ the last test he gave us was really easy. That might be the reason that he made it hard this time.)"라고 말한다. 즉 여학생은 '이번 시험이 어려워진 게 학생들이 지난번 시험을 쉽게 생각했기 때문일 것'이라 생각하며 시험이 어려워진 이유를 유추하고 있다. 따라서 정답은 (B)이다.

[23-26] Listen to a conversation between a student and a teacher. (S: student, T: teacher)

S Hi, Mr. Jordan. How are you?
T I'm fine, Billy. What's going on?
S Well, I have a doctor's appointment on Wednesday. I'm going to miss the test.
T Are you sure you can't change the appointment?
S I tried, but they won't be able to see me for another few months. I was wondering if I could take the exam early.
T That's fine, but you have to promise me you won't tell the other students what's on the exam.
S Of course I won't do that.
T Okay, I believe you. Why don't you meet me after school on Tuesday? Can you take the test then?
S Sure, that sounds good. I better start studying!
T Okay, Billy. See you soon.

번역 **학생과 선생님의 대화를 들으세요.**

학생 안녕하세요, Jordan 선생님. 잘 지내시죠?
교사 그래, Billy. 어쩐 일이니?
학생 음, 제가 수요일에 병원에 가야 해서요. 그날 시험을 못 볼 것 같습니다.
교사 진료 날짜를 바꾸지 못하니?
학생 바꿔 보려고 해봤는데요, 그러면 몇 달이나 지나야 진료가 가능해요. 시험을 좀더 일찍 볼 수 있을지 여쭤보려고 왔습니다.
교사 그건 괜찮다만, 단 다른 학생들에게 시험 문제가 뭐였는지는 절대 얘기하지 않는다고 약속해야 한다.
학생 그럼요, 말하지 않을 거예요.
교사 좋아, 믿으마. 화요일 방과 후에 오면 어떻겠니? 그때 시험을 볼 수 있겠니?
학생 네, 좋습니다. 공부 시작해야겠습니다.
교사 좋아, Billy. 곧 보자.

doctor's appointment 의사와의 진료 약속 **miss** (약속 등을) 지키지 못하다, ~하지 못하다

23. 남학생의 문제는 무엇인가요?

(A) 시험 보는 게 두렵다.
(B) 화요일 방과 후에는 만날 수 없다.
(C) 다른 학생들에게 시험에 관해 얘기하고 싶다.
(D) 시험일에 병원 진료가 있다.

정답 및 해설 **[주제를 묻는 문제]** 선생님과 학생의 대화이다. 학생이 선생님께 찾아와서 "수요일에 병원에 가야 해서 그날 시험을 못 볼 것 같다(I have a doctor's appointment on Wednesday. I'm going to miss the test.)"라며 자신의 문제를 밝히고 있다. 진료 날짜를 바꿀 수 없냐는 선생님의 질문에 몇 달이나 지나야 시간이 난다고 대답하고 있으므로 정답은 (D)이다. (A)는 언급되지 않은 내용이고, (B), (C)는 대화 내용과 상반되므로 오답이다.

24. 선생님은 시험을 일찍 보는 것에 대해 뭐라고 하나요?

(A) 학생이 열심히 공부해야 한다.
(B) 시험이 더 어려울 것이다.
(C) 반 아이들도 일찍 시험을 보게 될 것이다.
(D) 반 아이들에게 시험에 관해 얘기하면 안 된다.

정답 및 해설 **[세부사항을 묻는 문제]** 학생은 진료 날짜를 바꿀 수 없다고 말하면서 "시험을 좀더 일찍 볼 수 있겠냐(I was wondering if I could take the exam early.)"라며 찾아온 용건을 밝힌다. 이에 선생님은 시험을 일찍 보게 해 줄 수는 있지만 "단 다른 학생들에게 시험 문제가 뭐였는지는 절대 얘기하지 않는다고 약속해야 한다(~ but you have to promise me you won't tell the other students what's on the exam.)"라고 당부한다. 따라서 정답은 (D)이다.

25. 남학생에 관해 사실은 무엇일까요?

(A) 선생님의 신뢰를 받고 있다.
(B) 약속에 대해 거짓말을 하고 있다.
(C) 반 아이들과 친구가 되지 못했다.
(D) 운동을 하다가 다쳤다.

정답 및 해설 **[추론 문제]** 선생님이 시험을 일찍 보는 대신 다른 학생들에게 시험 문제에 대해 절대 얘기하지 말라고 당부하자 학생은 "당연히 말하지 않을 것이다(Of course I won't do that.)"라고 대답한다. 학생의 대답에 선생님이 "믿겠다(Okay, I believe you.)"라고 한 것으로 볼 때 '남학생은 선생님의 신뢰를 받고 있다'는 것을 알 수 있다. 따라서 정답은 (A)이다.

26. 남학생은 방과 후에 무엇을 할까요?

(A) Jordan 선생님에게 이메일을 보낸다.
(B) 친구와 함께 시험에서 컨닝을 한다.
(C) 진료 예약을 변경한다.
(D) 화요일에 볼 시험을 위해 공부한다.

정답 및 해설 **[예측 문제]** 선생님은 남학생이 시험을 일찍 볼 것을 허락한다. 그리고 나서 "화요일 방과 후에 시험을 볼 수 있겠냐(Why don't you meet me after school on Tuesday? Can you take the test then?)"라고 묻자 학생은 가능하다며 "공부를 시작해야겠다(I better start studying!)"라고 대답한다. 이를 볼 때 학생은 '곧 있을 화요일 시험을 위해 공부를 할 것'이라고 짐작할 수 있다. 따라서 정답은 (D)이다.

[27-30] Listen to part of a discussion in a history class. (T: teacher, S: student)

T So we've been learning about life in early America, but we haven't discussed the change that affected America and the rest of the world. This event is known as the Industrial Revolution. If it hadn't been for that, then the world wouldn't be as it is today. Yes, Violet, what's your question?

S Mr. Maskell, is it true that the Industrial Revolution was just the invention of cars and trains?

번역 **역사 수업 시간에 이뤄지는 토론의 일부분을 들으세요.**

교사 지금까지 초기 미국 생활에 대해 배우면서 미국과 그 밖의 다른 나라들에 영향을 미친 변화에 대해서는 아직 다루지 않았죠. 이 사건을 산업 혁명이라고 합니다. 만약 산업 혁명이 일어나지 않았더라면 세계가 오늘날과 같지는 않았을 겁니다. 네, Violet, 질문이 뭐죠?

학생 Maskell 선생님, 산업 혁명이 단지 자동차와 기차의 발명을 말하는 게 맞나요?

T Hmm, well, no, not exactly. Cars and trains were invented and manufactured as a part of the Industrial Revolution. See, the Industrial Revolution was bigger than that. It started in the 18th century in England and quickly spread. It started because of machine-based manufacturing. All that means is that goods could be made quickly and easily using machines.

S Well, it's true that today's things are usually made in factories, but I'm not sure I understand how that changed our country.

T You see, this change led to the growth and development of the American middle class and our modern cities. Because of the amount of factories being built, people flocked from the countryside to the cities in order to find work. You must understand—the Industrial Revolution changed everything. Goods were cheaper and more available, transportation grew and people were able to get around, electrical appliances were manufactured and sold across the country, people started working in different sorts of jobs... this was truly an important change. You can thank the Industrial Revolution for the kind of life you have today.

교사 음, 글쎄요, 아니에요, 그 말은 정확하지 않아요. 산업 혁명의 한 부분으로서 자동차와 기차가 발명되고 제작된 건 사실이에요. 그렇지만 산업 혁명은 그보다는 훨씬 더 규모가 크답니다. 산업 혁명은 18세기에 영국에서 시작되었고 급속히 확산되었습니다. 산업 혁명은 기계 중심의 제조업으로부터 시작되었습니다. 그 말은 곧 기계를 사용함으로써 상품을 빠르고 쉽게 생산할 수 있게 되었다는 겁니다.

학생 음, 요즘 물건들이 대개 공장에서 만들어진다는 건 사실이에요, 하지만 그게 어떻게 우리 나라를 변화시켰는지는 확실히 잘 모르겠습니다.

교사 있죠, 이러한 변화는 미국 중산 계층과 현대 도시의 성장과 발전을 이끌었습니다. 공장이 많이 건축되면서 사람들이 일자리를 찾아 시골에서 도시로 몰려들었습니다. 산업 혁명은 모든 걸 변화시켰다고 이해하면 됩니다. 물건 가격은 싸졌고 좀더 쉽게 구할 수 있게 되었으며, 운송량이 늘어나고 사람들의 이동이 (쉽게) 가능해지고, 전기 제품이 제조되어 전국에 걸쳐 판매되었으며, 사람들은 다양한 분야의 직종에서 일하기 시작했죠. 이건 정말 중요한 변화입니다. 오늘날 우리가 살고 있는 생활 방식은 다 이 산업 혁명 덕분인 거죠.

Industrial Revolution 산업 혁명 (*1760년경 영국에서 시작됨) **manufacture** 제조하다, 제작하다 (***manufacturing** 제조업)
spread 퍼지다, 만연하다 **goods** 상품, 물품; 물자 **middle class** 중산층, 중류 계급 **flock** (많은 수가) 모이다, 떼지어 가다 / 오다
transportation 수송, 운송 **get around** 돌아다니다 **electrical appliances** 전자 제품

27. 선생님과 학생은 주로 무슨 얘기를 하나요?
(A) 미국 중산층의 성장
(B) 산업 혁명이 미국을 어떻게 변화시켰는지
(C) 역사 전체에서의 미국의 성장과 발전
(D) 미국인들이 시골을 떠나 도시로 이동한 방법과 그 이유

정답 및 해설 **[주제를 묻는 문제]** 역사 선생님이 "우리가 초기 미국 생활에 대해 배웠지만 미국이나 그 밖의 다른 나라에 영향을 미쳤던 변화에 대해서는 토론하지 않았다(~ but we haven't discussed the change that affected America and the rest of the world.)"라고 말하면서 이 사건을 '산업 혁명'이라고 설명한다. 이후 산업 혁명이 미국에 끼친 영향들에 대해서 구체적으로 설명하고 있다. 따라서 핵심어인 '산업 혁명'과 '미국'을 모두 포함한 (B)가 정답이다. 역사 전체에서의 미국의 성장과 발전이라고 한 (C)에는 핵심어인 '산업 혁명'이 빠졌으므로 정답이 될 수 없고, (A)와 (D)는 세부적인 내용에 불과하므로 전체를 아우르는 주제로 볼 수 없다.

28. 선생님이 미국 중산층을 언급한 이유는 무엇인가요?
(A) 미국 중산층이 나라 전역으로 이동한 이유를 설명하려고
(B) 미국 중산층이 산업 혁명을 시작했다는 것을 증명하려고
(C) 산업 혁명이 미국 중산층에 영향을 미쳤음을 보여주려고
(D) 미국 중산층은 이 산업 혁명의 영향을 받지 않았음을 시사하려고

정답 및 해설 **[수사학적 구조를 묻는 문제]** 선생님은 산업 혁명이 끼친 영향을 설명하면서, 기계를 이용해 상품을 빠르고 쉽게 만들 수 있었다고 하자 학생은 "요즘 물건들이 대개 공장에서 만들어지는 것은 사실이지만 그것이 어떻게 우리 나라를 변화시켰는지 확실히 이해가 안 된다(~ but I'm not sure I understand how that changed our country.)"라고 말한다. 그러자 선생님은 "이 변화가 미국 중산층과 현대 도시의 성장과 개발로 이어졌다(~ this change led to the growth and development of the American middle class and our modern cities.)"라고 설명한다. 이를 볼 때 선생님이 미국 중산층을 언급한 것은 '산업 혁명이 끼친 영향을 설명하기 위해서'라고 볼 수 있다. 따라서 정답은 (C)이다.

29. 선생님 말씀에 따르면, 산업 혁명이 끼친 영향은 무엇인가요?
(A) 미국인들이 보다 유럽인처럼 되어 갔다.
(B) 사람들이 여러 전자 제품들을 사용하지 않았다.
(C) 사람들이 시골에서 도시로 이동했다.
(D) 상품이 기계로 만들어졌기 때문에 더 비쌌다.

정답 및 해설 **[세부사항을 묻는 문제]** 선생님은 산업 혁명이 끼친 영향을 설명하면서 "공장이 많이 지어졌기 때문에 사람들은 일자리를 찾아 시골에서 도시로 모여들었다(Because of the amount of factories being built, people flocked from the countryside to the cities in order to find work.)"라고 말한다. 따라서 정답은 (C)이다.

30. 자동차와 기차의 개발에 관해 추론할 수 있는 것은 무엇인가요?
(A) 여학생이 예전에 공부한 분야가 아니다.
(B) 독특하고 새로운 방식으로 미국에서 일어난 일이다.
(C) 기계를 사용하지 않고 발생하였을 것이다.
(D) 산업 혁명이 아니고서는 불가능한 일이었을 것이다.

정답 및 해설 **[추론 문제]** 학생이 "산업 혁명이 단지 자동차와 기차의 발명뿐이었냐(~ is it true that the Industrial Revolution was just the invention of cars and trains?)"라고 질문하자 선생님은 아니라고 답하면서 "자동차와 기차는 산업 혁명의 일부분으로서 발명되고 제조되었다(Cars and trains were invented and manufactured as a part of the Industrial Revolution.)"라고 설명한다. 이를 볼 때 '자동차와 기차의 개발은 산업 혁명 없이는 가능하지 않았을 것'이라고 추론할 수 있다. 따라서 정답은 (D)이다.

[31-34] Listen to a lecture in an English class.

W Well, class, as you know, this week we're going to start reading *The Adventures of Huckleberry Finn* by Mark Twain. Before we start reading, I want to give you a little background about this book. It was published in the United States in 1885 and it's now one of the most famous American novels. It was one of the first American novels to be written in the vernacular. Do you know what that means? Well, it means that the book was written in the language of the common people. It doesn't use the fancy language of upper-class poets and writers. Instead it uses the language of the people it was written about. The book is told from the voice of Huckleberry Finn, a young boy growing up on the Mississippi River. In fact, most of the book takes place beside this river, which is the largest in the United States. The book is about Huck and his friend Jim who is a former slave. I'd tell you about their adventure, but soon you'll read the book, so I don't want to spoil it for you. The book was written 20 years after slavery ended, but it takes place in a time when slavery in America still existed. Mark Twain plays with racial views and ideas in the book. I'd like you to think about these ideas as we read. Ask yourself what points Mark Twain might be making about slavery and race.

번역 **영어 수업에서의 강의를 들으세요.**

여 자, 여러분, 알다시피, 이번 주부터는 Mark Twain이 쓴 〈허클베리 핀의 모험〉을 읽을 겁니다. 읽기 전에 이 책에 관한 배경 설명을 잠깐 할게요. 이 책은 1885년 미국에서 출판되었고 현재 가장 유명한 미국 소설 가운데 하나입니다. 또 토착어로 쓰인 최초의 미국 소설 가운데 하나였습니다. 이게 무슨 의미인지 아나요? 음, 그 말은 곧 이 책은 일반적인 평범한 사람들의 언어로 쓰여졌다는 뜻이에요. 상류층 시인이나 작가들의 화려한 언어를 쓰는 대신 이 책에 나오는 사람들이 쓰는 언어를 사용했다는 겁니다. 이 책은 미시시피 강에서 자란 허클베리 핀이라는 소년의 목소리로 쓰여졌습니다. 사실, 이야기의 대부분은 미국에서 가장 긴 강인 미시시피 강 주변에서 벌어집니다. 이 책은 허클베리 핀과 원래는 노예였던 그의 친구 짐에 관한 이야기입니다. 여러분들에게 그들이 겪은 모험에 대해 들려줄 테지만 곧 여러분들이 읽게 될 테니까 미리 누설하지는 않겠습니다. 이 책은 노예제가 종식된 지 20년이 지나서 쓰이긴 했으나, 미국에 노예 문화가 여전히 존재하던 시기를 배경으로 합니다. Mark Twain은 이야기 속에 인종적 측면이나 그와 관련한 견해들을 다루고 있습니다. 읽으면서 이 점에 대해 생각해보길 바랍니다. Mark Twain이 노예와 인종 문제에 관해 어떤 점을 시사하고 있는지 자문해 보세요.

vernacular (특정 지역이나 집단이 쓰는) 말, 토착어 fancy 일류의, 고급의; (필요 이상으로 복잡한) upper-class 상류계급의, 상류층의 spoil 망치다, 버리다 slavery 노예, 노예 제도 racial 인종의, 민족의; 인종 간의, 민족 간의

31. 화자는 주로 무슨 얘기를 하나요?
(A) 허클베리 핀과 짐이라는 이름의 노예와의 우정
(B) Mark Twain이 쓴 〈허클베리 핀의 모험〉의 배경
(C) 미시시피 강이 〈허클베리 핀의 모험〉에 미친 영향
(D) Mark Twain이 쓴 〈허클베리 핀의 모험〉에 나오는 인물들

정답 및 해설 **[주제를 묻는 문제]** 선생님이 학생들에게 〈허클베리 핀의 모험〉이라는 책에 대해 수업하고 있다. 이번 주에는 Mark Twain의 〈허클베리 핀의 모험〉을 읽을 것이라고 말한 후 "읽기 전에 이 책의 배경을 조금 말해 주겠다(Before we start reading, I want to give you a little background about this book.)"라고 한다. 이어서, 출판 시기, 사용된 언어의 의미, 배경이 된 장소 등에 대해 세부적으로 설명한다. 따라서 정답은 (B)이다. (A), (C), (D)는 부분적으로 언급되기는 하였으나 수업의 전체 주제로는 볼 수 없다.

32. 선생님 말씀에 따르면, 〈허클베리 핀의 모험〉의 특별한 점은 무엇인가요?
(A) 1885년에 출판되었다.
(B) 토착민의 언어로 쓰여졌다.
(C) 마크 트웨인이 썼다.
(D) 노예 제도가 끝난 후 쓰여졌다.

정답 및 해설 **[세부사항을 묻는 문제]** 선생님은 〈허클베리 핀의 모험〉이 현재 가장 유명한 미국 소설 중 하나라고 설명한 후, "그 책은 토착어로 쓰인 최초의 미국 소설 중의 하나였다(It was one of the first American novels to be written in the vernacular.)"라고 말한다. 따라서 정답은 (B)이다. (A), (C), (D)는 맞는 내용이기는 하지만 소설의 사실 정보일 뿐 특별한 점으로 언급된 것은 아니므로 정답이 될 수 없다.

33. 선생님이 미시시피 강에 대해 말한 이유는 무엇인가요?
(A) 책의 내용이 일어나는 곳이 어디인지 설명하려고
(B) 어떻게 소년들에게 문제가 생기게 되었는지를 보여주려고
(C) 학생들이 허클베리 핀이 도망간 이유를 이해하는 데 도움을 주려고
(D) 강에서의 여행이 모험이라는 점을 증명하려고

정답 및 해설 **[수사학적 구조를 묻는 문제]** 선생님은 〈허클베리 핀의 모험〉이 "미시시피강에서 자란 소년 허클베리 핀의 목소리로 쓰여진 책(The book is told from the voice of Huckleberry Finn, a young boy growing up on the Mississippi River.)"이라고 설명한다. 이어서 "사실 이야기의 대부분은 미국에서 가장 긴 미시시피 강 근처에서 발생한다(In fact, most of the book takes place beside this river, ~.)"라고 덧붙인다. 즉 선생님은 '이 책의 내용이 발생한 장소를 설명하기 위해서' 미시시피 강을 언급한 것이라고 볼 수 있다. 따라서 정답은 (A)이다.

34. 선생님은 학생들이 이 책을 읽으면서 무엇에 대해 생각해 보기를 원하나요?
(A) 마크 트웨인이 왜 이 책을 썼는지
(B) 허클베리 핀의 전반적인 목표가 무엇인지
(C) 허클베리 핀이 짐과 친구가 된 이유가 무엇인지
(D) 마크 트웨인이 노예 제도와 인종 문제를 어떻게 다루는지

정답 및 해설 **[세부사항을 묻는 문제]** 선생님은 〈허클베리 핀의 모험〉이 노예 제도와 인종에 대한 견해를 다루고 있다고 설명한다. 그리고 수업을 마무리 지으며 "책을 읽으면서 이 점에 대해 생각해보고, Mark Twain이 노예 제도와 인종 문제에 대해 어떤 점을 지적하는지 스스로에게 물어보라(I'd like you to think about these ideas as we read. Ask yourself what points Mark Twain might be making about slavery and race.)"라고 제안한다. 따라서 정답은 (D)이다.

[35-38] Listen to the following discussion in a math class. (T: teacher, S: student)

T I know you're expecting me to start the unit on geometry today by drawing a bunch of formulas and numbers on the board. I'm not going to do that.

S You mean you're not going to teach us about triangles?

번역 **수학 수업에서의 토론 내용을 들으세요.**

교사 여러분들은 아마도 오늘 기하학 수업 시간엔 선생님이 칠판에 여러 공식들이나 숫자를 적으면서 할 거라고 짐작할 텐데요, 오늘은 그렇게 하지 않을 겁니다.

학생 그럼 오늘 삼각형에 관해 수업하지 않으신단 뜻인가요?

T Well, I am, but first I'm going to tell you a little bit about Pythagoras, the man who is responsible for our ideas about geometry. OK, so, who was Pythagoras? And why are we talking about him in math class? Well, Pythagoras was a mathematician and philosopher who lived in Ancient Greece in the 6th century BC.

S Wow! That means he lived about 8,000 years ago!

T Exactly. It's a long time ago, right? Because he lived so long ago, we don't know that much about him. All of the information that we've got came from writers who wrote about him centuries after he actually lived. We know that he had many followers... religious followers, actually. That's uncommon for a mathematician. But honestly, we really don't know that much about his life. Some aren't even sure that Pythagoras came up with the Pythagorean Theorem. This theorem is the reason we're talking about Pythagoras in math class today.

S Mr. Blake, is that the theorem that helps us calculate the length and angles of triangles?

T That's right. Pythagoras came up with the idea that a-squared plus b-squared equals c-squared. I know that sounds complicated when I say it out loud, but when I write it out on the board you'll see that it's actually quite simple. You'll understand how to use the theorem by the end of class today.

교사 음, 하긴 할 거예요, 하지만 먼저 우리에게 기하학에 대한 일반적인 개념을 심어준 피타고라스에 대해 조금 설명을 하겠습니다. 좋아요, 그럼 피타고라스는 누구인가요? 우리는 왜 수학 시간에 이 사람 얘기를 하는 걸까요? 음, 피타고라스는 기원 전 6세기경 고대 그리스에서 살았던 수학자이자 철학자였습니다.

학생 와~ 그럼 8,000년 전에 살았단 말이네요?

교사 그래요. 정말 오래 전 일이죠? 피타고라스가 아주 오래 전 인물이기 때문에 그에 관해 아는 것이 많지 않습니다. 우리가 얻은 모든 정보는 그가 죽은 몇 세기 후에 피타고라스에 대해 글을 썼던 작가들로부터 온 것입니다. 피타고라스를 따르는 추종자들은 많았습니다, 주로 종교적인 추종자들이었죠. 수학자에게는 흔치 않은 일입니다. 하지만 솔직히 그의 인생에 관해서는 많이 알 수가 없습니다. 어떤 사람들은 심지어 피타고라스 정리가 피타고라스 본인의 아이디어였는지에 관해서도 확신을 못합니다. 오늘 우리가 수업 시간에 이 피타고라스를 논하는 것도 바로 이 피타고라스 정리 이론 때문입니다.

학생 선생님, 피타고라스 정리가 삼각형의 길이와 각도를 재는 데 유용한 이론인가요?

교사 맞아요. 피타고라스는 <$a^2+b^2=c^2$>이라는 이론을 만들었습니다. 선생님이 이렇게 말로 하면 굉장히 복잡하게 들리겠지만 칠판에 써 놓으면 무척 간단하다는 걸 알게 될 겁니다. 오늘 수업이 끝나면 이 이론을 어떻게 사용하면 되는지 알 수 있어요.

geometry (수학) 기하학 formula 공식, 식 be responsible for ~에 책임이 있다 mathematician 수학자 philosopher 철학자
follower 추종자, 신봉자 uncommon 흔하지 않은, 드문 theorem (수학에서의) 정리 calculate 계산하다, 산출하다
square 제곱하다

35. 교사와 학생은 주로 무슨 얘기를 하고 있나요?

(A) 피타고라스의 삶에 관한 얘기
(B) 피타고라스의 정리 이론을 사용하는 방법
(C) 피타고라스의 아이디어와 그의 종교적 추종자들
(D) 피타고라스가 수학 시간에 중요한 이유

정답 및 해설 **[주제를 묻는 문제]** 수학 선생님이 오늘 수업은 칠판에 공식이나 숫자를 쓰는 일반적인 수업 방식과 다르게 해보겠다고 말하면서 "먼저 우리에게 기하학에 대한 일반적인 개념을 심어준 피타고라스에 대해 말하겠다(~ Pythagoras, the man who is responsible for our ideas about geometry.)"라고 한다. 이어서 피타고라스에 대한 여러 설명이 이어지고 있는 것으로 보아 이 강의의 전체 주제는 (D)라고 할 수 있다. (A), (B), (C)는 부분적으로만 언급되었을 뿐으로 전체를 아우르는 주제는 될 수 없다.

36. 다음 중 피타고라스에 관해 사실인 것은 무엇인가요?

(A) 그에게는 그를 따르는 추종자들이 많지 않았다.
(B) 그는 6세기경 고대 로마에서 살았다.
(C) 그는 삼각형의 수치를 측정하는 방법을 고안해냈다.
(D) 역사학자들과 수학자들은 그의 삶에 관해 많이 알고 있다.

정답 및 해설 **[세부사항을 묻는 문제]** 학생이 "그것이 바로 삼각형의 길이와 각도를 계산하는 데 도움을 주는 〈피타고라스의 정리〉인가(**~ is that the theorem that helps us calculate the length and angles of triangles?**)"라고 질문하자 선생님은 그렇다고 대답하면서 "피타고라스가 <$a^2+b^2=c^2$>이라는 아이디어를 생각해냈다(**Pythagoras came up with the idea that a-squared plus b-squared equals c-squared.**)" 라고 설명한다. 이 내용을 통해 피타고라스가 '삼각형을 측정하는 방법을 생각해 냈다'는 것을 알 수 있다. 따라서 정답은 (C)이다.

37. 선생님은 피타고라스의 삶에 관해 뭐라고 하나요?
(A) 무척 오래 살았다.
(B) 그에 관한 정보가 많다.
(C) 여러 중요한 발견들을 많이 해냈다.
(D) 그가 생존하던 시기에는 그의 삶에 관한 기록이 없다.

정답 및 해설 **[세부사항을 묻는 문제]** 선생님은 "피타고라스가 매우 오래 전에 살았기 때문에 그에 대해서 많은 것을 알지 못한다(**Because he lived so long ago, we don't know that much about him.**)"라고 말한다. 이어서 "우리가 얻은 모든 정보는 그가 죽은 몇 세기 후에 피타고라스에 대해 글을 썼던 작가들로부터 온 것이다(**All of the information that we've got came from writers who wrote about him centuries after he actually lived.**)"라고 설명하고 있다. 그러므로 정답은 (D)이다. (A), (C)와 관련된 내용은 언급되지 않았고 (B)는 틀린 내용이다.

38. 선생님은 피타고라스 정리에 관해 무엇을 암시하나요?
(A) 수년이 지나면서 (이론이) 바뀌었다.
(B) 삼각형 수치 측정에만 도움이 된다.
(C) 보통 기하학 수업에서는 가르치지 않는다.
(D) 학생들이 배우기에 그다지 어렵지 않을 것이다.

정답 및 해설 **[추론 문제]** 선생님은 마지막에 "피타고라스의 정리 공식을 말로 설명하면 복잡하게 들릴지도 모르지만, 칠판에 쓰면 사실 상당히 간단하다는 것을 알게 될 것이다(**I know that sounds complicated when I say it out loud, but when I write it out on the board you'll see that it's actually quite simple.**)"라고 설명한다. 이를 볼 때 선생님은 피타고라스의 공식이 '학생들이 배우기에 그다지 어렵지 않을 것'이라고 생각하고 있음을 알 수 있다. 따라서 정답은 (D)이다.

[39-42] Listen to a teacher talking in a biology class.

W You've probably seen them running around your backyard, but do you really know anything about squirrels? Squirrels are mammals, just like dogs, elephants, and humans. They're part of a group of mammals called the Sciuridae. Many people think they're closely related to mice, but they're surprisingly more closely related to chipmunks, woodchucks, and prairie dogs. Squirrels are well-known for their big bushy tail.

What's amazing about squirrels is that they can live in almost any habitat in the world. There are squirrels that live in tropical rainforests and squirrels that live in deserts. Squirrels usually eat plants—they like to eat nuts and seeds—that's why squirrels are always pictured with acorns. Unlike some other animals, squirrels need to eat things that are high in protein. They can't survive by eating green leaves like a rabbit can. That's why they eat nuts. When it's difficult for squirrels to find food, they'll eat insects, eggs, and even small birds.

번역 **선생님의 생물 수업 강의를 들으세요.**

여 여러분들은 아마도 뒷마당에서 뛰어다니는 다람쥐들을 본 적이 있을 텐데요, 다람쥐에 관해 뭔가를 정말로 알고 있는 게 있나요? 다람쥐는 개나 코끼리, 그리고 인간과 같은 포유동물입니다. 다람쥐는 다람쥐과에 속하는 포유동물의 한 부류입니다. 다람쥐가 쥐과에 속한다고 생각하는 사람들이 많은데요, 놀랍게도 (쥐보다는) 북미산 얼룩 다람쥐나, 북미산 마멋, 프레리도그(*북미 대초원 지대에 사는 다람쥐과 동물)에 좀 더 밀접하게 연결되어 있죠. 다람쥐는 커다랗고 숱이 무성한 꼬리로 유명하지요.

다람쥐에 관해 놀라운 점은 이들이 세상 어느 곳에서도 서식할 수 있다는 겁니다. 열대 우림 지역에 사는 다람쥐도 있고 사막에 사는 다람쥐도 있습니다. 다람쥐는 주로 식물을 먹이로 하는데요, 견과류나 씨앗류를 좋아합니다. 다람쥐가 항상 도토리를 들고 있는 모습으로 그려지는 것도 그 때문입니다. 다른 동물들과 달리 다람쥐는 고단백질 음식물을 섭취해야 합니다. 토끼처럼 초록 잎만 먹고서는 살아갈 수가 없습니다. 그래서 견과류를 먹는 겁니다. 다람쥐는 먹잇감을 찾기가 어려워지면 곤충이나 알, 심지어는 작은 새들을 잡아먹기도 합니다.

Right, so, you might have noticed that squirrels are great climbers. Unlike most mice, squirrels can scurry up and down trees. They have large back legs and four feet, each with 4 or 5 toes. Most squirrels have thumbs, too, but they're not very useful. The squirrel's strong legs and claws help it to climb, along with its excellent sense of vision.

There are many different types of squirrels in the world and even in this country. Next time you see a squirrel, don't just think it's some animal trying to eat the food in your birdfeeder. Instead, remember that it's a unique creature, and a pretty cute one too.

자, 그리고, 여러분들은 아마도 다람쥐가 (나무 등의 무언가를) 잘 오르는 걸 봤을 겁니다. 대부분의 쥐들과 달리 다람쥐는 나무를 종종거리며 오르내릴 수 있습니다. 다람쥐는 커다란 뒷다리에 4개의 발이 있으며, 각각 4~5개의 발가락이 달려 있습니다. 대개의 다람쥐는 엄지손가락도 있습니다만 그다지 유용하게 쓰이지 못합니다. 다람쥐는 튼튼한 다리와 발톱, 그리고 시력이 상당히 좋아서 잘 기어오를 수 있습니다.

전 세계에는 여러 종류의 다람쥐들이 있으며 또 우리 나라에도 있습니다. 다음 번에 다람쥐를 보게 된다면 여러분들 새 먹이 장치에 있는 음식을 먹는 동물이라고만 생각하지 말고, 독특하고 아주 귀여운 생물이라는 점을 생각해 보도록 하세요.

squirrel 다람쥐 mammal 포유동물 Sciuridae 다람쥐과 related to ~와 관계 있는, ~와 친척인
bushy (털 등이) 숱이 많은, 텁수룩한; 덤불이 많은 habitat 서식지 tropical rainforest 열대 다우림 nut 견과, 나무 열매
seed 씨, 종자 acorn 도토리 protein 단백질 insect 곤충 scurry 허둥지둥 달리다, 총총걸음으로 달리다 toe 발가락, 발끝
thumb 엄지손가락 claw 발톱 sense of vision 시각 birdfeeder 새에게 먹이를 주기 위해 외부에 설치된 장치

39. 이야기의 주제는 무엇인가요?
(A) 다람쥐가 사는 장소
(B) 다람쥐가 겨울을 나는 방법
(C) 일반 다람쥐에 관한 놀라운 정보
(D) 다람쥐가 북미산 얼룩 다람쥐나 북미산 마멋에 속한 이유

정답 및 해설 **[주제를 묻는 문제]** 선생님은 학생들에게 다람쥐에 대한 강의를 하면서, 많은 사람들이 다람쥐가 쥐과에 속한다고 생각하지만 "놀랍게도 다람쥐는 북미산 얼룩 다람쥐나, 북미산 마멋, 프레리도그에 좀더 밀접하게 연결되어 있다(~ they're surprisingly more closely related to chipmunks, woodchucks, and prairie dogs.)"고 설명한다. 이어서 다람쥐의 서식지, 다람쥐의 먹이, 나무를 잘 기어오르는 특색 등을 자세히 언급한다. 이를 볼 때, 이 수업의 주요 목적은 '다람쥐에 관한 다양한 정보 제공'임을 알 수 있다. 따라서 정답은 (C)이다. (A)는 여러 정보들 중 하나일 뿐이고, (B), (D)는 언급되지 않았다.

40. 선생님이 정정해 준 다람쥐에 대한 잘못된 믿음은 무엇인가요?
(A) 다람쥐는 나무에서 산다.
(B) 다람쥐는 대단히 잘 기어오르는 동물이다.
(C) 다람쥐는 쥐와 대단히 밀접한 관계에 있다.
(D) 다람쥐는 씨앗류를 먹는 특이한 생물이다.

정답 및 해설 **[세부사항을 묻는 문제]** 선생님은 "다람쥐가 쥐과에 속한다고 생각하는 사람들이 많은데, 놀랍게도 (쥐보다는) 북미산 얼룩 다람쥐나, 북미산 마멋, 프레리도그에 좀더 밀접하게 연결되어 있다(Many people think they're closely related to mice, but they're surprisingly more closely related to chipmunks, woodchucks, and prairie dogs.)"라고 설명한다. 이를 볼 때, 다람쥐에 대한 잘못된 믿음은 '쥐와 대단히 밀접한 관계에 있다'는 것임을 알 수 있다. 따라서 정답은 (C)이다.

41. 다람쥐에 관한 내용을 통해 무엇을 추론할 수 있나요?
(A) 주로 교외 거리에 서식한다.
(B) 쥐나 생쥐와 밀접한 연관이 있다.
(C) 초록 잎사귀를 먹기 위해 토끼와 경쟁한다.
(D) 생존을 위해 희귀한 먹이도 기꺼이 먹는다.

정답 및 해설 **[추론 문제]** 선생님은 다람쥐는 주로 식물을 먹이로 하고 견과류나 씨앗류를 좋아한다고 설명하면서 "다람쥐는 먹잇감을 찾기가 어려워지면 곤충이나 알, 심지어는 작은 새들을 잡아먹기도 한다(When it's difficult for squirrels to find food, they'll eat insects, eggs, and even small birds.)"라고 설명한다. 이 내용을 근거로 '다람쥐는 생존을 위해 희귀한 먹이도 기꺼이 먹는다'고 추론할 수 있다. 따라서 정답은 (D)이다.

42. 선생님 말씀에 따르면 다람쥐가 잘 기어오르는 이유는 무엇인가요?

(A) 무척 빠르다.

(B) 유용한 엄지 손가락을 가지고 있다.

(C) 강한 다리와 발톱을 가지고 있다.

(D) 발에 4~5개의 발가락을 가지고 있다.

정답 및 해설 **[세부사항을 묻는 문제]** 선생님은 다람쥐가 나무를 잘 기어오른다고 말하면서 "다람쥐는 튼튼한 다리와 발톱이 있어서 잘 기어오른다 **(The squirrel's strong legs and claws help it to climb ~)**"라고 그 이유를 설명한다. 따라서 정답은 (C)이다. (A)는 언급되지 않았고, 엄지 손가락은 유용하지 못하다고 했으므로 (B)는 틀린 내용이고, (D)는 언급되었으나 잘 기어오르는 직접적인 이유로 드러나지는 않았다.

Unlock your potential with

Master **TOEFL Junior**